IMAGES
of America

MT. WASHINGTON

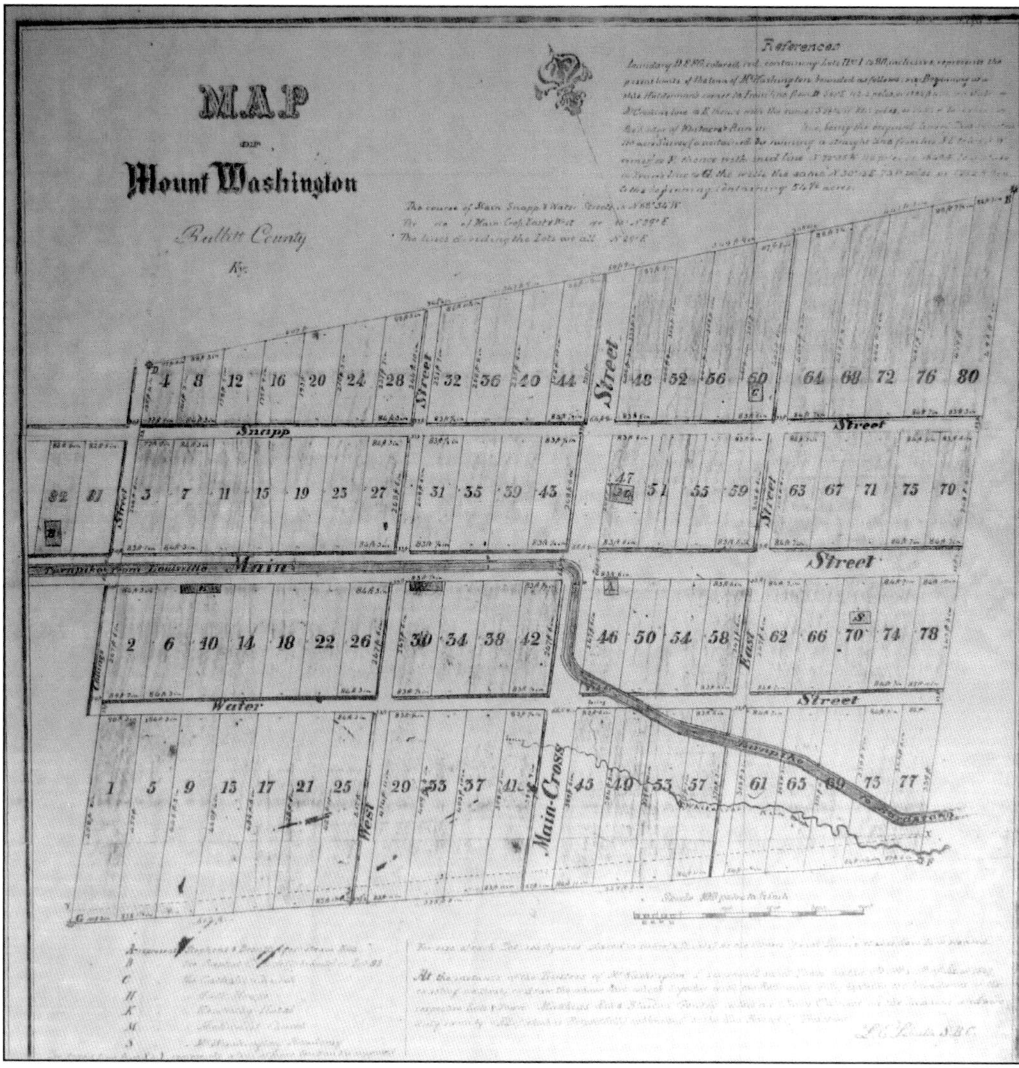

In 1847, L.E. Shultz surveyed the original plat of 82 lots that formed the city of Mt. Washington. He describes the boundaries of the city through landmarks—many that no longer exist, but some that survive to this day. He noted several key locations in town such as William Steven's gristmill at the crossroads and Spout Spring that ran through it. Also included are the locations of the Baptist, Methodist, and Catholic churches, the Kentucky Hotel and Charles Hall's hotel in addition to the acclaimed Mt. Washington Academy. (Courtesy of the Mt. Washington Historical Society.)

On the Cover: Stuyler Harris (second from left) was the quintessential Mt. Washington historian when the history of the city was still fresh in the minds of the first settlers. At 15, he started working at the Cyclone store located next to his home. After school, he went to work as head cashier for the Peoples Bank of Mt. Washington where he was an employee for 31 years. In 1964, Norville Harris and John Settles began their newspaper, the *Mt. Washington Star*, for which Stuyler wrote a weekly article about Mt. Washington history. (Courtesy of the Mt. Washington Historical Society.)

IMAGES
of America

MT. WASHINGTON

Bobby K. Darnell

ARCADIA
PUBLISHING

ISBN 978-1-4671-1348-9

Published by Arcadia Publishing
Charleston, South Carolina

Printed in the United States of America

Library of Congress Control Number: 2014957769

For all general information, please contact Arcadia Publishing:
Telephone 843-853-2070
Fax 843-853-0044
E-mail sales@arcadiapublishing.com
For customer service and orders:
Toll-Free 1-888-313-2665

Visit us on the Internet at www.arcadiapublishing.com

To Rhonda, whose inspiration gave me the courage to write this book

CONTENTS

ACKNOWLEDGMENTS

It is impossible to acknowledge, thank, or even remember every single person that I have crossed paths with in my journey learning about Mt. Washington's past; I apologize if I miss anyone. Everyone that has helped me, living, deceased, or those historians I never knew personally but know so well I appreciate from the bottom of my heart. I couldn't have done this without you.

I thank the good Lord above for leading me to become a historian and Charles Abel Long for inviting me to a Mt. Washington Historical Society meeting. After becoming a member, I realized no one was collecting historical information or photographs before they disappeared. My partners in crime are Jimmy Breeden and Dale Salmon, who have truly been of great assistance and made this so fun and fascinating. I give my thanks to David Strange and his amazing crew at the Bullitt County History Museum and good friends and fellow Society members Betty Lutes, Gayle and Eleanor Troutman, and Lloyd and Arbidella Dooley. Stuart Tichenor, Mildred Brown, and Dorothy Dean Porter have been most gracious with their assistance. Much appreciation to Kaycee Salmon for her special talents. Although I never knew them, Stuyler Harris, Leda Barnes, and Statira Mathis provided information that is immeasurably valuable. Hopefully, I've given due credit to all others through courtesy lines.

Also, a big thanks to Jesse Darland from Arcadia Publishing for being patient with this rookie writer. It has been a great experience.

Introduction

Mt. Washington came to be in a unique variety of circumstances. In the late 1700s, Revolutionary War soldiers with land grants raced to lay claim to the most valuable acreage they could find. David Leach was one of those whose hundreds of acres included the future site of Mt. Washington. Pioneers traveling on the Wilderness Road who veered off the path near McCulloughs Run on Salt River looking for a more direct route to Louisville subsequently ventured through a small borough called Hell's Kitchen. There a fur trader ran a tavern that catered to rough characters. The possibility of Indian attacks was still certainly a threat. Eventually the Indians were chased out of the area and roads were forged from Bardstown to Louisville and from Shepherdsville to Shelbyville and Taylorsville. That area near Hell's Kitchen where the roads met was soon labeled the Crossroads.

Joseph Hough, a merchant and Bullitt County deputy sheriff, bought 100 acres surrounding the Crossroads in 1812 with his wife, Catherine, and son Christopher. Tragedy led to the formation of the city of Mt. Washington. Joseph died in 1813, leaving his wife alone with Christopher who had an unknown medical condition. Catherine remarried David Drake and renounced her widow dower. David became Christopher's guardian and to adequately provide for his special care they sold 50 of the 100 acres at the Crossroads in 1818 to be divided into 82 lots, creating a city called Mt. Vernon. Within a year, most of the lots had been sold and many resold. Large, two-story homes started rising along Main Street, or the Louisville/Bardstown Turnpike, along with numerous businesses and a school. Just south of the Crossroads was a unique area where several springs met, including the Spout Spring that supplied water year-round for manufacturing. William Stevens started one of the first businesses in that area with his gristmill and wool-carding machine that provided lumber for construction and wool for the manufacture of clothing. Godfrey Wolf had a tannery that employed several locals, contributing to the town's self-sustainability. Many of the Harris, Swearingen, and Hall families who had farms outside of the community moved into the city, and the Baptist, Methodist, and Catholic congregations built churches within city limits.

The first form of government came in 1822 when trustees were appointed, but it was not until 1834 that the town was officially chartered by the state. Between those dates a problem arose that took some time before it was resolved. The city had petitioned for a post office, but to their dismay, found there was already a Mt. Vernon established in the state. To proceed, a name change was necessary, which was a difficult decision for many. The town was originally named Mt. Vernon to honor Pres. George Washington and his estate. Keeping in line with honoring the president, they decided on the name Mt. Washington, and as the city is situated at a high elevation, it was fitting. The transition took several years; the earliest known document mentioning Mt. Washington is from 1828, but an 1838 document still refers to the area as Mt. Vernon. Many maps continued to designate Mt. Washington as Mt. Vernon well into the 1800s.

The city grew leaps and bounds in the 1800s, surviving the Civil War without any serious damage and out-populating all other cities in Bullitt County. By the late 1800s, Mt. Washington was well established and vying for a railroad to be built through or near the city, but Shepherdsville received that honor. It was quite a blow to the city, and Shepherdsville, the county seat, benefitted greatly from the decision. The city also fought hard to get electric rail car transportation from Louisville and was rejected. But as roads improved, the traffic through Mt. Washington increased. As many as five hotels were located in the area and the Masonic lodge, built in 1853, featured a large room with a stage where locals would present plays, politicians would speak, and musicians and actors would entertain traveling guests and locals alike. Maccabee Hall would be built at the Crossroads in 1905 and become the popular event space.

In 1925, the new and improved Jackson Highway, which was essentially Bardstown Road, was paved. This improvement brought traffic and business into the city that changed the landscape dramatically and extended businesses farther north on Main Street.

In the early 1900s, the population declined somewhat and the town population grew little, remaining a quiet, scenic community until the early 1950s when large plants like General Electric and International Harvester were established. These new businesses, among others, initiated the arrival of hundreds of new residents, mostly from farming communities, looking for better jobs. Mt. Washington was a perfect blend of the country and the big city. Mt. Washington has come a long way from its humble origins but retains its small town feel and continues to grow and thrive.

One

At the Crossroads

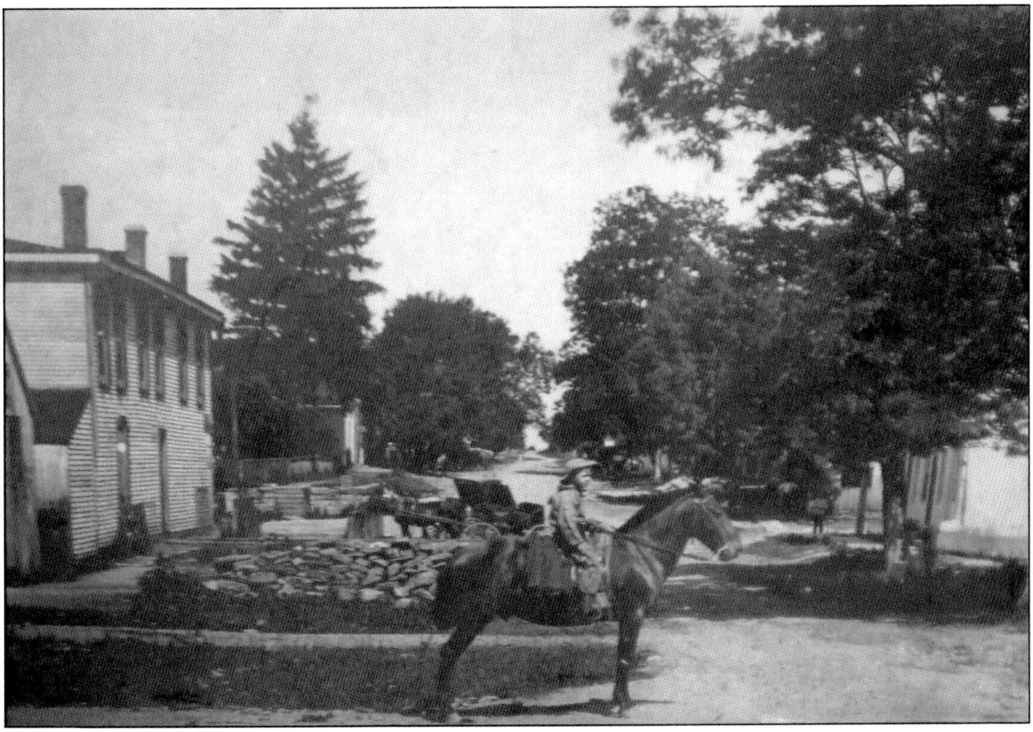

Thurston Long on his horse, Deck, looks north on Main Street, the major business district of Mt. Washington. The bulk of the businesses in the early days were located within this block, which included two hotels, a mansion, a blacksmith shop, food and dry goods stores, a Masonic lodge, and a lawyer's office. Beginning from the Crossroads north on Main Street to Frogtown, it is a short jaunt west on Highway 44, a stroll on South Main Street, and a glimpse of East Highway 44. (Courtesy of Mark and Lisa Rouse.)

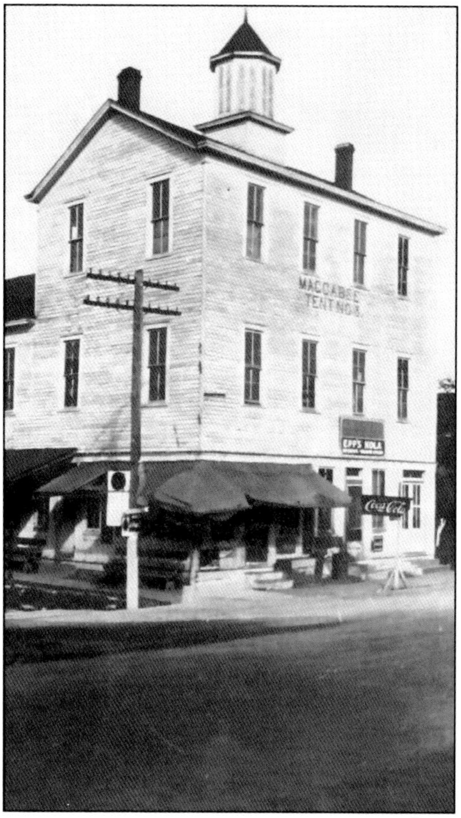

The Fraternal Order of Maccabees of Mt. Washington was established in 1903, and property was purchased at the corner of Main Street and Highway 44. Construction began under the supervision of William A. King and was finished around 1906. The official name for the building was Tent Three, but it was known as Maccabee Hall. Several businesses leased space on the first floor, including German Branham's restaurant, Kenny Snyder's clothing store, Preston Parrish's barbershop, and Dr. Asa. C. Overall's office. The third floor was used exclusively by the Maccabees as their meeting room and offices. The second story had a stage (below) that was used on numerous occasions and was the delight of the community. Locals would have plays they called "minstrels" and enjoyed watching their neighbors perform. Pictured here is Mary William's troupe that entertained often at the Maccabee. On November 18, 1940, a blaze broke out between Branham's restaurant and Snyder's clothing store, which ultimately leveled the entire building and the old Methodist church. The town did not have a fire department, and by the time the Jeffersontown firefighters made it to Mt. Washington it was too late. (Courtesy of the Mt. Washington Historical Society.)

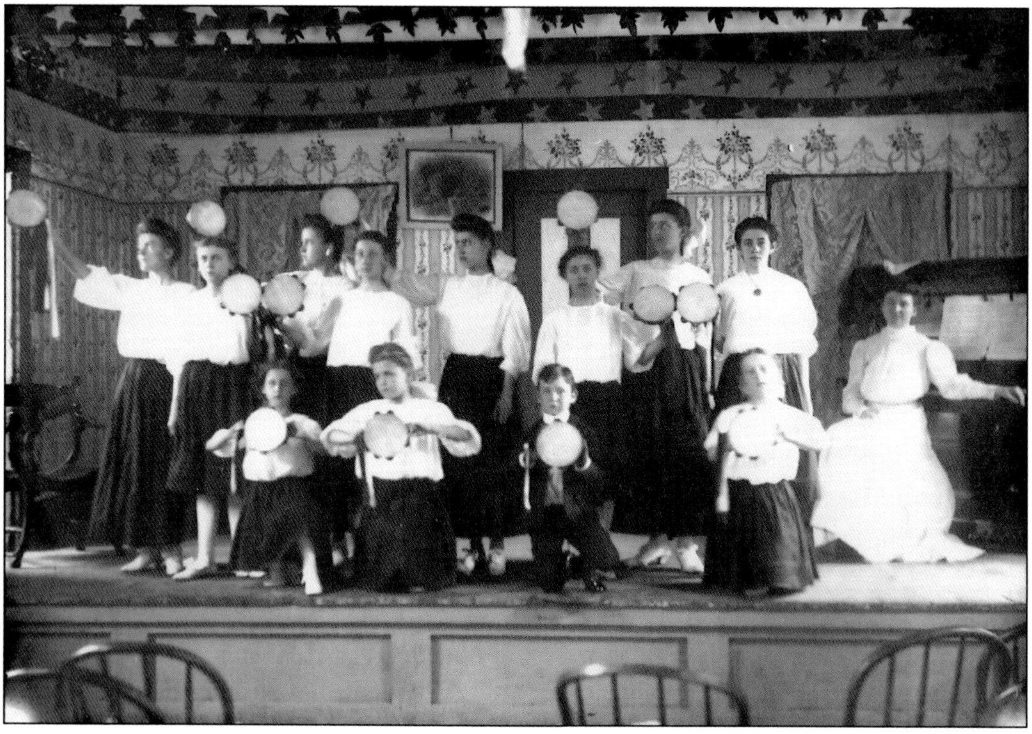

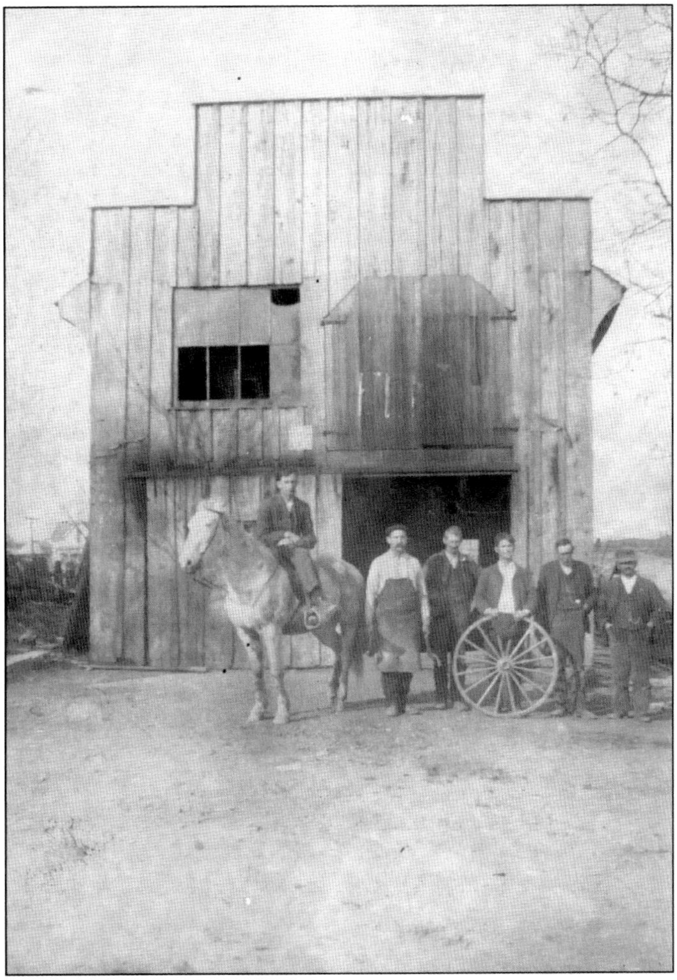

Brothers Charlie and Tom Parrish ran their blacksmith shop at the corner of Main Street and Highway 44 from the late 1800s until the 1920s when the shop was moved to Snapp Street near Tom's home. Charlie was an expert carriage maker, and Tom, a talented blacksmith, shoed horses. The shop featured an elevator to transport the carriages built on the second floor. Tom had the distinction of being the last remaining blacksmith in Bullitt County. Charlie passed away in 1929, but Tom continued to work until he was in his 80s. Will Judd (pictured below, center) was an outstanding worker at the shop for several years. (Courtesy of the Mt. Washington Historical Society.)

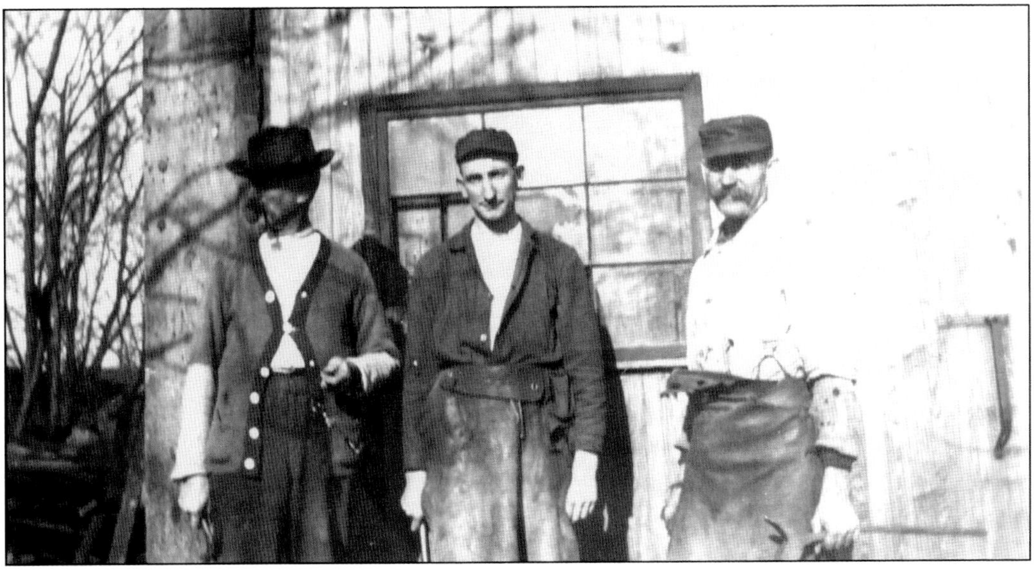

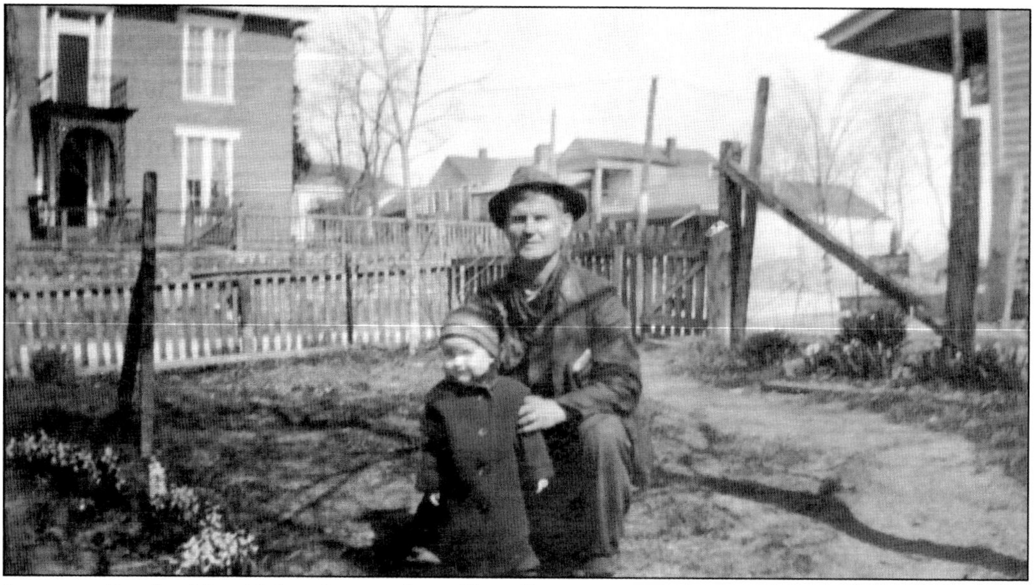

Just over Stuyler Harris's head was where Elmo Jasper ran a grocery after William and Almer Barnes moved their grocery-and-goods business across the street. Elmo would later move across the street into the John Ellaby (Sullivan's Bakery) building. The building was well aged even at the turn of the century. Dr. Smith Hobbs and his son Dr. Nick Hobbs ran their practice from the narrow two-story building with a porch on the left. Both buildings were constructed prior to the Civil War. (Courtesy of the Mt. Washington Historical Society.)

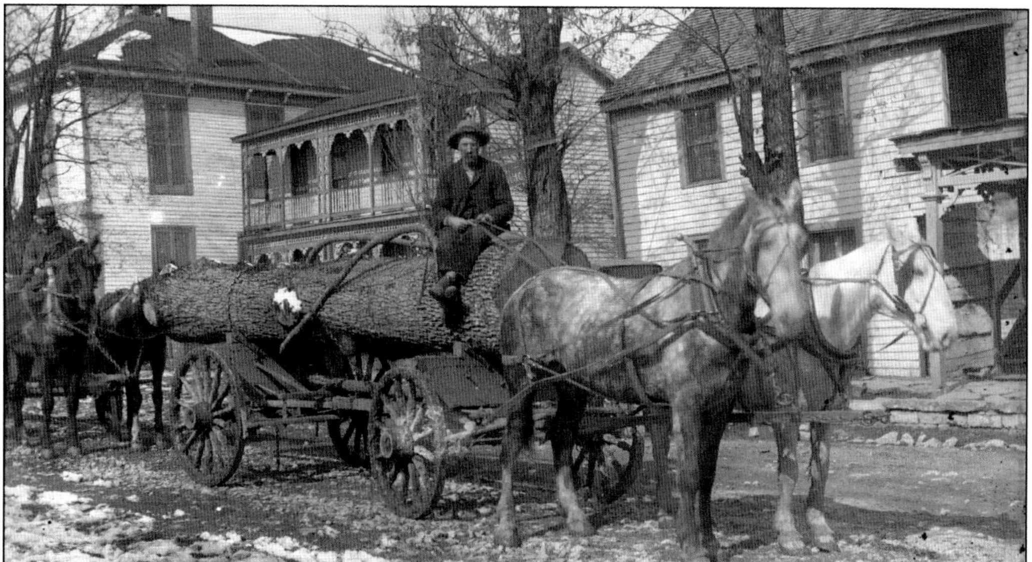

The lumber needed to construct a town could be found in great abundance around Mt. Washington, and the majority of the trees in the surrounding forests are poplar, insect-resistant and durable. The load pictured here would have been heading just down the street to Marshall Collier's sawmill to be cut into lumber for construction or furniture. There were several talented woodworkers in the area, and many of their creations reside in local homes today. The earliest mill was William Steven's saw and gristmill located near the southwest corner of the Crossroads. (Courtesy of the Mt. Washington Historical Society.)

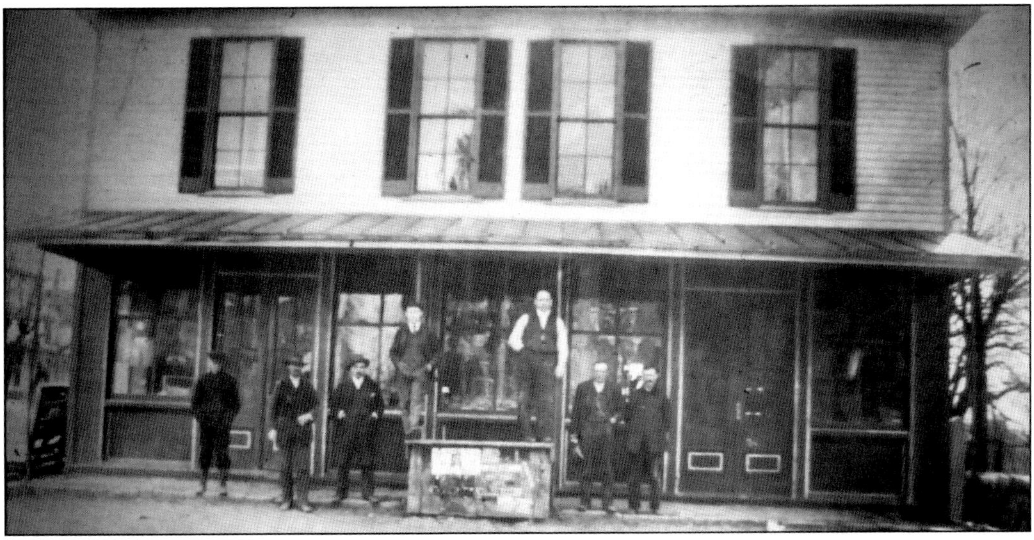

Cyclone started in 1885 as a stock-owned company managed by Albert Miller. The store provided a variety of goods, including groceries, household goods, and hunting and fishing equipment. In 1906, James "Buddy" Gentry bought the store outright, and in 1913 sold it to Clarence Porter and Hubert Wiggington. Porter bought out Wiggington's share a few years later. In 1937, Porter was involved in a fatal automobile accident and the business was handed down to his son William Franklin. Franklin ran the business until his passing, and his son Larry took over operation of the business. The business was dissolved in 2013 after 127 years. (Courtesy of the Mt. Washington Historical Society.)

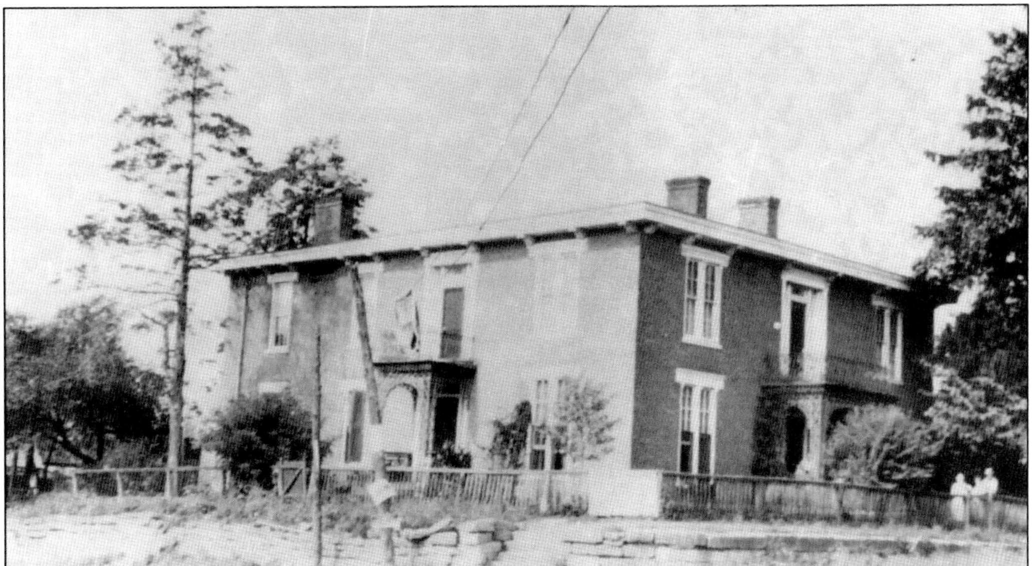

This Italianate mansion was built by master carpenter Henry J. Barnes in the late 1870s, and he lived there until his death in 1910. The bricks for the home were a foot thick and fired in a kiln on property he owned next to the Mt. Washington Cemetery, which he also owned. A black man by the name of Bill Thomas helped with the carpentry and masonry. Many of Henry's family members lived in the upstairs apartments at one time or another, including his brother William, with whom he once built covered bridges. (Courtesy of Stuart Tichenor.)

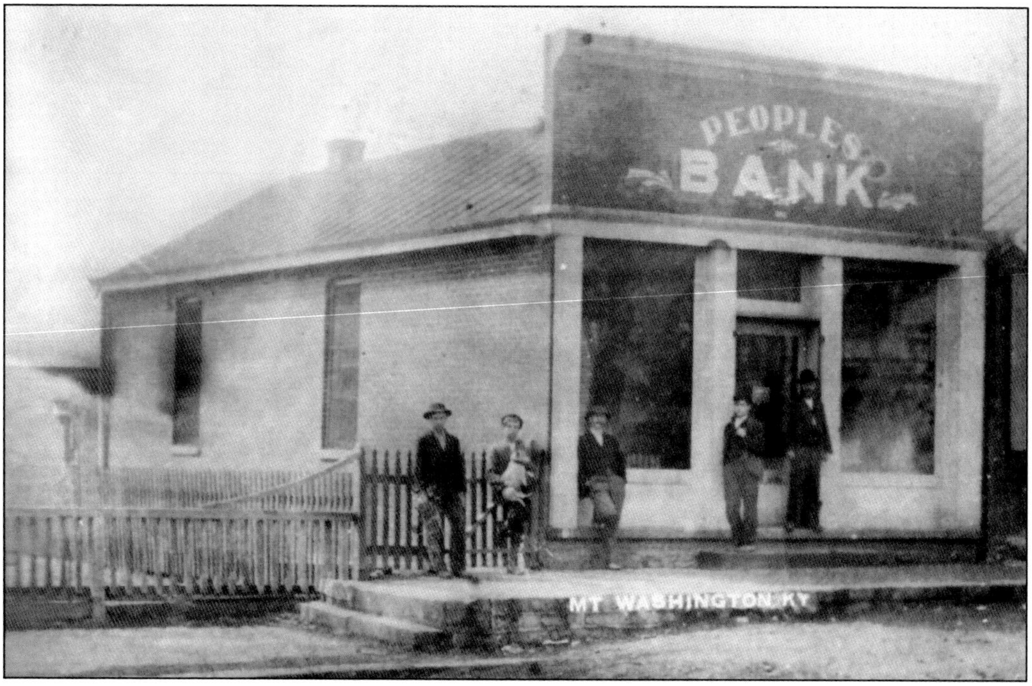

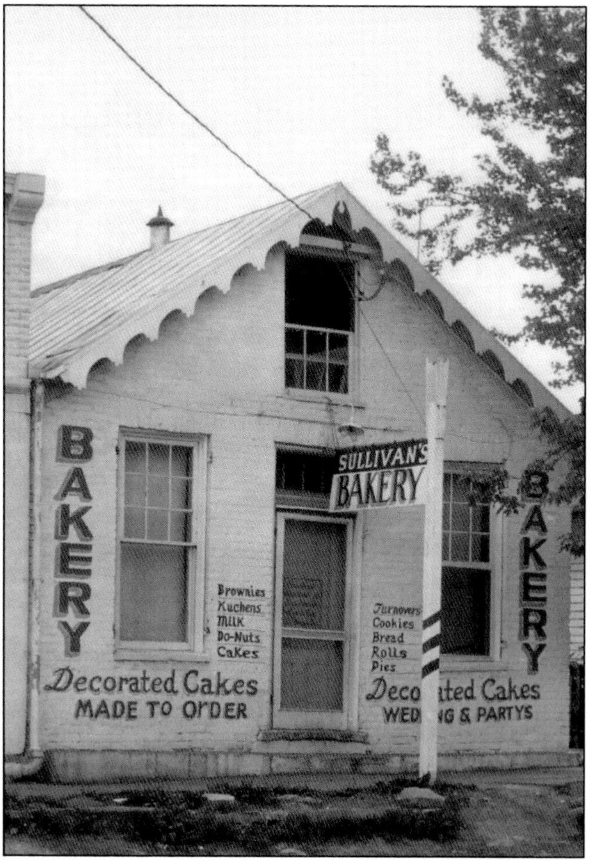

The Mt. Washington Peoples Bank began in the rear of the Cyclone store in 1901. Property was purchased beside Henry J. Barnes home, and a bank building was erected in 1903. They were an affiliate of the Bank of Shepherdsville at that time, but in 1909, they became an independent. Bert Hall was the bank's first president and William L. McGee its cashier. The building served until 1953 when a new bank building was constructed on a nearby location. (Courtesy of the Mt. Washington Historical Society.)

This building has a storied history. It was built before 1857 and the earliest known business it housed was the law office of John Ellaby. It was also Bertie Snyder's clothing and millinery store, an ice cream shop, and a restaurant. Elmo Jasper moved his grocery there from across the street around 1908, but it will always be best known as Frank Sullivan's bakery. The building was torn down and replaced with a more modern one in 1969. (Courtesy of Frank Sullivan.)

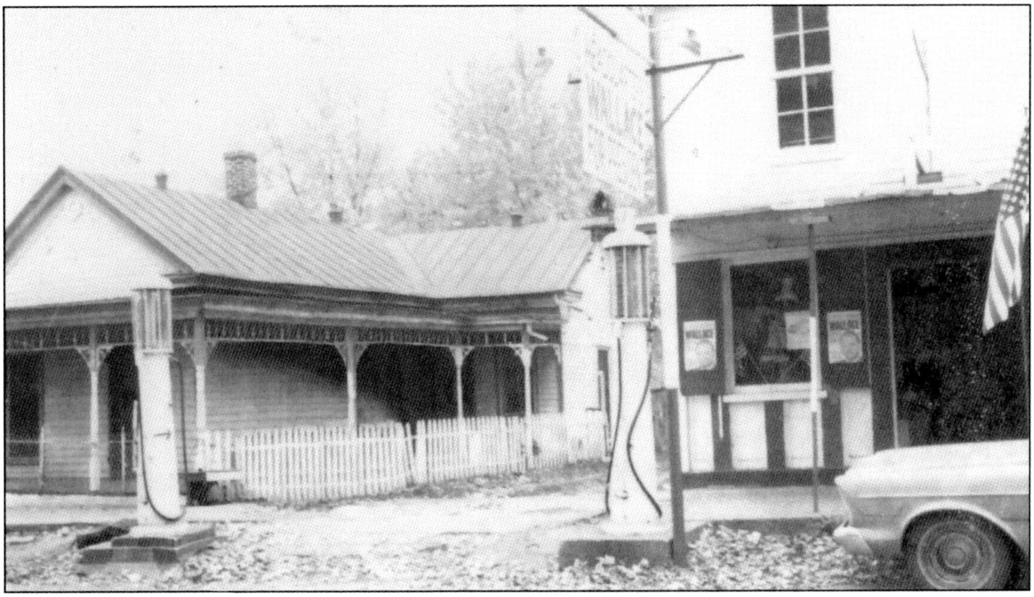

This home, nestled between John Ellaby's building and the Barnes Brothers' store, belonged to Elizabeth "Bettie" Barnes. She was the widow of Timoleon Barnes, who was killed in a logging accident in 1864 near Main Street and Flatlick Road. She raised two young sons, William and Almer, with the help of nearby family members. William and Almer would eventually buy the building next to their mother's home after starting their grocery business just across the street. (Courtesy of Trulavern Couch.)

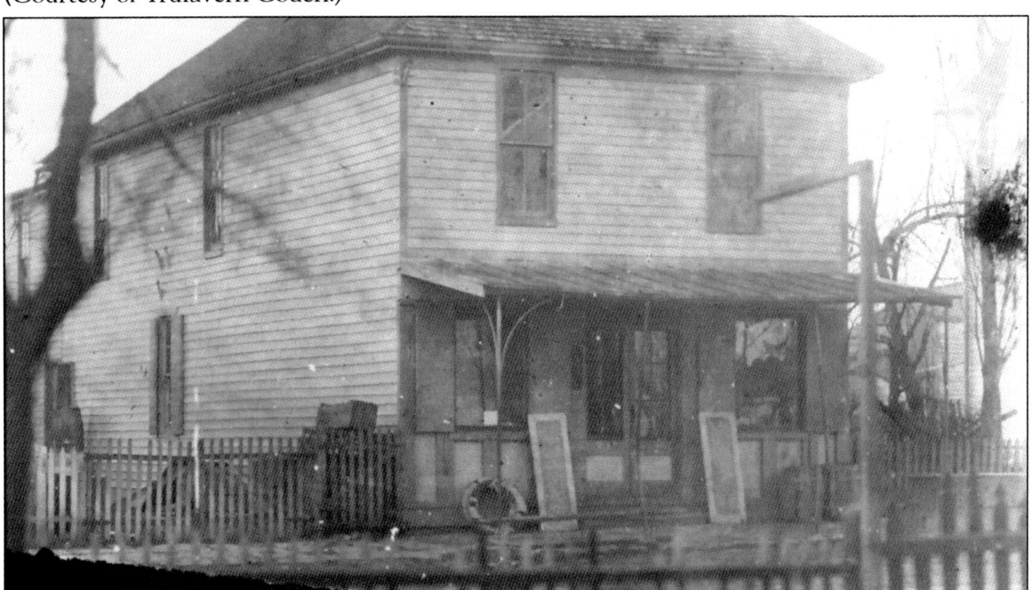

This antebellum building was used by Lucian Minor Parrish to build furniture and caskets. It then housed the Ceres Co-operative general store in the late 1800s. Around 1900, brothers William and Almer Barnes bought the store. William died in 1914, and Almer continued to run the store with the help of his son Harold "Jack" Barnes. Almer retired when his daughter Bernice married J. Edgar Fisher. Edgar and Bernice ran the store until 1961. (Courtesy of the Mt. Washington Historical Society.)

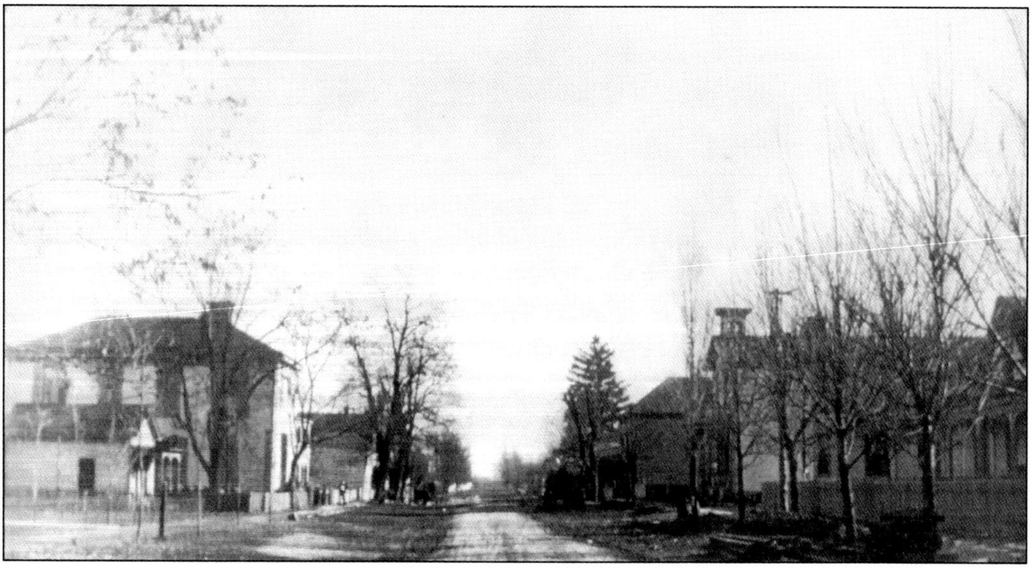

This street scene on Main Street looks south toward the Crossroads, captured in front of the present-day Peoples Bank of Mt. Washington. This was the major business district of town where most of the activity happened. On the right, James "Buddy" Gentry's beautiful home can be seen in addition to the Settle Hotel and the Barnes Brothers' store. On the left sits Dr. William W. Coleman's small office building and the Masonic Hall. Henry J. Barnes's first home and the Lewis/Carlton Hotel are next door. (Courtesy of the Mt. Washington Historical Society.)

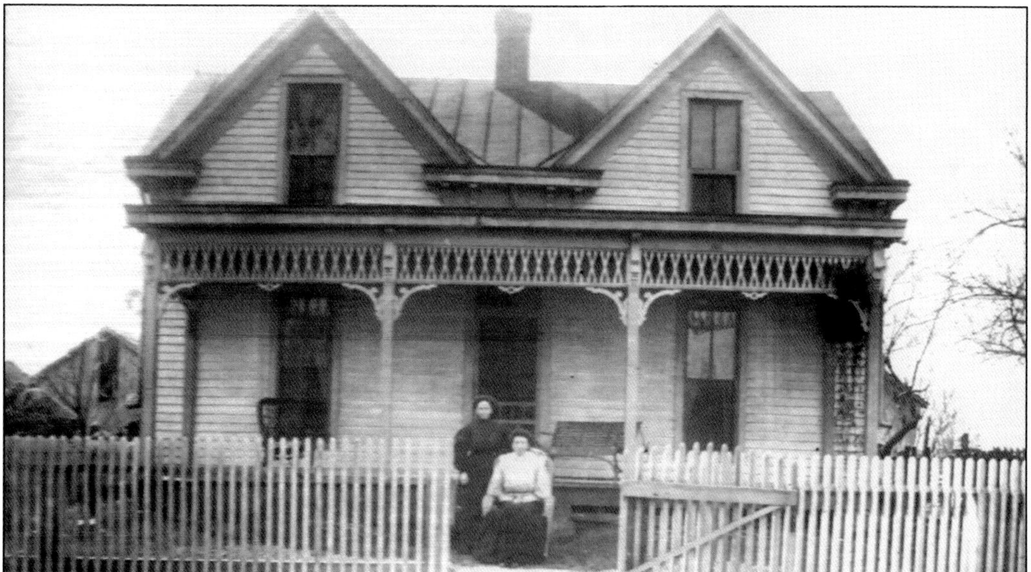

This beautiful Civil War–era home had quite a few occupants before the turn of the 20th century. Mrs. Reuben Porter, John Hough, Nick Pratt, and Quentin Gentry once resided there. Quentin's son James "Buddy" Gentry lived there for several years, and his wife, Zella, continued to live in the home after James passed in 1947 until the late 1960s. James was a former owner of the Cyclone store, and Zella was a descendent of the Bell family that owned Bell's Mill. She was also an avid painter; many of her paintings hang in the homes of locals today. (Courtesy of Chris Rothman.)

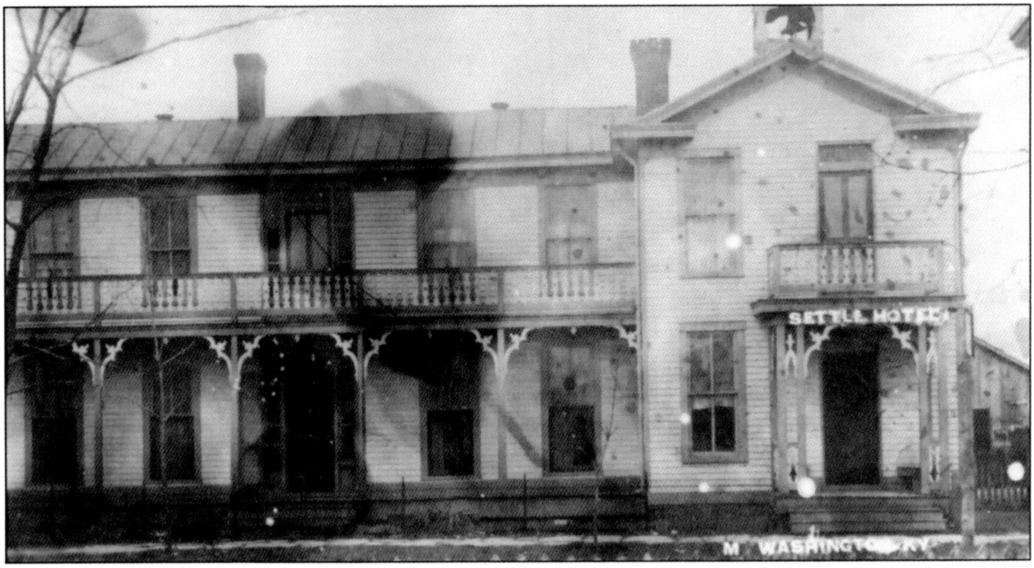

This hotel, best known as the Settle Hotel, was built sometime in the 1830s by Charles Hall. James Wright was its next owner. Reuben and Kate Settle bought the hotel around 1870 and Adam Settle and his sister Bettie took over operations after their parents' deaths. The hotel then went through several owners, including Henry Biven, Maurice Harris, and William Shelburne, shown (below) inside the hotel in this image from 1927. The hotel had a beautiful dining hall and once contained a saloon. An ice cream parlor was a huge attraction, and Mattie Tichenor ran a restaurant in the hotel. Before the dawn of automobiles, the hotel experienced tremendous success. Travelers would have to stop midway on their travels, and there was also a large livery barn for farmers taking their livestock and animals to market. Business declined sharply in the 1930s, but continued due to several independent businesses and apartments. Its last owner was B.F. "Bull" Roberts, who ran a pool hall. (Courtesy of the Mt. Washington Historical Society.)

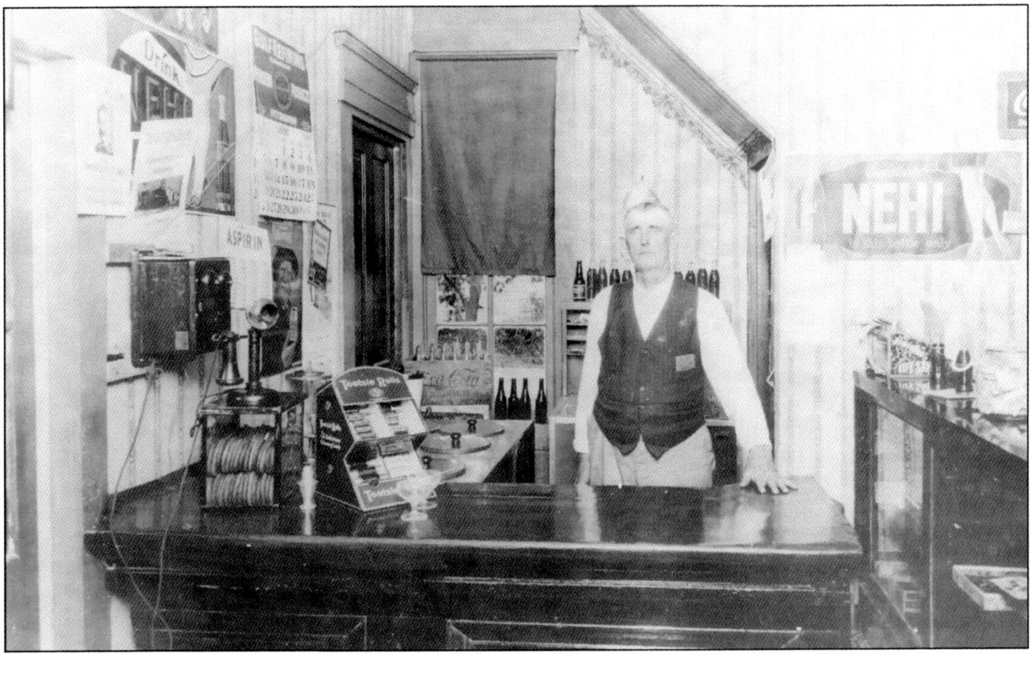

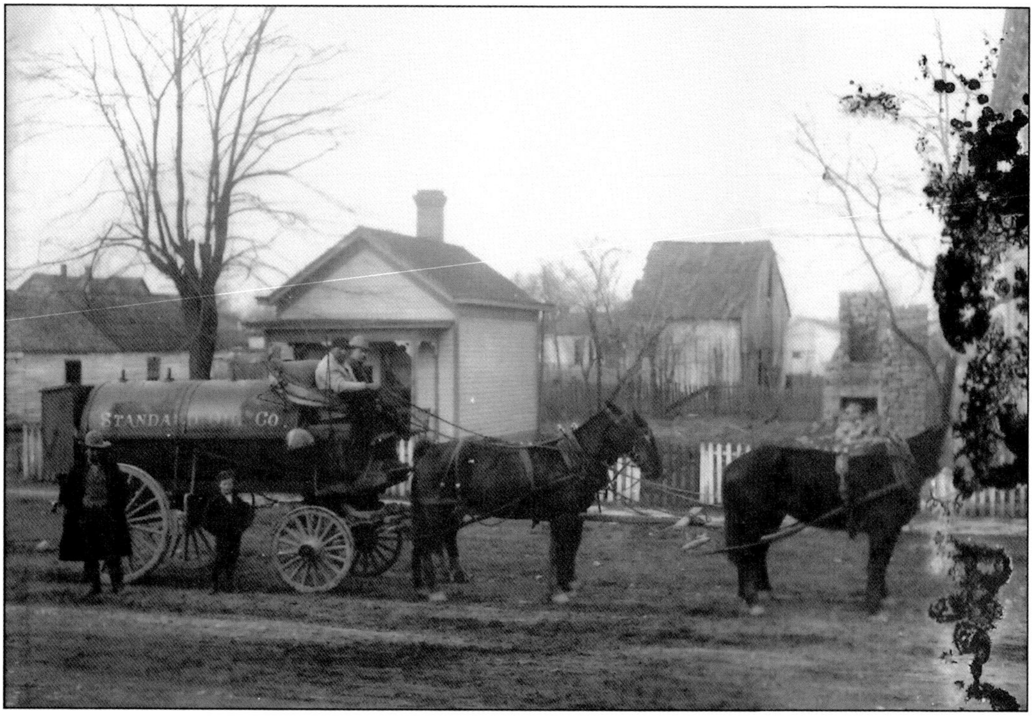

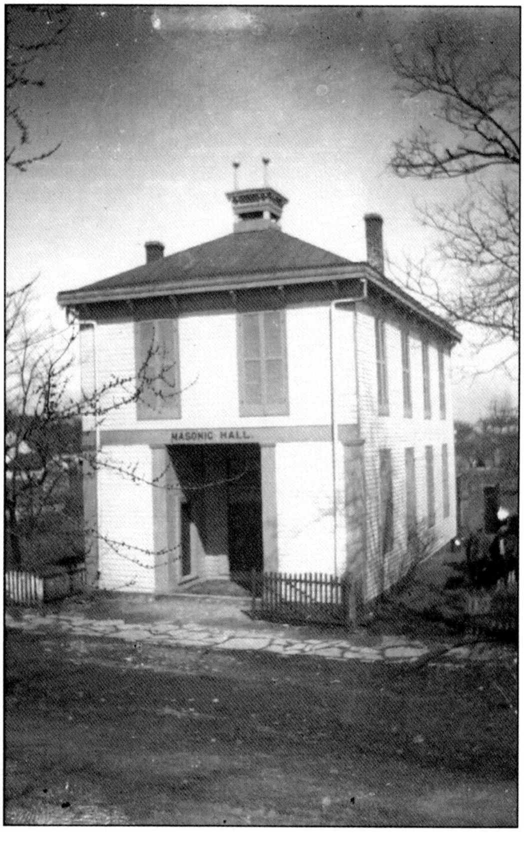

Dr. W.W. Coleman's office (behind tanker) was built shortly before his death in 1910. He practiced in Mt. Washington from the late 1800s until his passing. The building stood vacant for many years and was eventually torn down and acquired by the Standard Oil Company in the early 1920s. Take note of the remains of two large fireplaces to the right of the building. They were once part of a large two-story home owned by Reuben and Kate Settle. (Courtesy of the Mt. Washington Historical Society.)

Salt River Lodge No. 180, Free & Accepted Masons was chartered on August 29, 1849, and the Masonic lodge building on Main Street was erected in 1853. The Reverend George L. Rogers was its first master. The building served the Masons until 1974 when a new lodge was built. The upper floor of the lodge was used for meetings, plays, and political speeches until Maccabee Hall was built. The lower level was used for OES fundraising suppers and eventually leased to various businesses, including Long's grocery. (Courtesy of the Mt. Washington Historical Society.)

This house was built by Henry J. Barnes in the mid-1800s, likely as his first home with his bride, Susan Hall Snapp. The house was nondescript and rather plain in its original stages. Around 1920, the size of the house was doubled with the addition of a near duplicate section on to the front and a beautiful two-story balcony. Part of the lower right section served as the city's post office from the early 1900s to the 1940s. It has served as a residence and the location of several businesses over the years. Pictured here in the foreground are Emma Mell Harris and her niece Stuart Troutman. (Courtesy of Stuart Tichenor.)

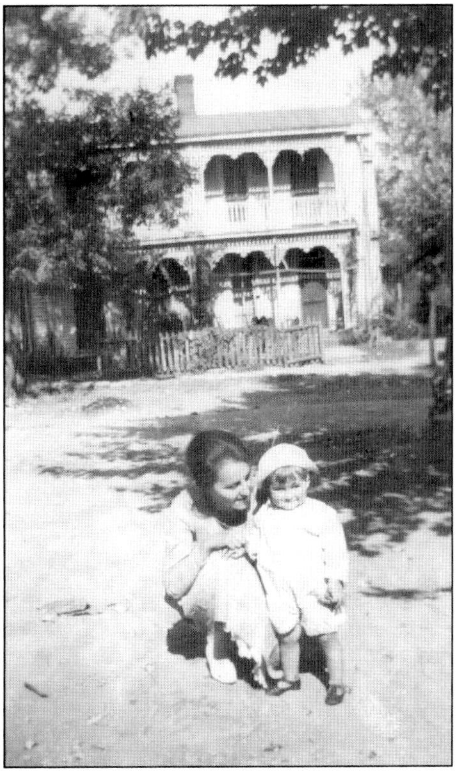

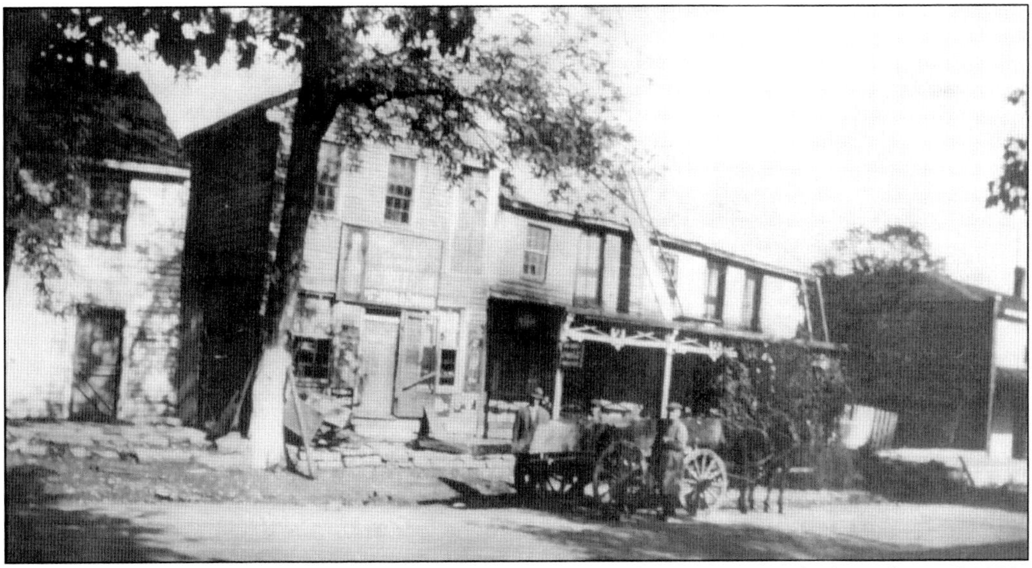

Josephine Lewis ran this establishment, known as the "Mother Lewis Hotel," from the mid-1800s until her death on January 1, 1905. Her son Jerome "Rome" Lewis assisted her with the business. It was a popular stop for travelers, and many locals would stay over after attending plays or political speeches at the Masonic lodge next door. It featured rooms, a dining room, and a saloon. The Carlton family bought it after Josephine's death and ran it until the 1920s. They added a pool and billiards room that only increased the hotel's popularity. (Courtesy of the Mt. Washington Historical Society.)

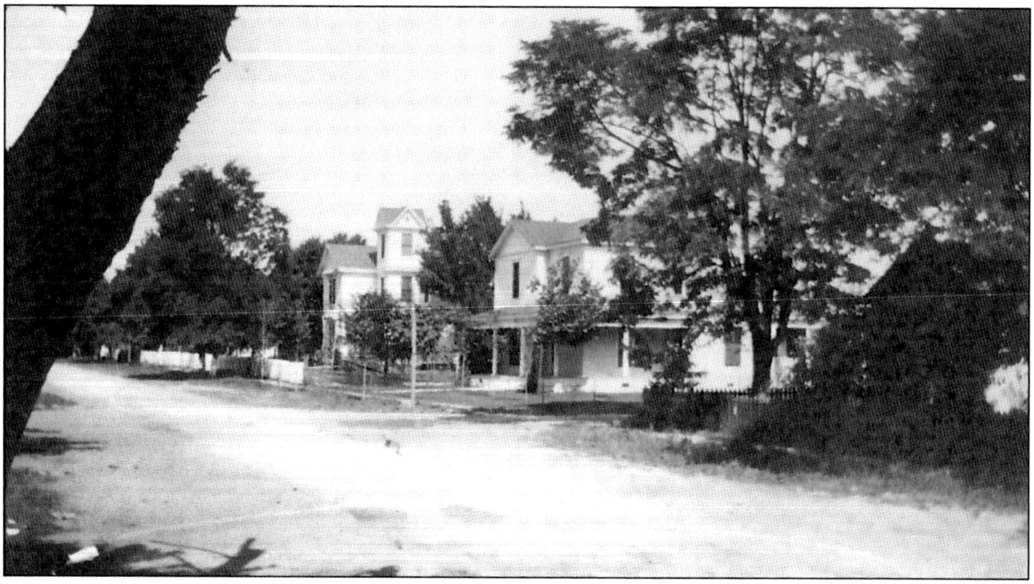

This image captures the front of the Barnes Brothers' store on Main Street looking north around 1915. The house on the right belonged to Shelt Brookshier's. Shelt was an entrepreneur and horse breeder. The Methodist parsonage is to the left. The new Methodist church would be built just past the parsonage in 1920. (Courtesy of the Mt. Washington Historical Society.)

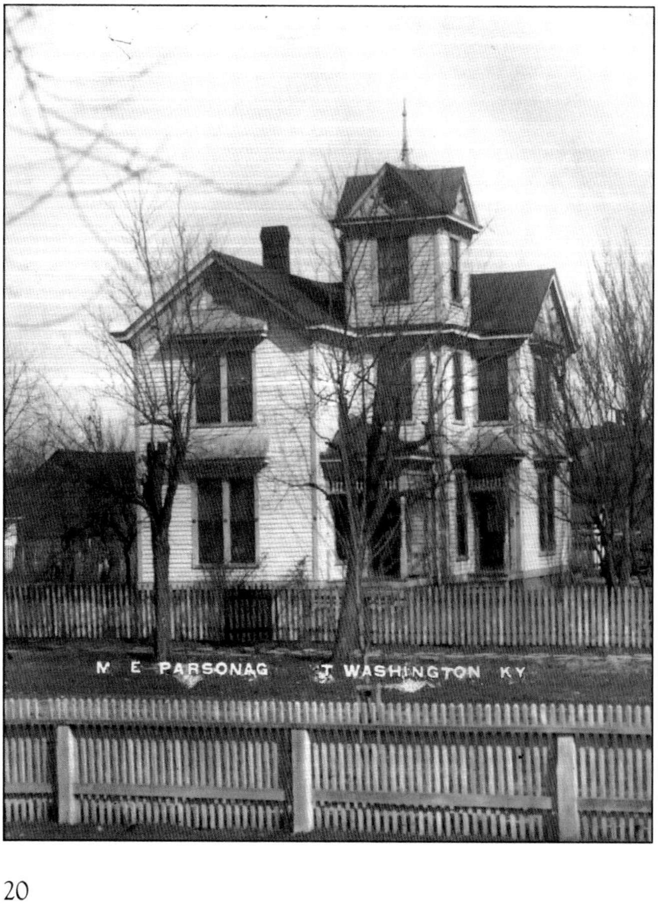

The Methodist parsonage on North Main Street was one of the most beautiful and unusual houses in town. It featured a small third-story room reminiscent of Gothic architecture. The exact date of its construction is unknown, but it preceded the second Methodist church built in 1920. The first Methodist church was located on Highway 44. The second was built on the left-hand lot of the parsonage. It was torn down and a more modern parsonage replaced it sometime in the early-to-mid-1950s. (Courtesy of the Mt. Washington Historical Society.)

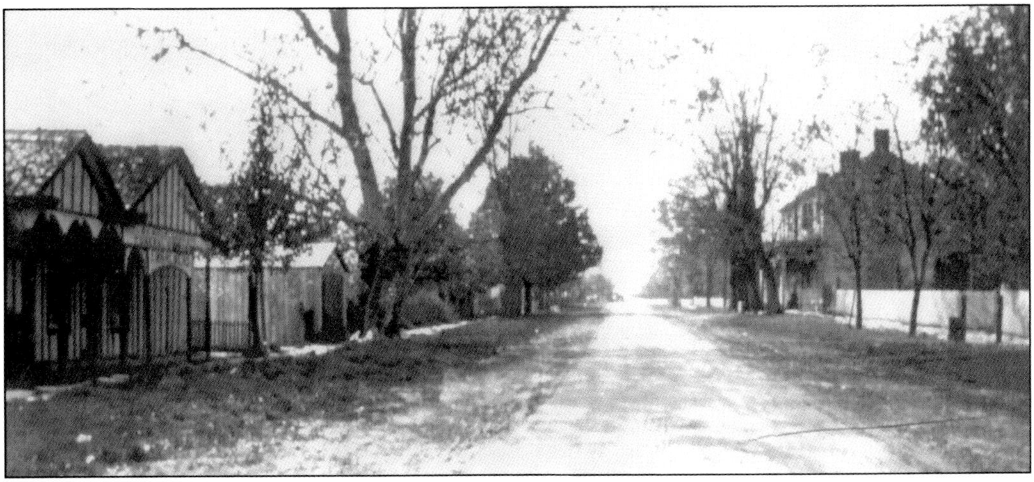

The unique buildings on the left are McFarland's undertaker shop and carriage house. Lucian Minor Parrish also made caskets in the shop. In its later years, it served as a small shop that carried everyday objects, such as magazines. Just behind these shops stood the John Wesley Harris/ Donahue house (not shown). Marion Burdette's garage is further on the left, and he was the first citizen in Mt. Washington to own an automobile, a Buick. In a few years, the McFarland Dodge dealership would be built just past Burdette's garage. The McFarland Funeral Home is on the right. (Courtesy of the Mt. Washington Historical Society.)

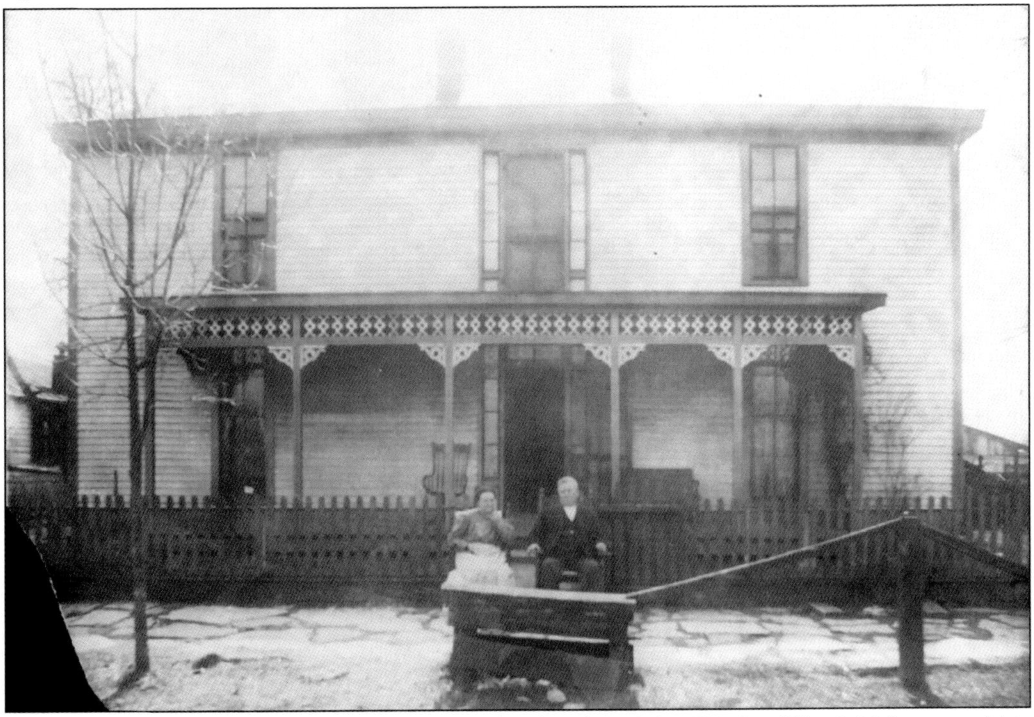

This home had an open door policy for much of its life. John Wesley "Shady" Harris and his wife, Mary Ann Miller, were cordial hosts for many of their neighbors and passersby along Main Street during the early 1900s. Frank and Martha Parrish continued that tradition in the 1920s with nearby family and friends. Many families moved in and out until the Donahue family took residence. (Courtesy of Stuart Tichenor.)

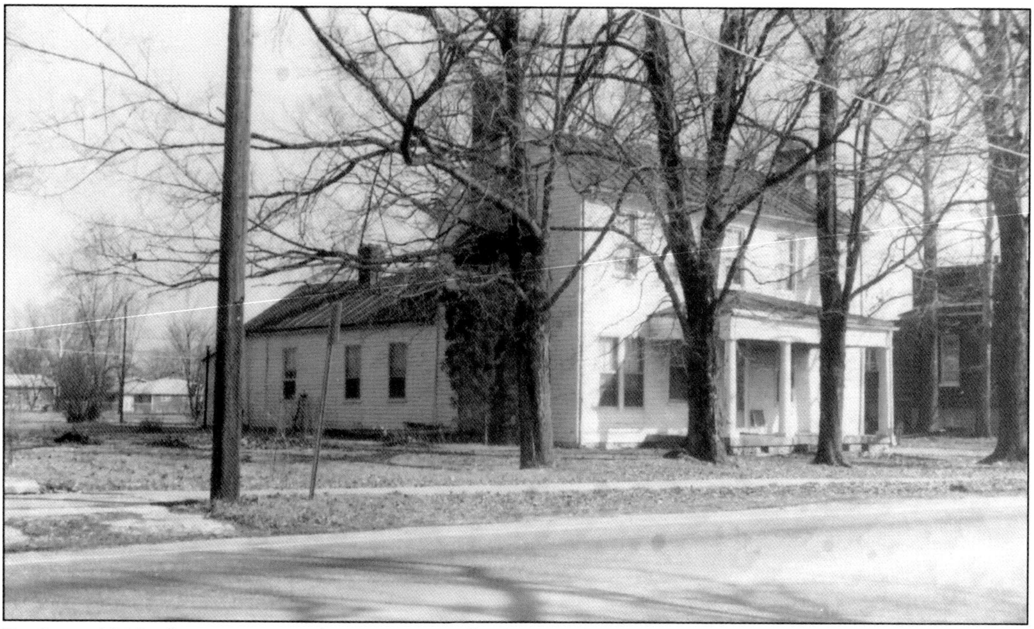

Built in 1840, this attractive home originally featured a two-story balcony with beautiful trim and woodworking that was replaced by a more modern porch with a concrete floor around 1920. Adam Milby, Quincey Hall, and Dr. W.H. Swearingen were just a few that lived there, but most will remember it as Horace and Edna McGee's home where numerous citizens learned to play a musical instrument with Edna's tutoring. (Courtesy of the Mt. Washington Historical Society.)

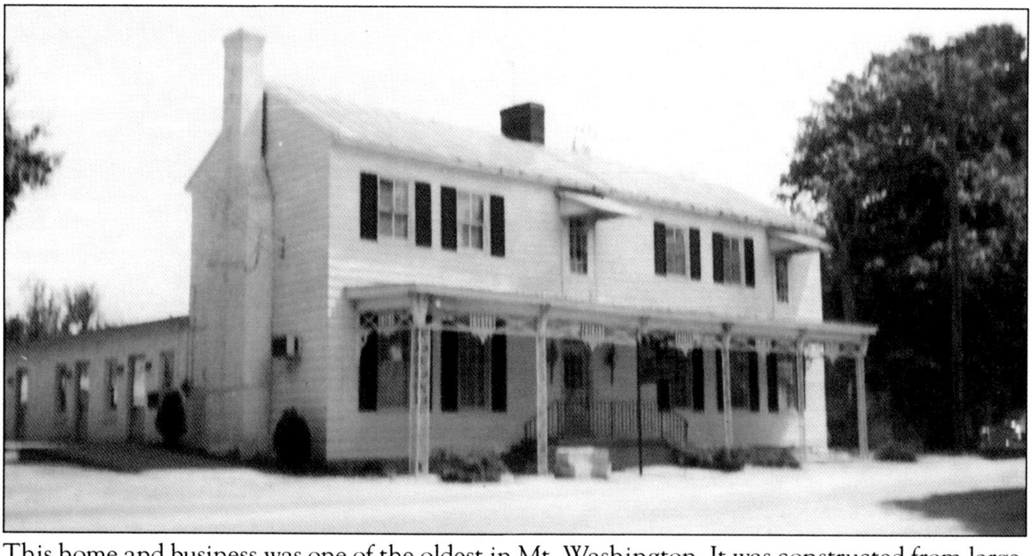

This home and business was one of the oldest in Mt. Washington. It was constructed from large, hand-hewn logs and featured a unique springhouse underneath the home. One of the earliest occupants was the Hamilton family, possibly related to future owner Sam Carothers's wife, Elizabeth Hamilton. Sam became involved in the funeral business and worked as an embalmer. His daughter Mary married W. Stanford McFarland, who turned part of the home into a funeral parlor. Thus began the McFarland Funeral Home. Their sons William H. and Sam continued the business, as did William's son Grigsby. The building was later converted to other businesses and apartments. (Courtesy of Gayle and Eleanor Troutman.)

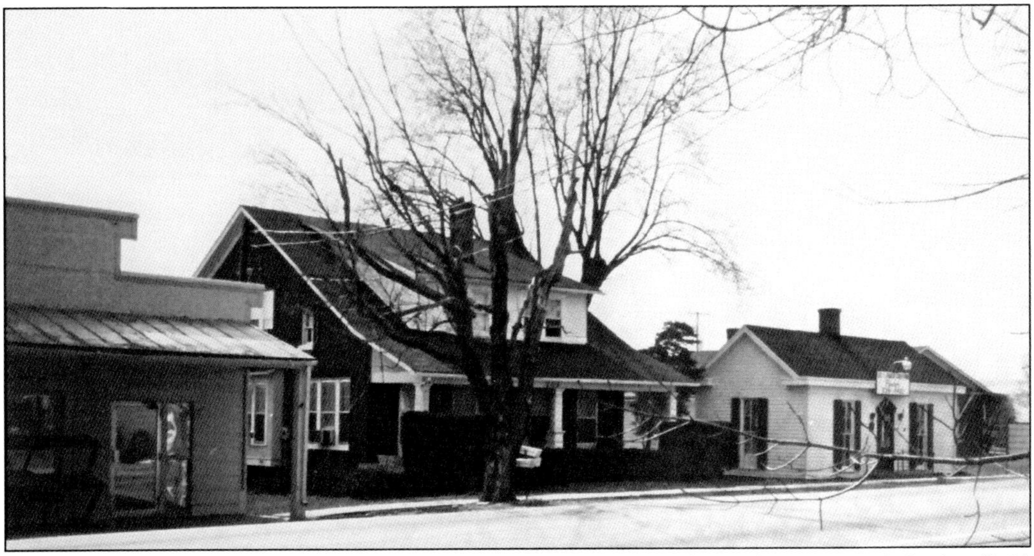

Across Main Street from the McFarland Funeral Home sits Stuyler and Leo Harris's duplex (left) and John S. Harris's home (right), which were built on property where the Kentucky Hotel once stood. Not much is known about the hotel, although it may have also been an all-female private school run by a Professor Brown, according to historian Statira Mathis. The hotel is marked on an 1847 map of the city, and accounts record that it burned before the Civil War. (Courtesy of Lloyd and Arbidella Dooley.)

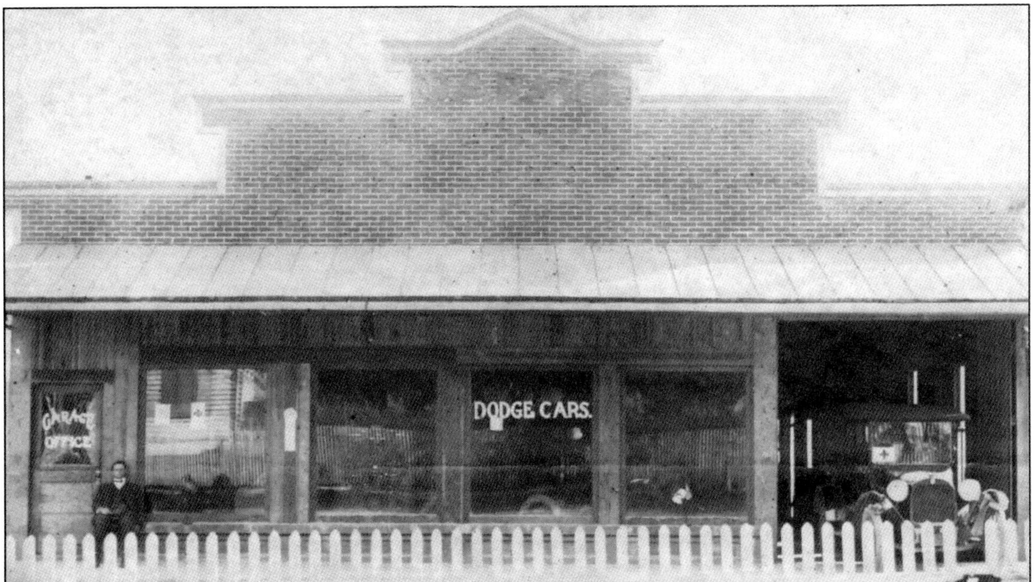

The first known auto dealership in Mt. Washington was owned and operated by William and Sam McFarland beginning in the 1910s. It was located across from their other business, the McFarland Funeral Home. Maynard Jasper leased it in the mid-1920s as a Hudson-Terraplane Dealership before Leo Harris leased it as an Essex dealership. The building housed several businesses afterwards, including The Sycamore Inn Restaurant and Phil Lockett's autobody repair business. It was best known as "the Fruit Stand," a grocery run by Sidney Griffin. (Courtesy of Gayle and Eleanor Troutman.)

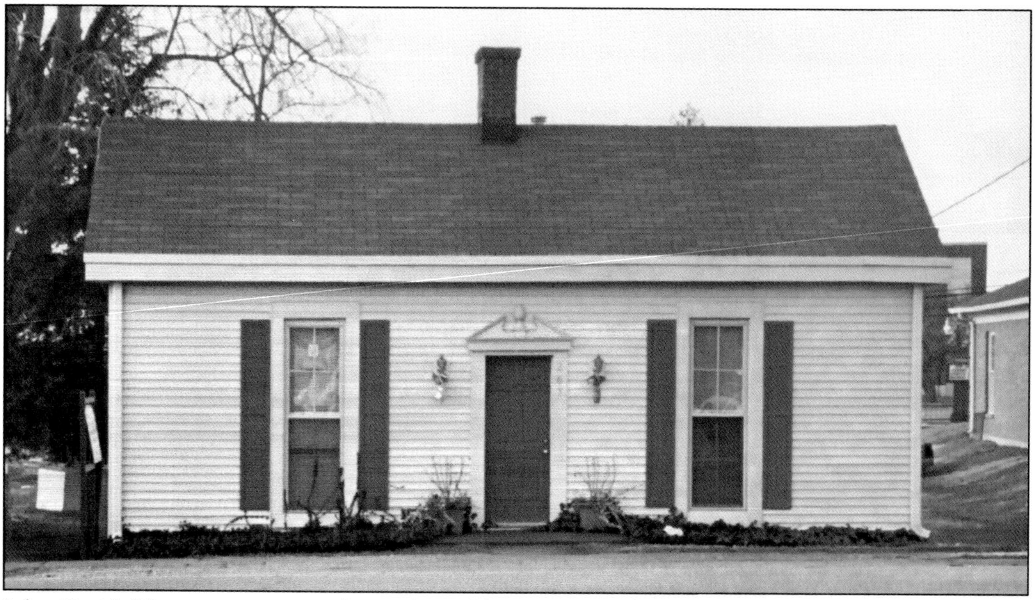

John Smith Harris, a carpenter by trade and longtime resident of Mt. Washington, lived in this home with his wife, Alice, and his daughter Birty. One afternoon in 1893, John took some family matters into his own hands. William Turner, a deputy sheriff, had made some unseemly remarks about the wife of one of John's cousins, and John nearly blew Turner's arm off with his shotgun. He was exonerated when it was discovered that Turner had his own gun drawn. (Courtesy of Lloyd and Arbidella Dooley.)

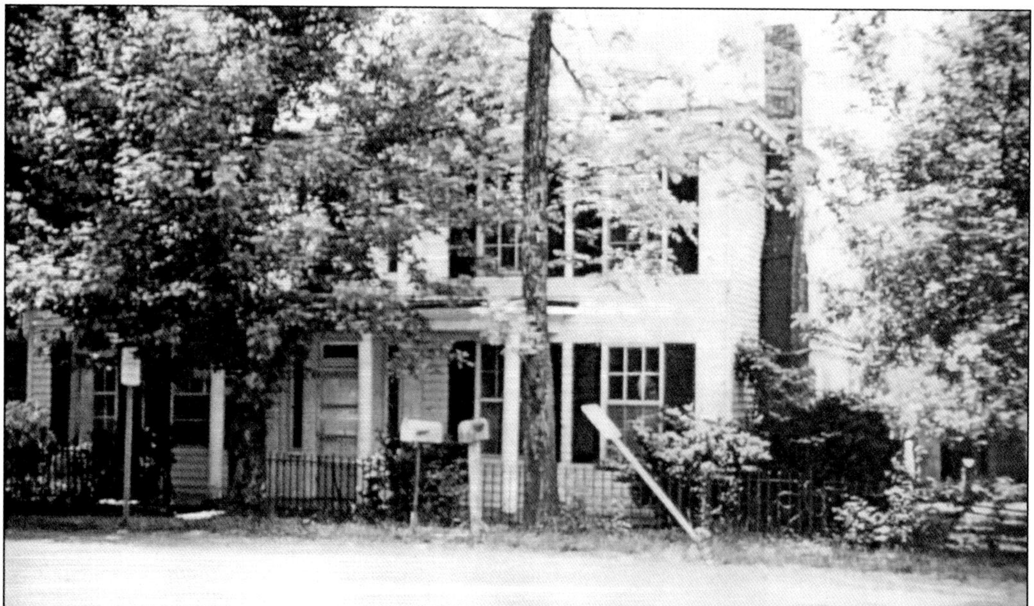

This picturesque home built in the Civil War era was once owned by S.T. Lloyd, a prominent landowner and farmer. His property and estate were auctioned in 1885, and Dr. H.F. Crenshaw bought the home and lived there until his death in 1905. Dr. Lloyd Settle came to Mt. Washington in that same year and bought the home to use as his office. He lived there until the mid-1940s. (Courtesy of the Mt. Washington Historical Society.)

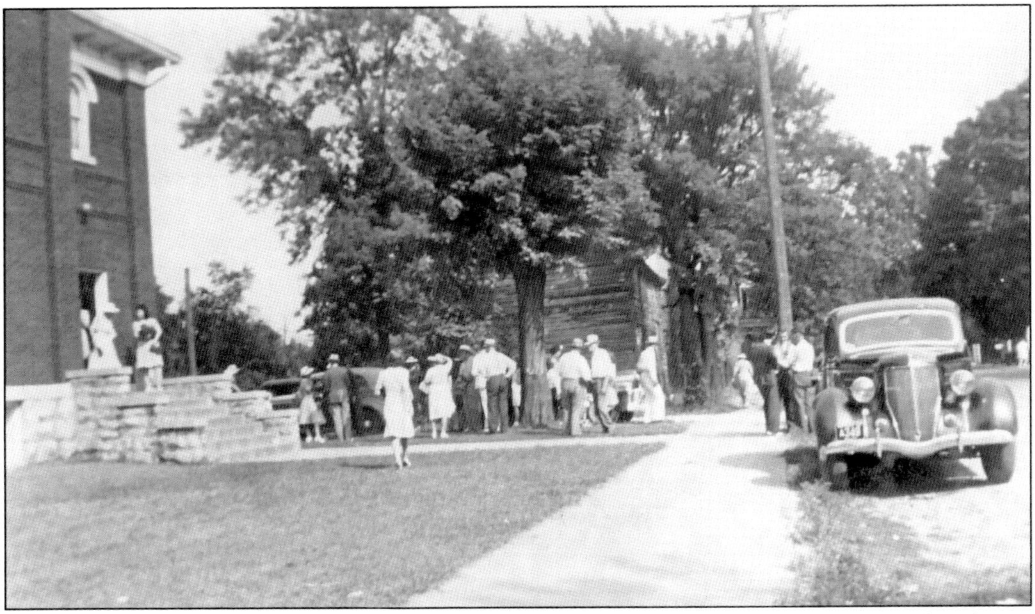

This street scene was captured in front of the Baptist church looking southeast. The church was commemorating its 100th anniversary in 1938. Just beyond the trees was the Squire Fidler/Lizzie Bridwell log cabin, one of the first structures erected in the city. (Courtesy of Mildred Brown.)

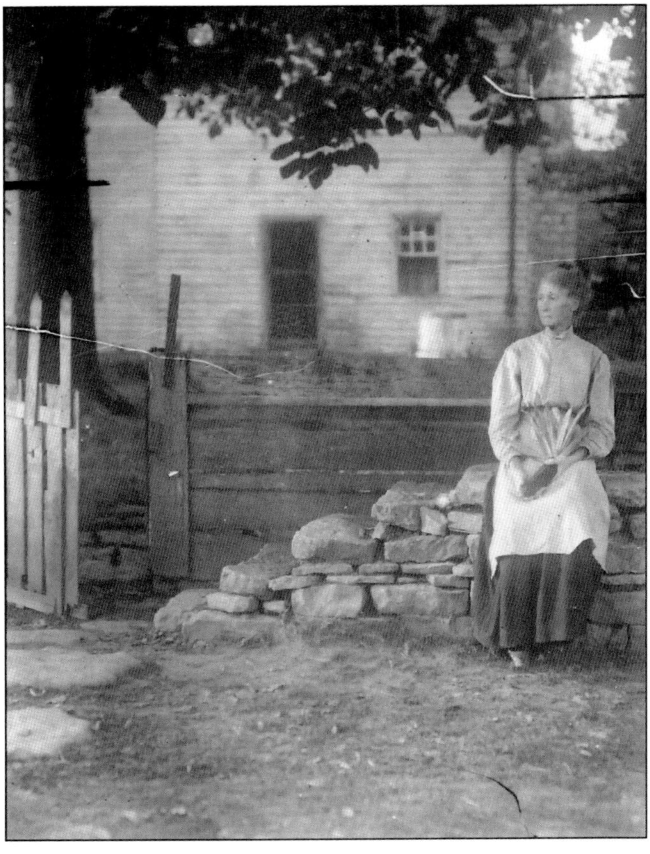

Pictured here is the first or one of the first houses built in Mt. Washington sometime in the late 1700s. This log cabin sat near Main Street and was once the home of Squire Fidler, who made Kentucky long rifles. After Squire moved to Indiana, a woman by the name of Elizabeth "Lizzie" Bridwell lived there from the late 1800s until the late 1930s. Several families lived there until the property was donated to the Lion's Club to build a park. The cabin was disassembled and rebuilt in Cherry Valley in Prospect, Kentucky. (Courtesy of the Mt. Washington Historical Society.)

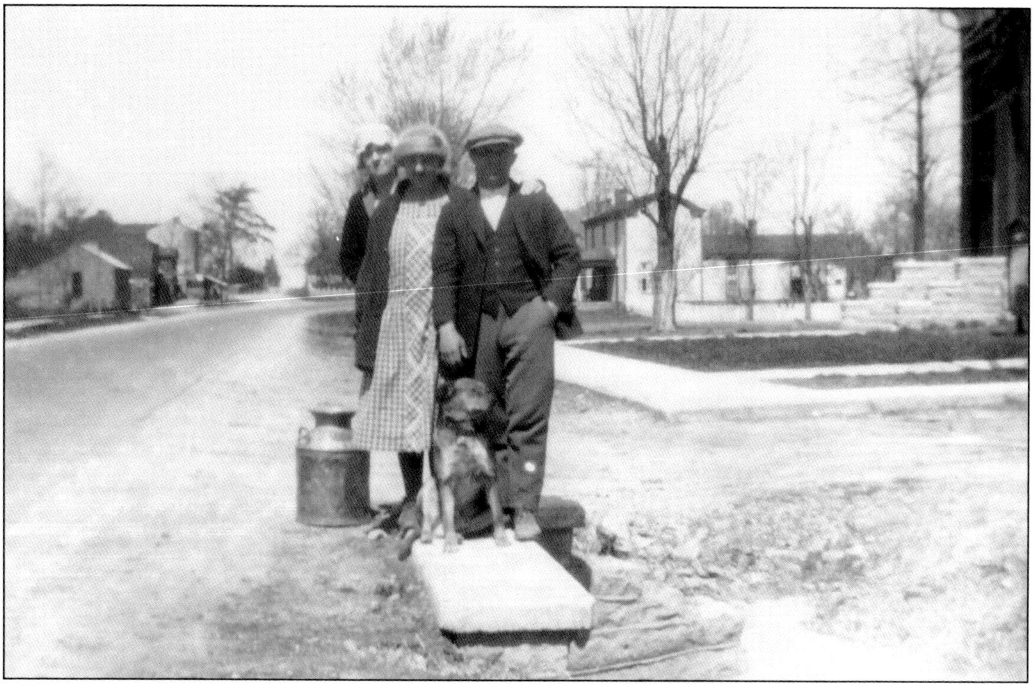

This threesome is bringing milk back from one of the creameries just north on Bardstown Road, a daily routine in those days. Looking north on Main Street from the Baptist church was a mix of small and large elaborate homes in addition to Fox's blacksmith shop at the corner of Main Street and Flatlick Road. Some of the town's finest citizens lived in this stretch at one time, including Bert Hall, William Threlkeld, and William P. Barnes. (Courtesy of Lloyd and Arbidella Dooley.)

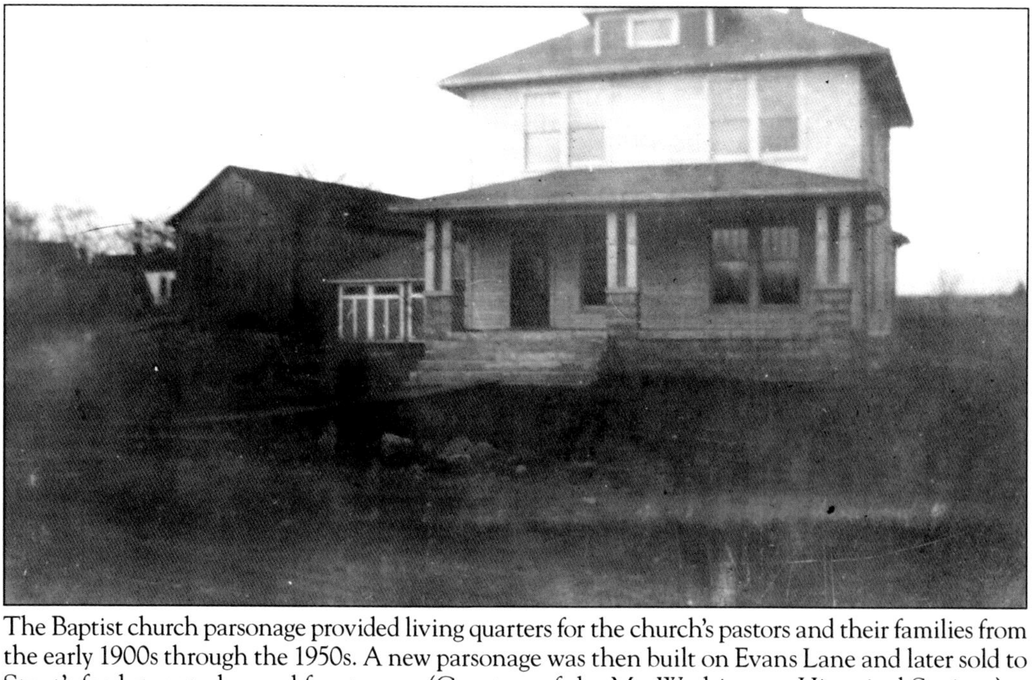

The Baptist church parsonage provided living quarters for the church's pastors and their families from the early 1900s through the 1950s. A new parsonage was then built on Evans Lane and later sold to Stout's feed store to be used for storage. (Courtesy of the Mt. Washington Historical Society.)

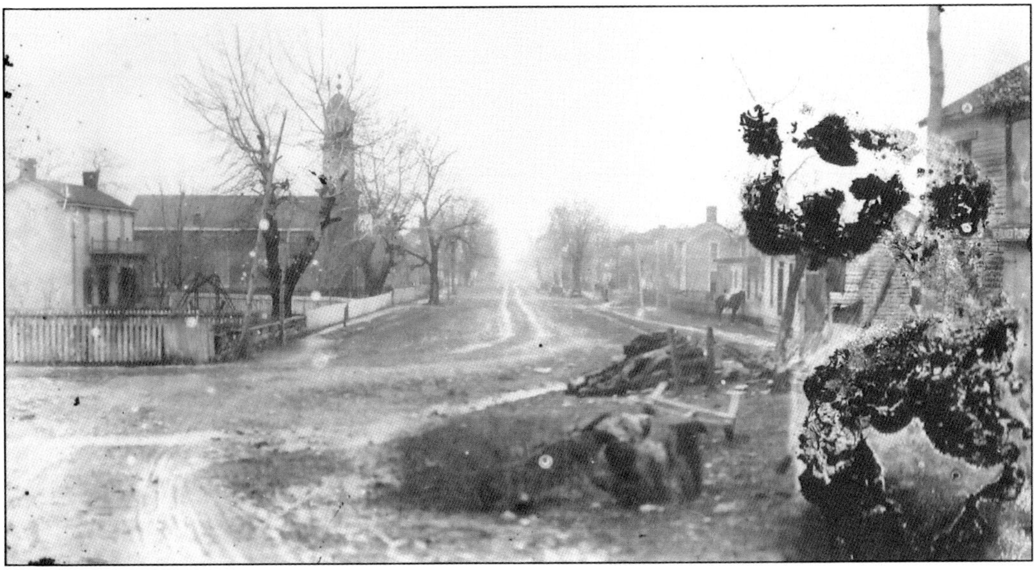

This c. 1905 photograph taken from Flatlick Road looking south down Main Street shows the John Showalter home on the left (which was also the former residence of teacher Ann Goodwin), followed by the Baptist Church. Directly on the right and only partially shown was the complex of William and Philip Fox's blacksmith and carriage shop. The next house on the right was the home of Dr. Collins, followed by the home that has the horse hitched in front of it where William Carothers and later W.P. Barnes resided. The two-story house following them with the unusual overhang was the home of John Gentry. (Courtesy of the Mt. Washington Historical Society.)

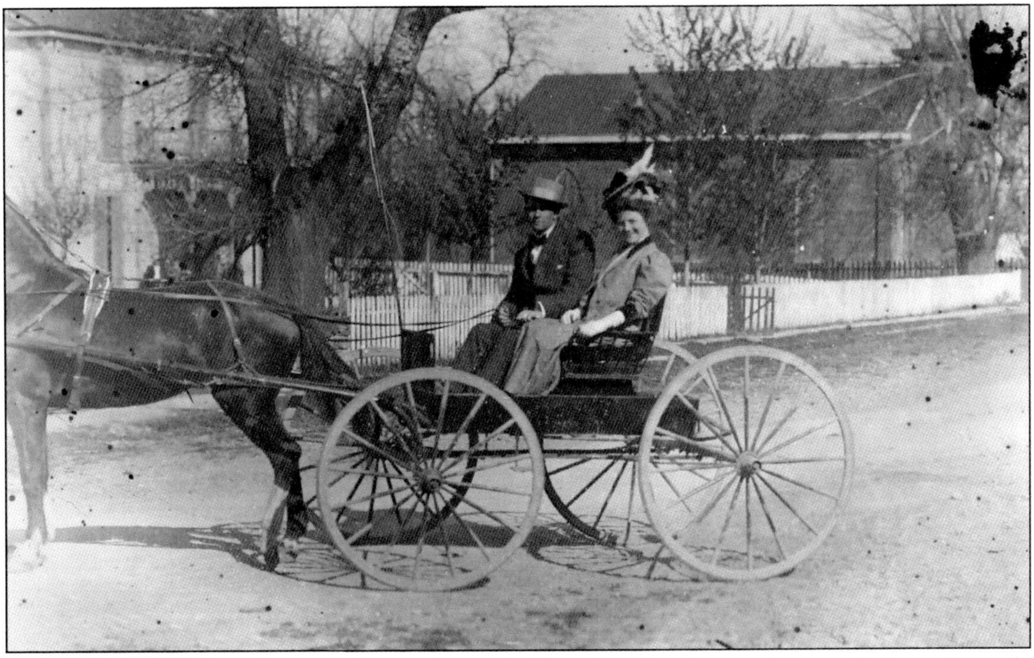

There is nothing like a buggy ride on a beautiful Sunday after church. This well-dressed couple is clearly enjoying themselves. The old Baptist church is in the background. It is likely that this carriage was built either by the Fox blacksmith shop behind them or down the street at Parrish's blacksmith shop. (Courtesy of the Mt. Washington Historical Society.)

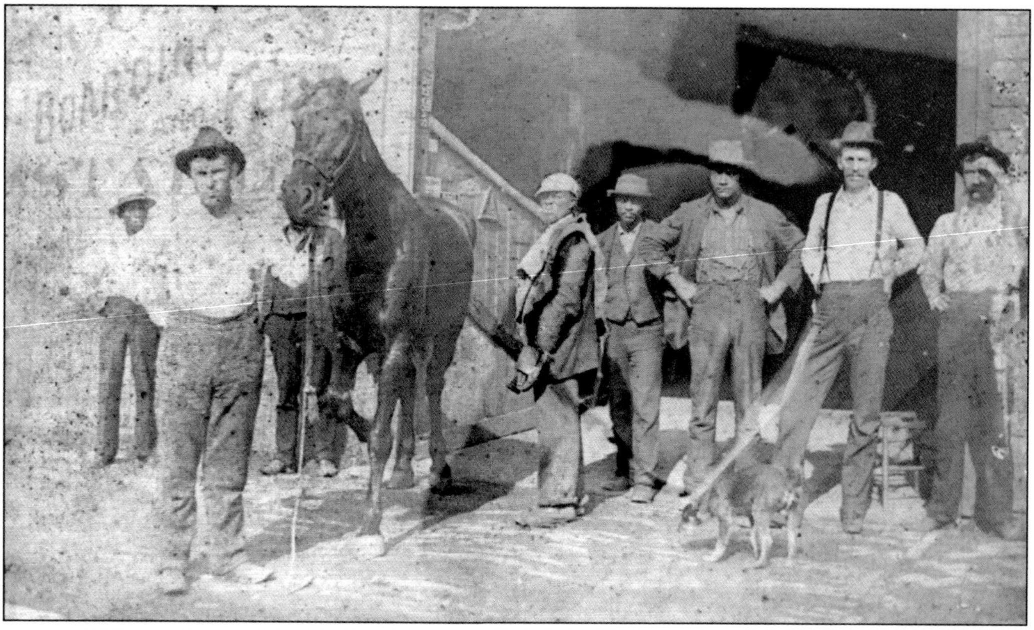

Around 1911, as the need for blacksmiths dwindled, John W. Long bought one of the Fox buildings at the corner of Main Street and Flatlick Road, opened a boarding stable for horses, and sold feed. John (right) was a member of the prominent Long family from Fairmount, near Fern Creek. As the blacksmith business waned, so did the heyday of the horse and buggy. John sold the business in 1920 and moved to Louisville. (Courtesy of Chris Rothman.)

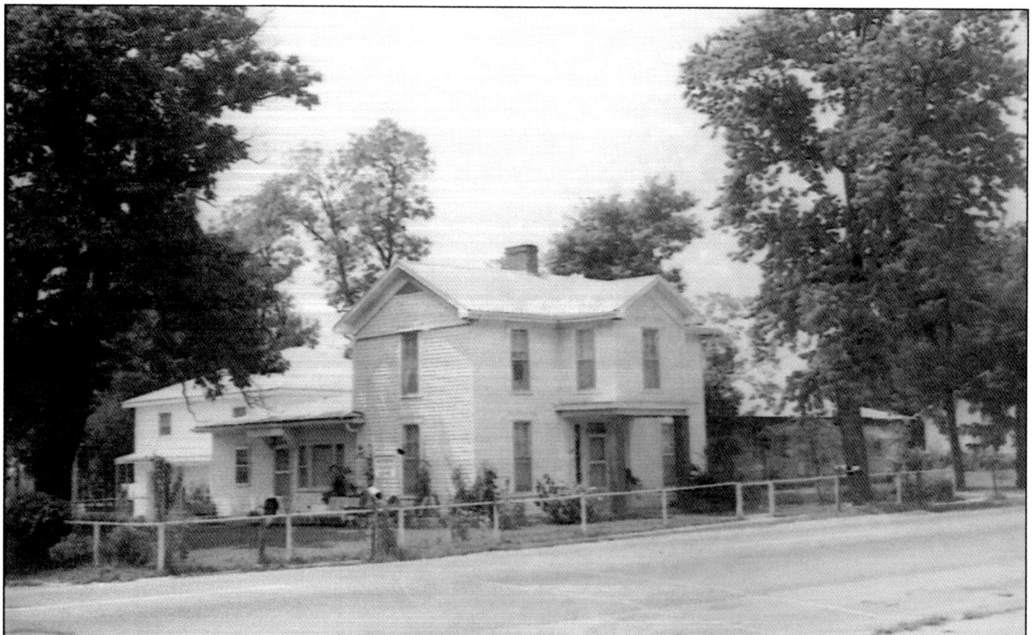

This home was occupied by John Gentry during the early-to-middle-1900s. Built prior to 1900, it featured an overhanging second-story room on the front of the house. The Ridgeway family lived there also, before Leon Coulter and family moved in sometime during the 1960s and opened a small restaurant and ice cream business in the rear. (Courtesy of Carolyn Quebbeman.)

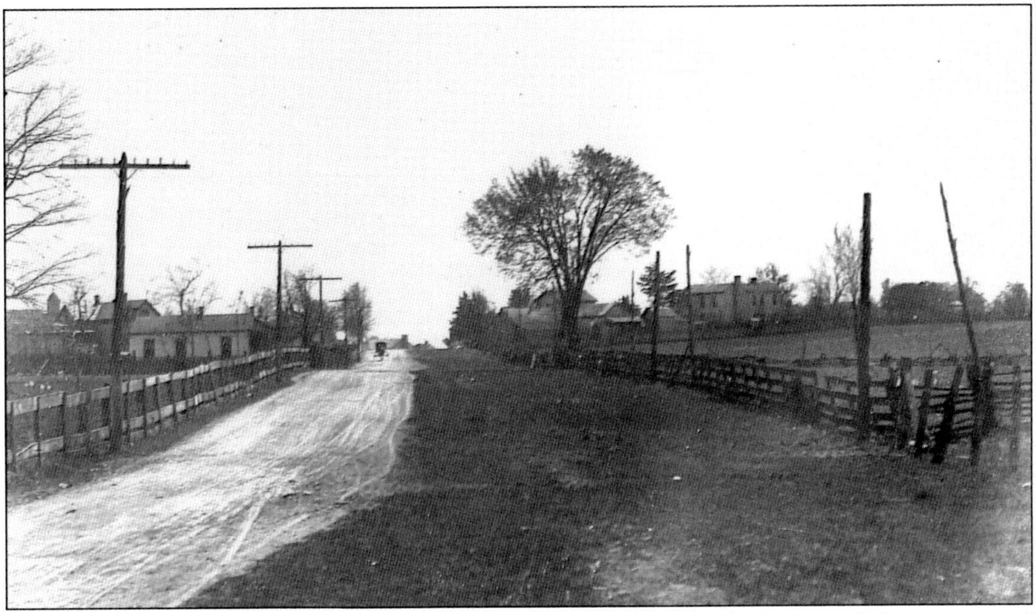

This rare c. 1905 scene on North Main Street near Fairlane Drive looks toward the junction of Main Street and Flatlick Road. On the left is William Crenshaw's home. Others are too difficult to identify, but visible well in the distance to the left is the steeple of the Baptist church. Only farmland is to the right until Flatlick Road, where there is a complex of houses and barns. One house would be W.P. Wigginton's home, facing Main Street, which had an attractive stone fence in front of it. By 1927, Wiggington's son Hubert built a grocery next to the home. Somewhere in this area, there was a Baptist church for blacks. The large home in the background on the right is the pre–Civil War Grigsby/Barnes/Fisher home. (Courtesy of the Mt. Washington Historical Society.)

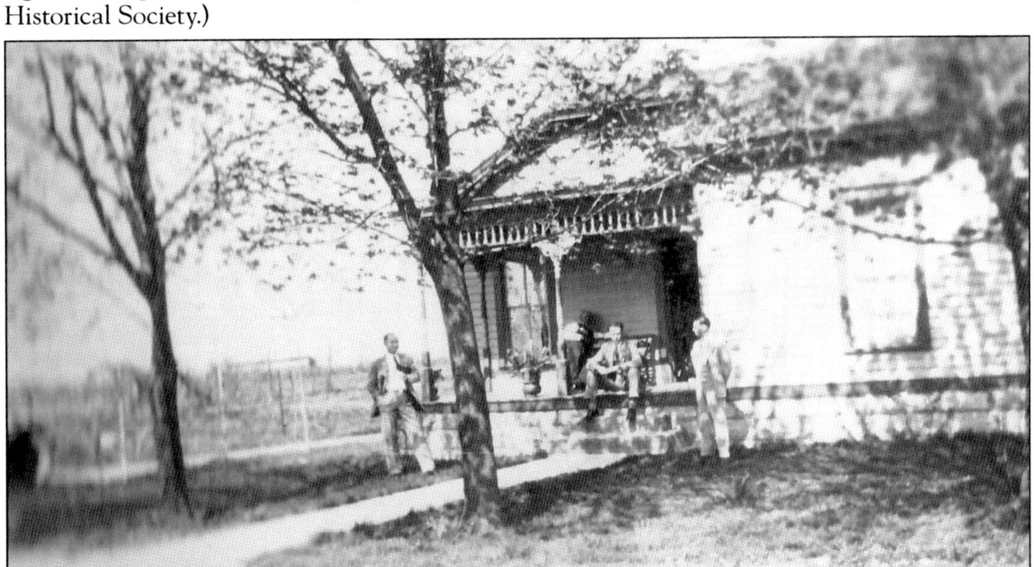

William Edward and Arzula Crenshaw lived in this home on North Main Street until Arzula's death in 1925. At the time, it was the only house on that side of the street until the Threlkeld mansion. Haskall Deacon owned the house in the 1950s and may have been related to Crenshaw. Both Crenshaw's brother and Deacon had a son named Coleman. (Courtesy of Stuart Tichenor.)

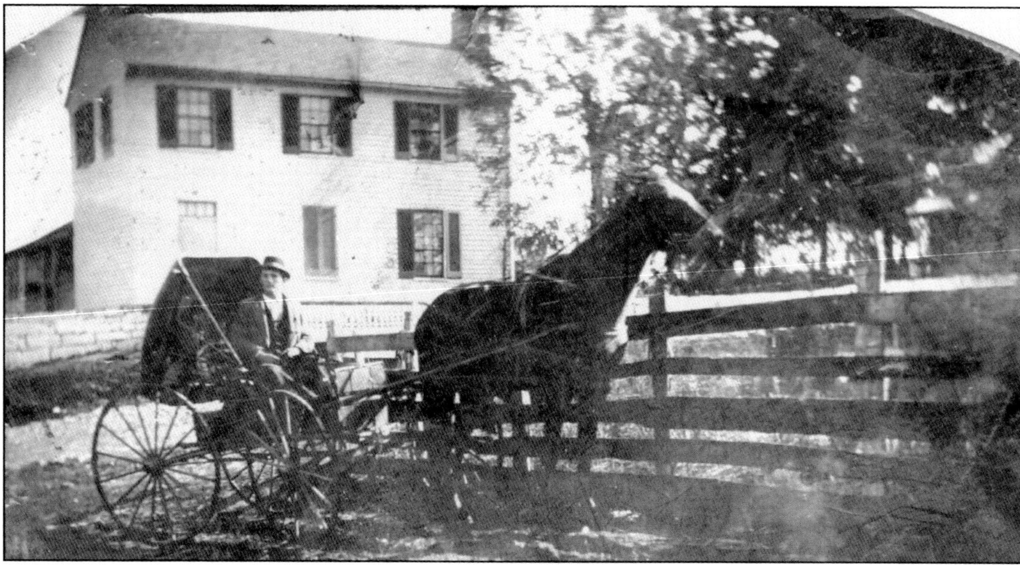

One of the most prominent and well-known historical homes in Mt. Washington is the Grigsby/ Barnes/Fisher Home at the junction of Main Street and Flatlick Road, which was called Manslick Road when the house was built in the early 1800s. Obed Swearingen owned the property, which was then purchased by James Calvin Grigsby in 1861. James's daughter Lula married Almer Barnes and they resided there; their daughter Bernice married J. Edgar Fisher and made it their residence also. Edgar's daughter Joy still lives there, making for over 154 years of the same family's ownership and occupation. (Courtesy of Leda Barnes.)

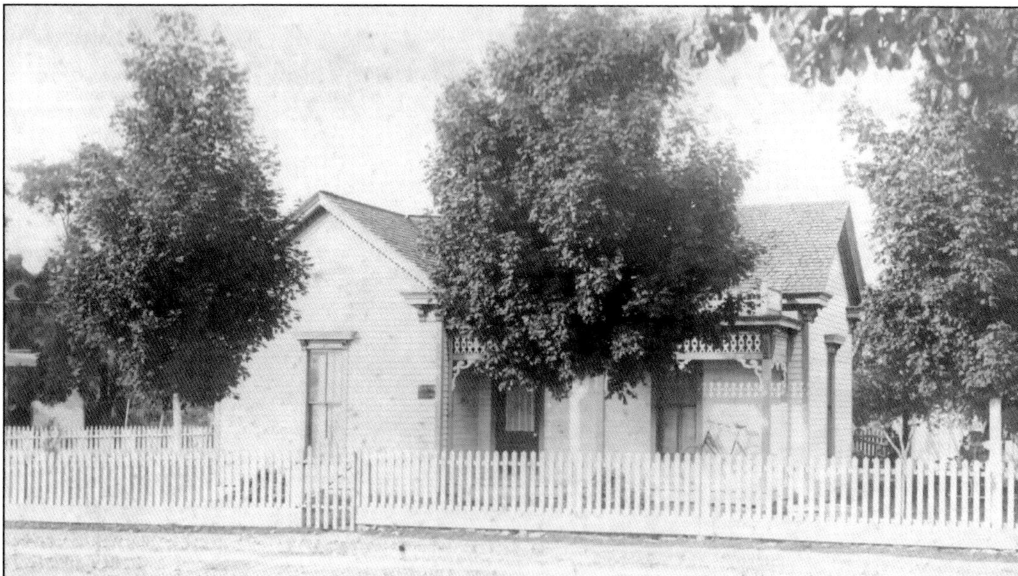

Dr. William W. Coleman with his wife, Viola, and children lived in this home located across from Flatlick Road on Main Street. He also owned property that was later developed by James Coleman into a subdivision, which he named for himself. The land was previously referred to as the Coleman Woods, which included a few ponds that earned the area the nickname "Frogtown." The Coleman home was replaced by a Standard Station in the 1950s, and many of Dr. Coleman's descendants continue to live in the community. (Courtesy of Donny and Josh Coleman.)

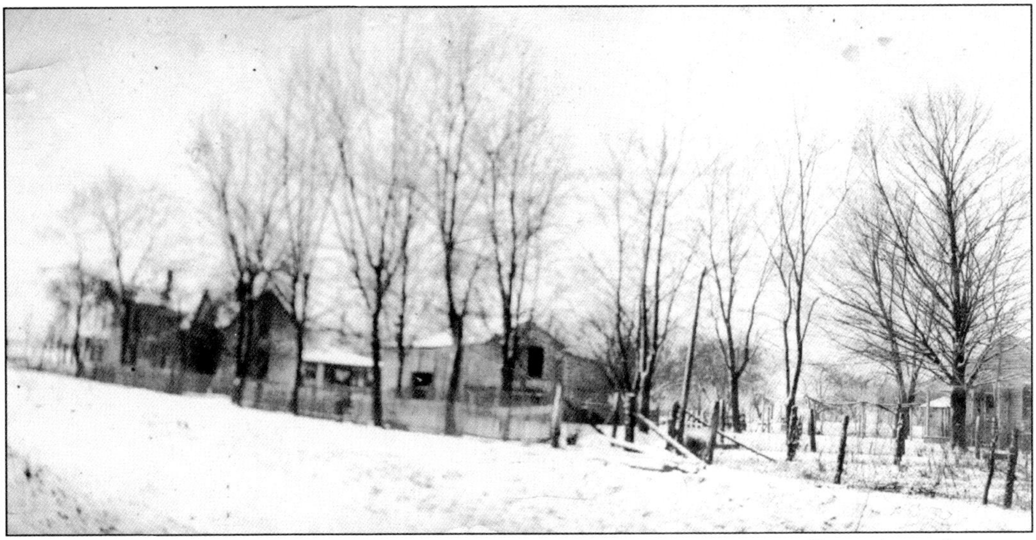

Pictured here around 1925 is Frogtown, so named due to the many small ponds in the area. On the right was Charlie Long's home and farm. Next would be William Levi Harris's farm; he moved from his grand home on Stringer Lane around 1907. The next home belonged to Frank Carrithers Porter and is followed by the home of Hubert Wigginton. Not pictured, but to the left is the mansion that William Threlkeld built in 1876. (Courtesy of Leda Barnes.)

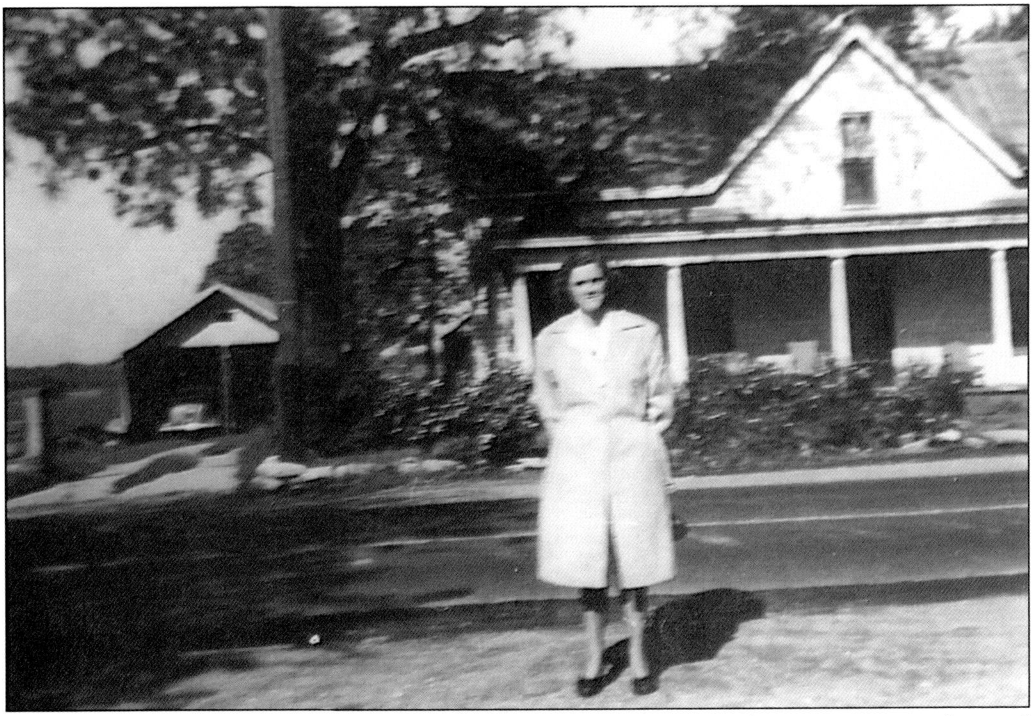

William Levi Harris sold the Harris homestead on Stringer Lane to his son Wayne and moved into this home on North Main Street around 1907. It included a large farm that stretched to Flatlick Road and featured a dairy along with numerous other barns and buildings. Harris died in 1914, and John Goins bought the home a few years later and lived there until 1939. The farm was then sold to Ernest Lee Ryan Sr. (Courtesy of Leda Barnes.)

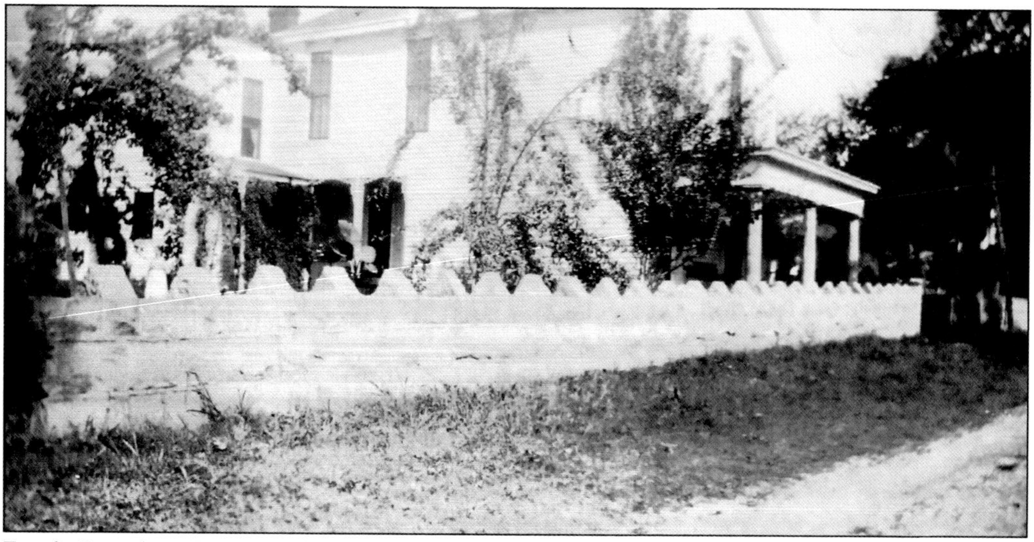

Frank Carrithers Porter and his wife, Fannie, moved from their home located in Sugar Valley to this magnificent home on North Street in Frogtown. The massive house featured 13 rooms, seven porches, and two staircases. The couple's sons became prominent merchants, farmers, and landowners. Their son Clarence became the owner and proprietor of the Cyclone store. (Courtesy of Louise Porter.)

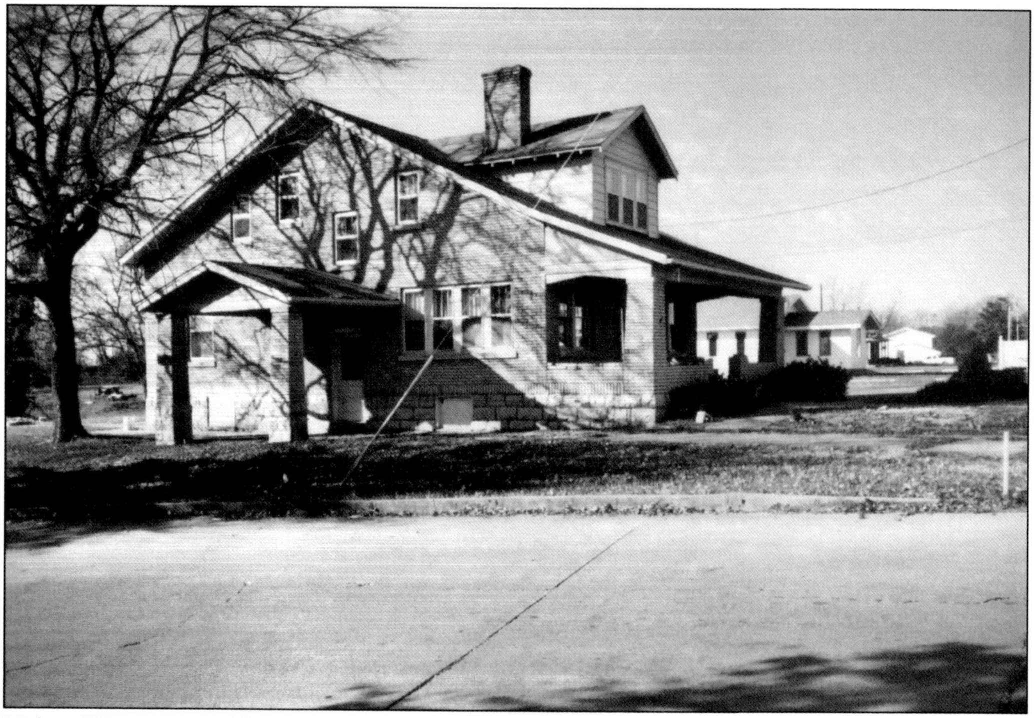

Hubert Wigginton and his wife, "Lizzie," lived in this 1920s-style home, possibly built by Wigginton's close relative Clarence Porter. Hubert was known by everyone, as he worked in the retail and grocery business in Mt. Washington from the early 1900s until his death in 1969. His son Lindsay continued to run the business for several more years. The Lion's Club bought the house and dedicated it to J.E. Fisher for meetings and fundraisers. (Courtesy of Jimmy Breeden.)

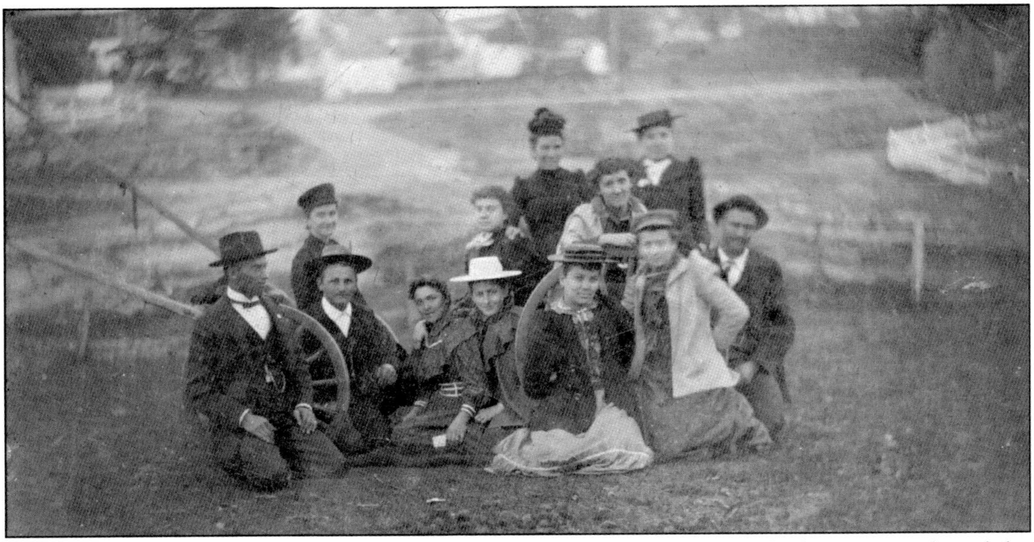

This view from atop "Kitten Ridge" from the late 1800s looks east towards the Crossroads and the South Main Street area. Marshall Collier's mill site would be just to the left before he erected a building that would have been below this group of people. Pictured here crouching behind the plow is Maurice A. Harris. Many historical buildings can be seen faintly in the background, including the Cyclone store, John T. Harris home, and the Lloyd House. (Courtesy of Stuart Tichenor.)

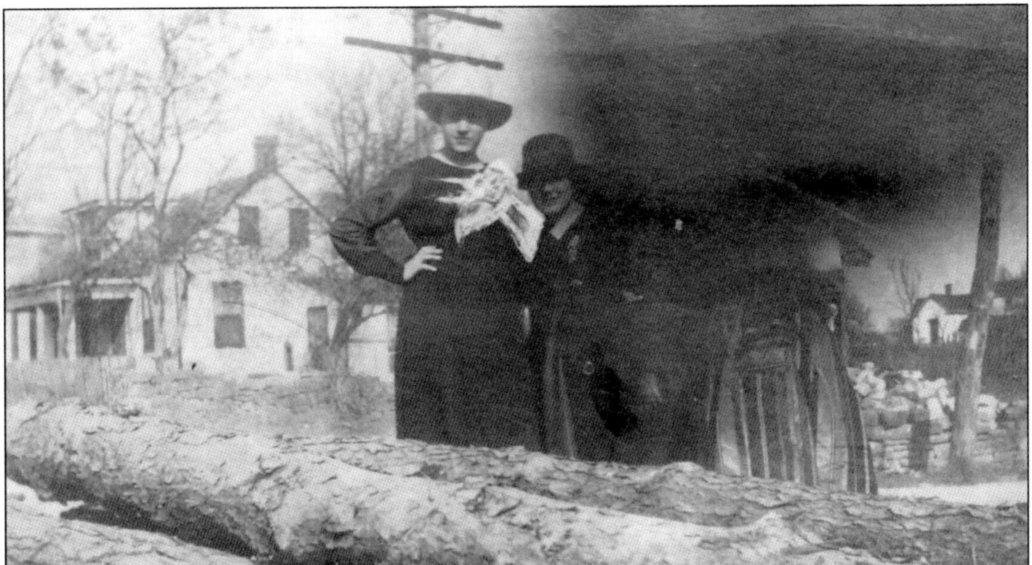

The home of John T. and Catherine "Kate" (Wise) Harris was built around 1855. John left to prospect in Colorado about 1858 and made a substantial amount of money when he disappeared suddenly and was never heard from again. His wife and three children, John Smith Harris (a well-known carpenter), Robert (later a respected medical physician in New Albany, Indiana), and Ruth continued to live in the house. Ruth married Lewis "Lucy" Harris and lived in the home with their two sons, Stuyler (a prominent historian), and Leo. In the 1940s, well-known grocer Thurston Long owned the Harris home. (Courtesy of Lynn Martin.)

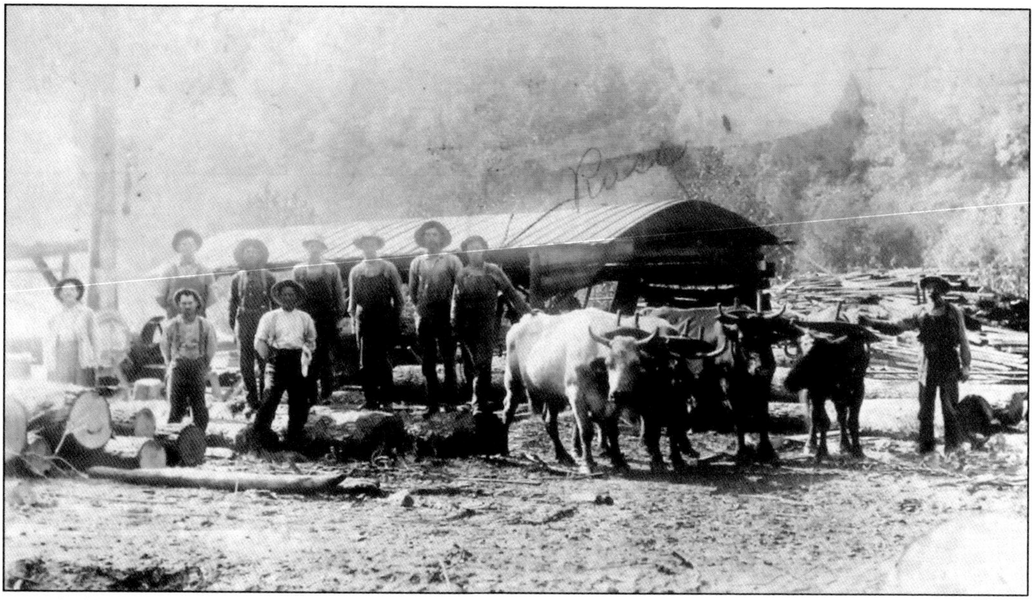

Marshall Collier ran a sawmill at the corner of Highway 44 and Water Street from the late 1800s to 1946. Virtually all of the homes and furniture built in Mt. Washington between 1880 and 1920 used lumber from his mill. Shortly before he sold the business to Robert "Eggy" Bridwell, he turned it into a gristmill for grain. The area was a hotbed for industry in the 1800s due to the abundance of water from underground springs. Before electricity was available the mill was run by steam power. (Courtesy of the Mt. Washington Historical Society.)

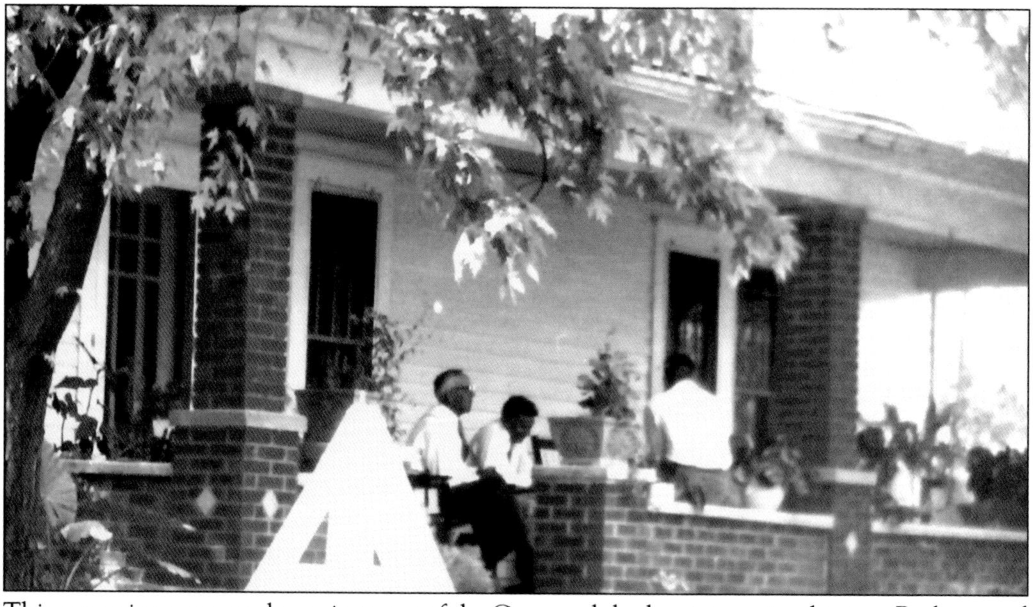

This attractive two-story home just west of the Crossroads had an interesting history. Built around 1920, it was owned by Susie Swearingen, but she never lived in it. She may have had it built to lease rooms as it was divided into apartments; local teachers were the most common tenants including Lindsay Jones and his wife, Ann. It was sold to Bluford Crenshaw who also never lived there, then passed to his son-in-law Tom Porter who resided there with his wife, Lora, and family for many years. (Courtesy of Louise Cornell.)

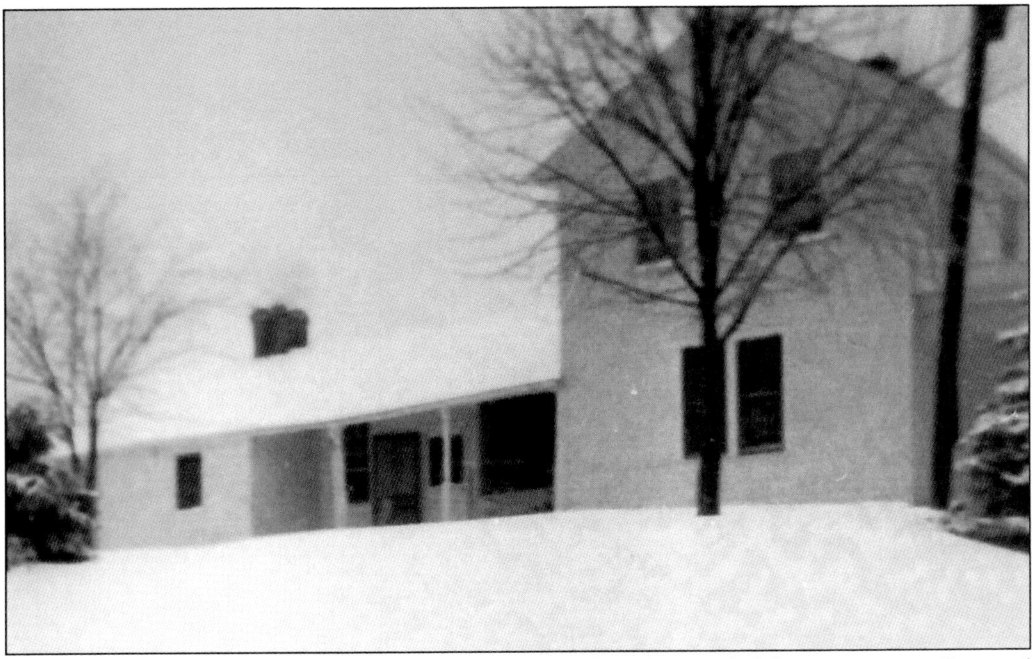

This was the home of Judge Robert "Bob" McAfee where he resided for many years. Situated on Kitten Ridge, it was a dominant house to the smaller homes nearby that were occupied by members of the Harris and Parrish families. Bob was married to Mabel Harris, who grew up near there. The home has had many modifications, including the relocation of the front door to the side due to the widening of Highway 44. It is only a few steps from the front door to the road. (Courtesy of Leda Barnes.)

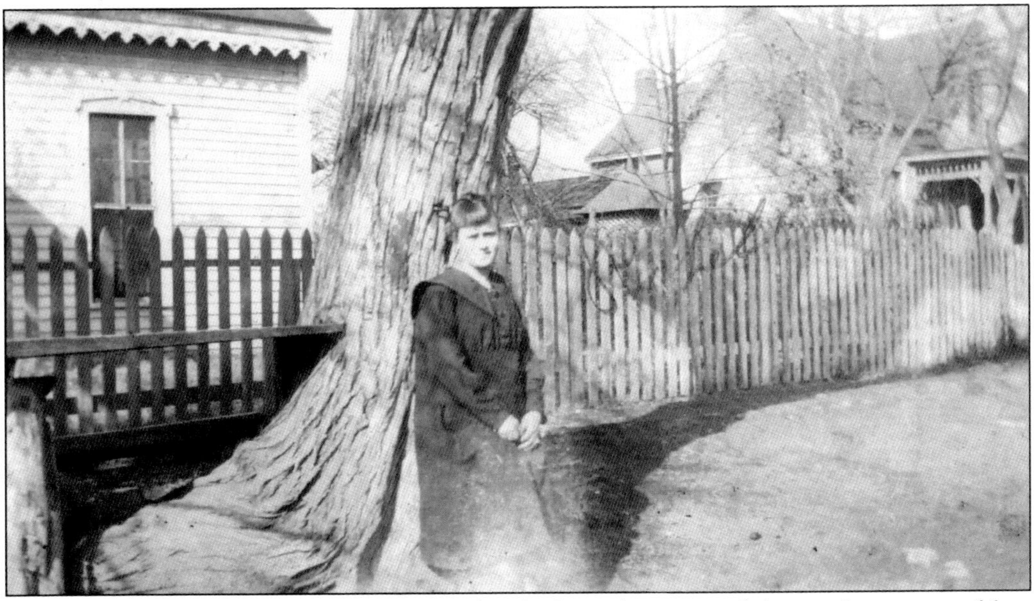

The home on the right with intricate woodwork along the eves and the porch was one of four pre–Civil War homes just west of the Crossroads on Highway 44. Guy Goins and family lived in the home in the early-to-mid-1900s. He drove a school bus for the Mt. Washington High School for several years. (Courtesy of Leda Barnes.)

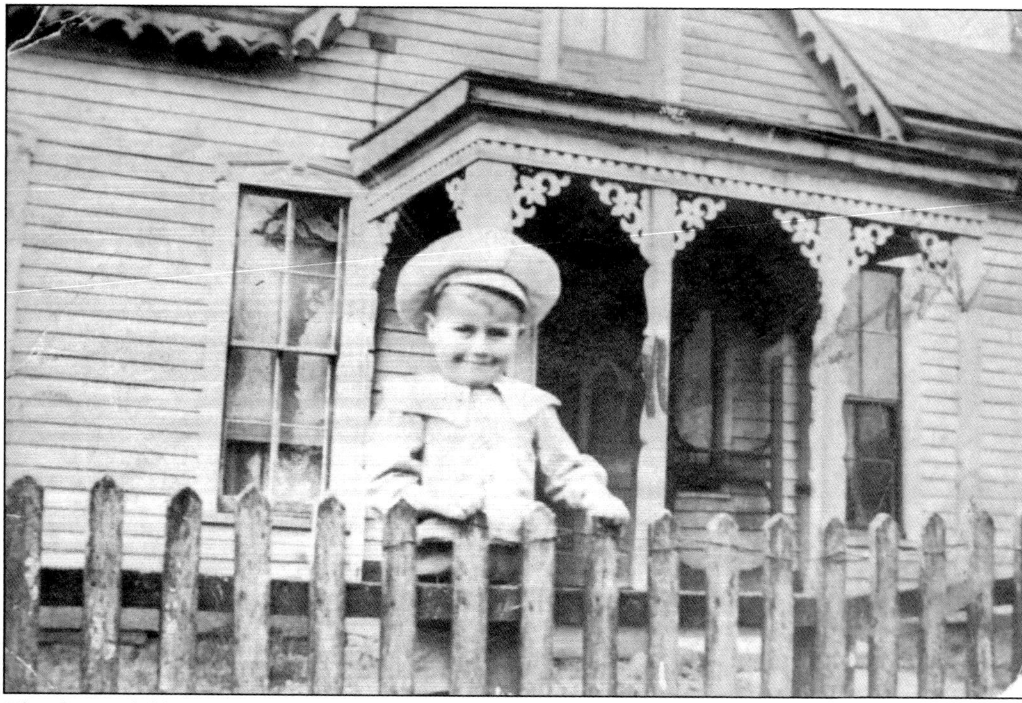

This beautiful home just west of the Crossroads predates the Civil War and was occupied by a very special man, Lucian Minor Parrish, and his wife, Mary (Shoptaugh) Parrish. They had several children that became important members of the community. Lucian was a furniture maker but his main occupation was making hundreds of caskets. Vernon Dickey bought the home after Mary passed away in 1920. Then his daughter Elizabeth married W.A. Lutes and they resided there for many years. Lutes's grandson Chad Jones and family live there at present, keeping the house in the family's possession for over 90 years. (Courtesy of Leda Barnes.)

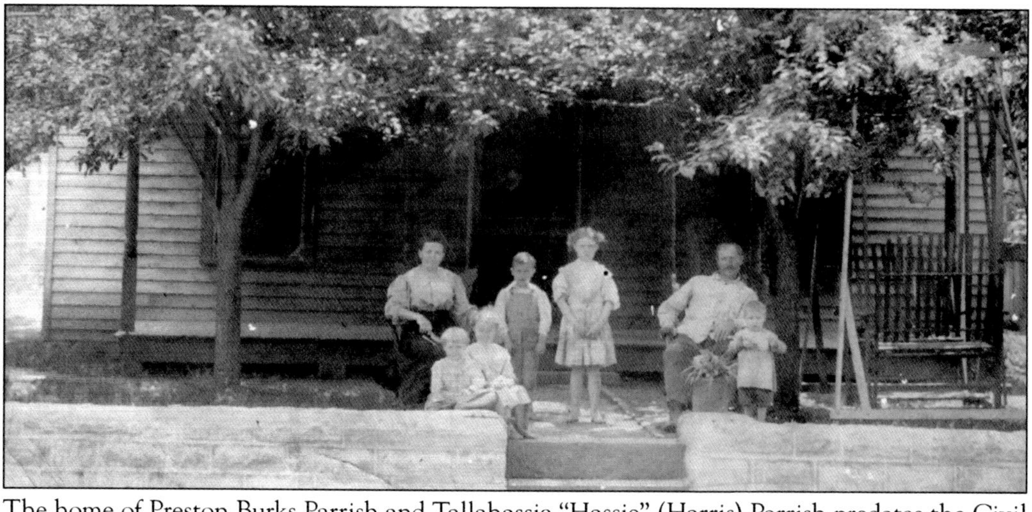

The home of Preston Burks Parrish and Tallahassie "Hassie" (Harris) Parrish predates the Civil War. The floor joists were planed logs from poplar trees, which were resistant to termites and bugs. Still standing, the little home was in a community of Parrishes and Harrises. Preston was a jack-of-all-trades skilled at painting, tinning, and barbering. He was a constable of Mt. Washington, and his barbershop was located in Maccabee Hall. (Courtesy of Leda Barnes.)

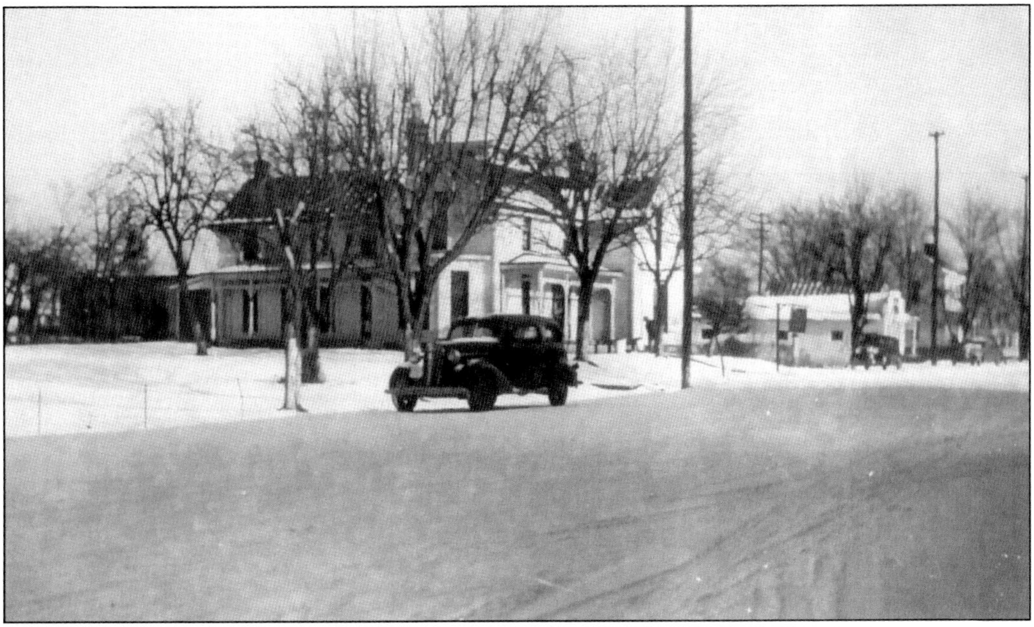

Looking down the left hand side of south Main Street during the 1940s reveals there were quite a few homes and businesses on that stretch. The Maccabee Hall would have been directly to the photographer's left with Henry Biven's home and Garner Dooley's tavern just past it. Myrtle Hall's little home can be seen with the Lloyd House in the distance. (Courtesy of the Mt. Washington Historical Society.)

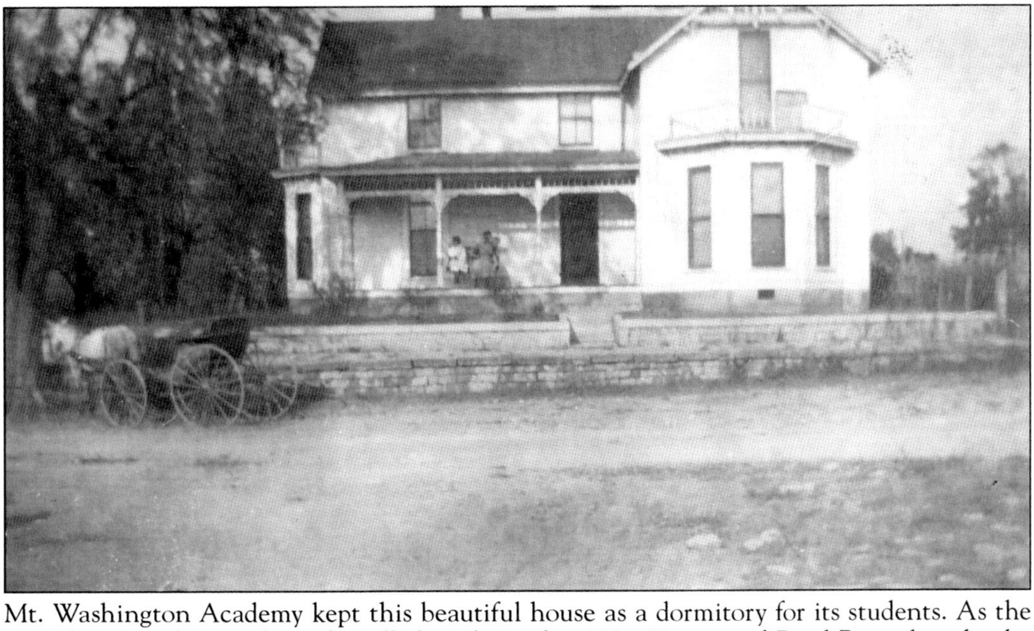

Mt. Washington Academy kept this beautiful house as a dormitory for its students. As the attendance at the Academy dwindled in the early 1900s, Henry and Pearl Biven bought the home and lived there for numerous years. A front room was leased to Dr. E.N. Rush, a dentist. Former Mt. Washington High School principal William Anderson bought the home, and it was later sold to Marvin Porter and torn down for his Chevrolet dealership expansion. (Courtesy of the Mt. Washington Historical Society.)

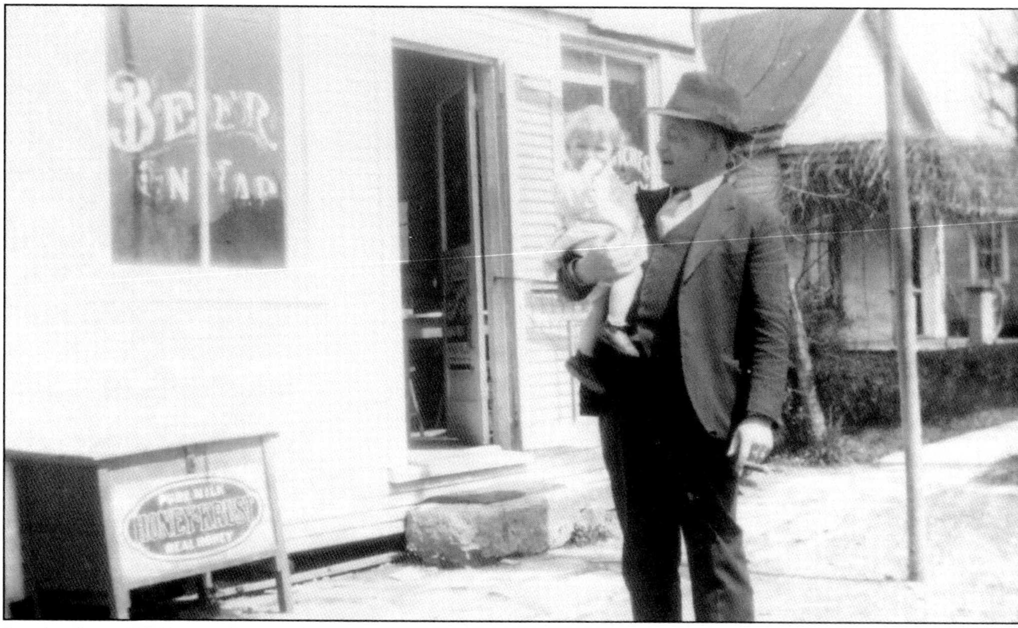

In the late 1930s to the mid-1940s, Garner Dooley ran a small tavern near his home on South Main Street. It was a popular watering hole for many of the locals and offered 3.2 beer, a watered-down optioned designed to prevent overindulging. Behind the pub was Mt. Washington's first illuminated croquet court, an extremely popular activity at the time. Pictured is Dr. George B. Hill with one of Garner's daughters he delivered. (Courtesy of Lloyd and Arbidella Dooley.)

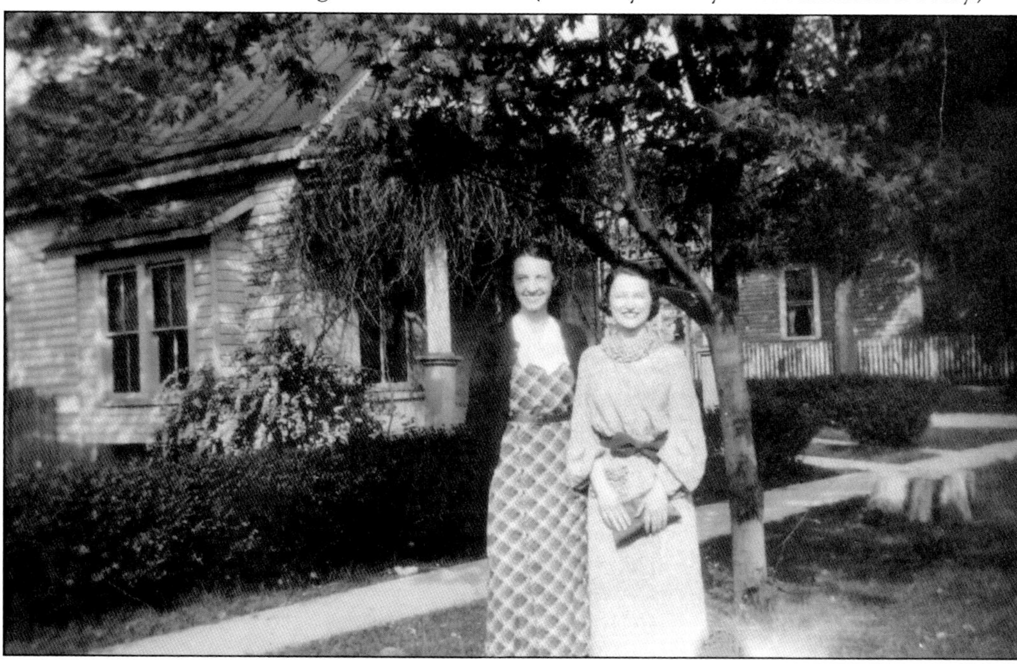

This was the first home of Garner and Bertha Dooley where their first child, Betty Jane, was born. Myrtle Hall, a widow, resided there for many years. Later, Marvin Porter bought the property, and his wife, Ruth, ran an antiques business from the home. The two ladies in the photograph were schoolteachers, one being Sarah Davidson (at right). (Courtesy of Lloyd and Arbidella Dooley.)

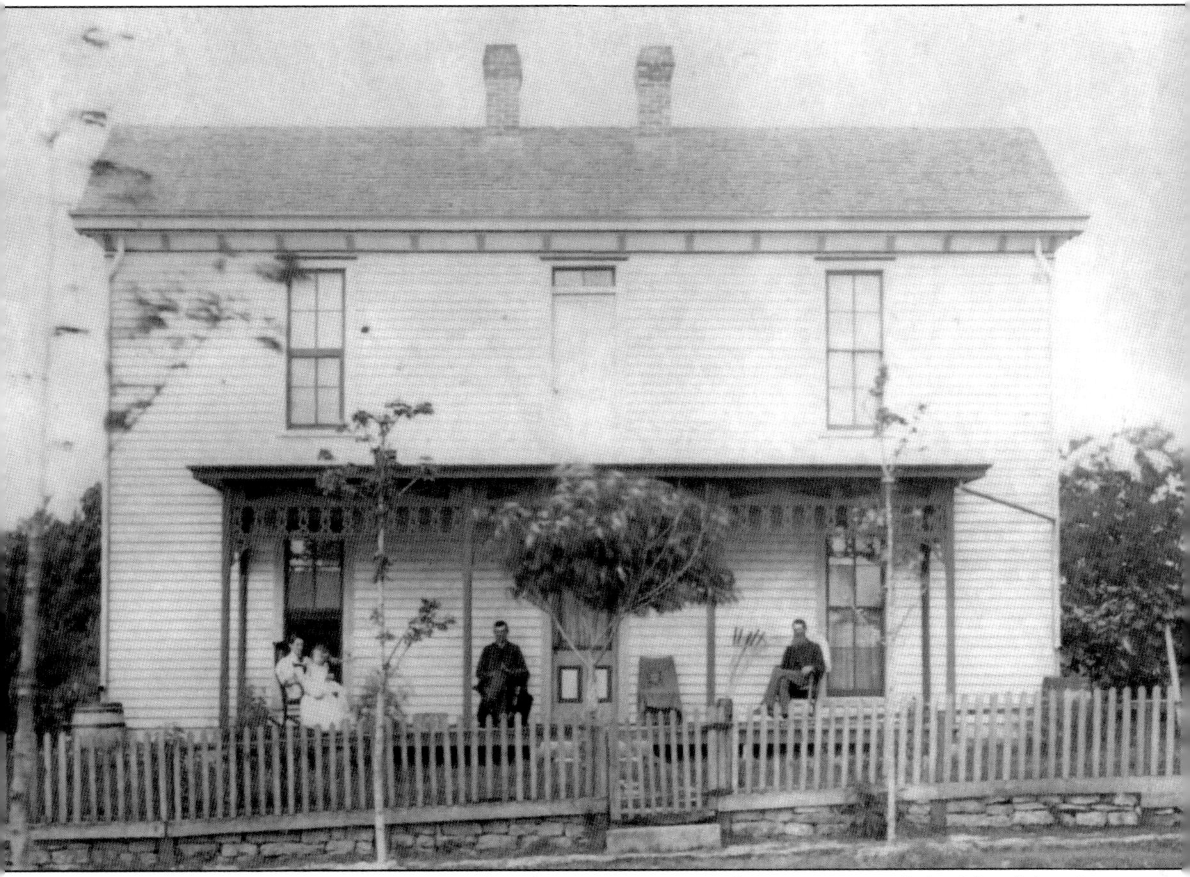

James Lloyd built this home for his family in 1880. Several generations of the Lloyd family, including the Dooley and Rothman families, resided there. Kenneth Lutes donated the house to the Mt. Washington Historical Society in honor of his wife, Anita, in 1989. The house was added to the National Register of Historic Places in 1993. It is currently known as "The Lloyd House Museum" and furnished in turn-of-the-century decor. Sitting on the porch are from left to right, James Lloyd, his son Thomas, and Thomas's wife, Mattie, holding their daughter Lula Lee. (Courtesy of Lloyd and Arbidella Dooley.)

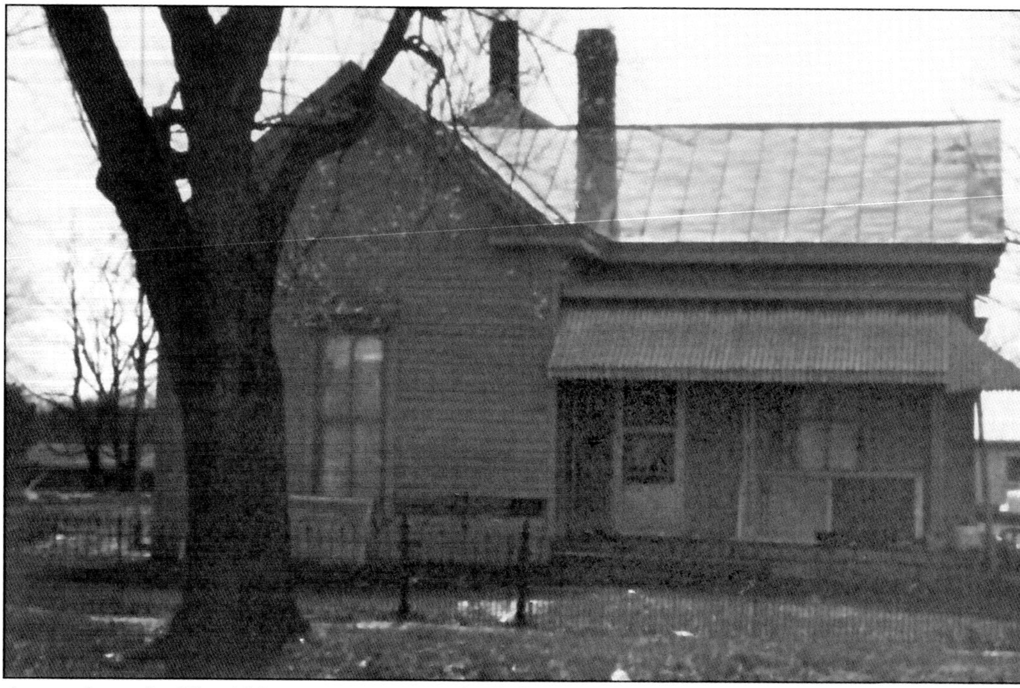

Across from the Lloyd House was a quaint little home that belonged to the Fox/Bridwell family for about a century. The pre–Civil War home was occupied in the early 1900s by popular local business owner Sam Fox along with his mother, Sarah, and sister Almira. His father, Philip, once ran a blacksmith shop where his store was located. Margaret Woodden, a descendant of the family, and her husband, Bob, were one of the last families to live there. (Courtesy of Lloyd and Arbidella Dooley.)

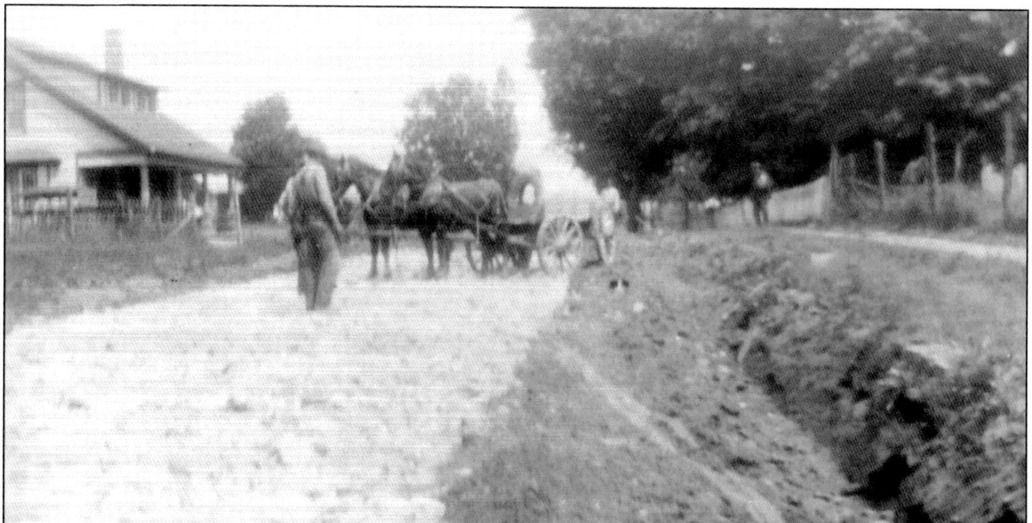

In 1925, Main Street was rerouted and paved, straightened down the stretch known today as South Main Street. Before, Main Street turned west at the Cyclone store before turning left again on College Drive and continuing south towards Bardstown. This section would have been a dead end a short distance from the front of the Lloyd House, where this photograph was taken. (Courtesy of Lloyd and Arbidella Dooley.)

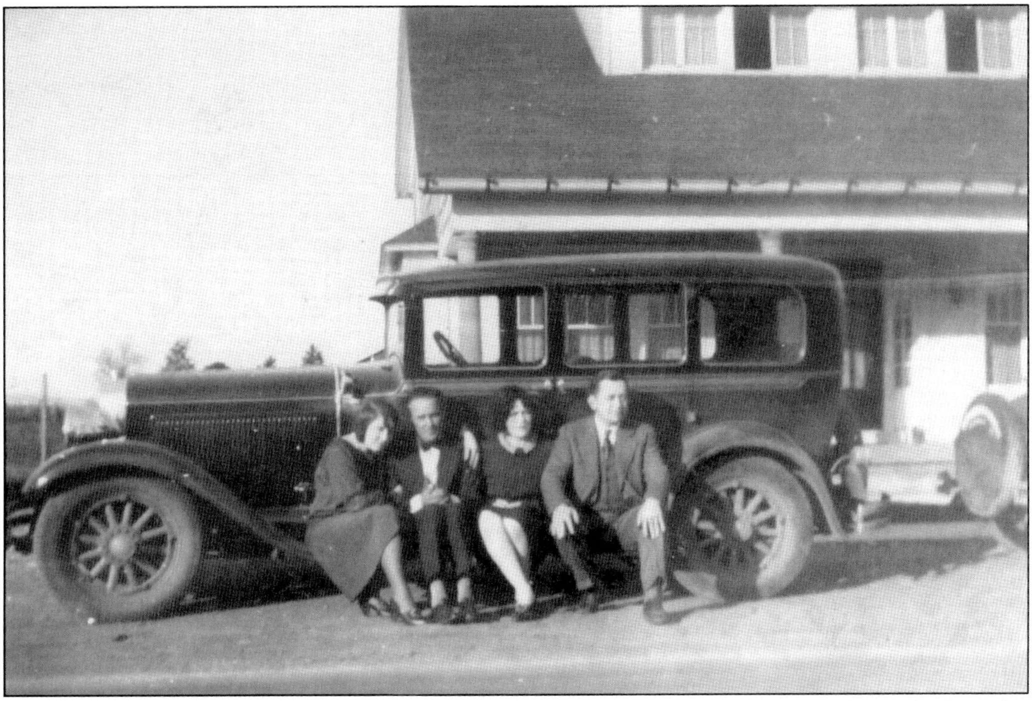

When Dr. George B. Hill moved to Mt. Washington around 1923, he had this home built at the corner of South Main Street and Porter Avenue. For unknown reasons, he sold the new home to Marvin Porter in 1927 and had William A. King build him a new house (below) down the street from his previous home on South Main Street. Dr. Hill used the basement for his office. (Courtesy of Leda Barnes.)

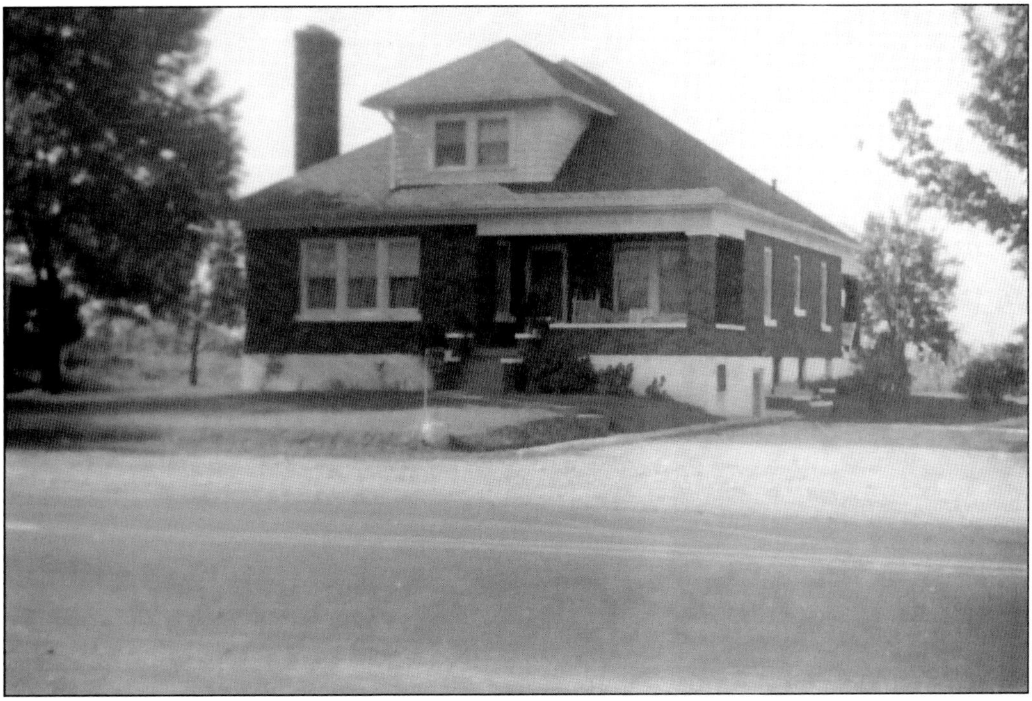

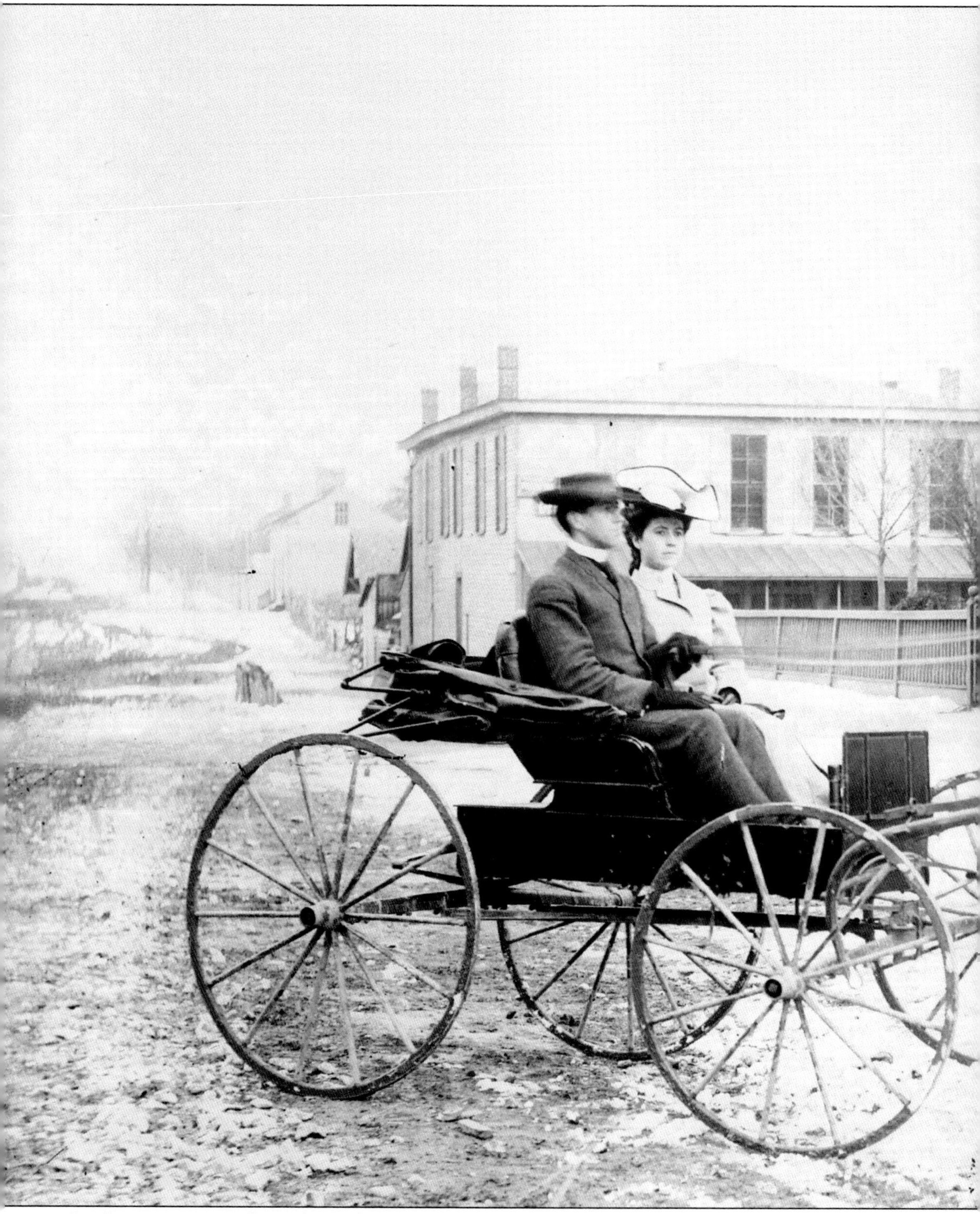

In this street scene from the early 1900s, a well-dressed couple takes in some fresh air near the Crossroads in their handsome carriage on a cold, snow-covered day. Henry J. Barnes's mansion can be seen to the right with the Cyclone store in the foreground. South Main Street in the distance

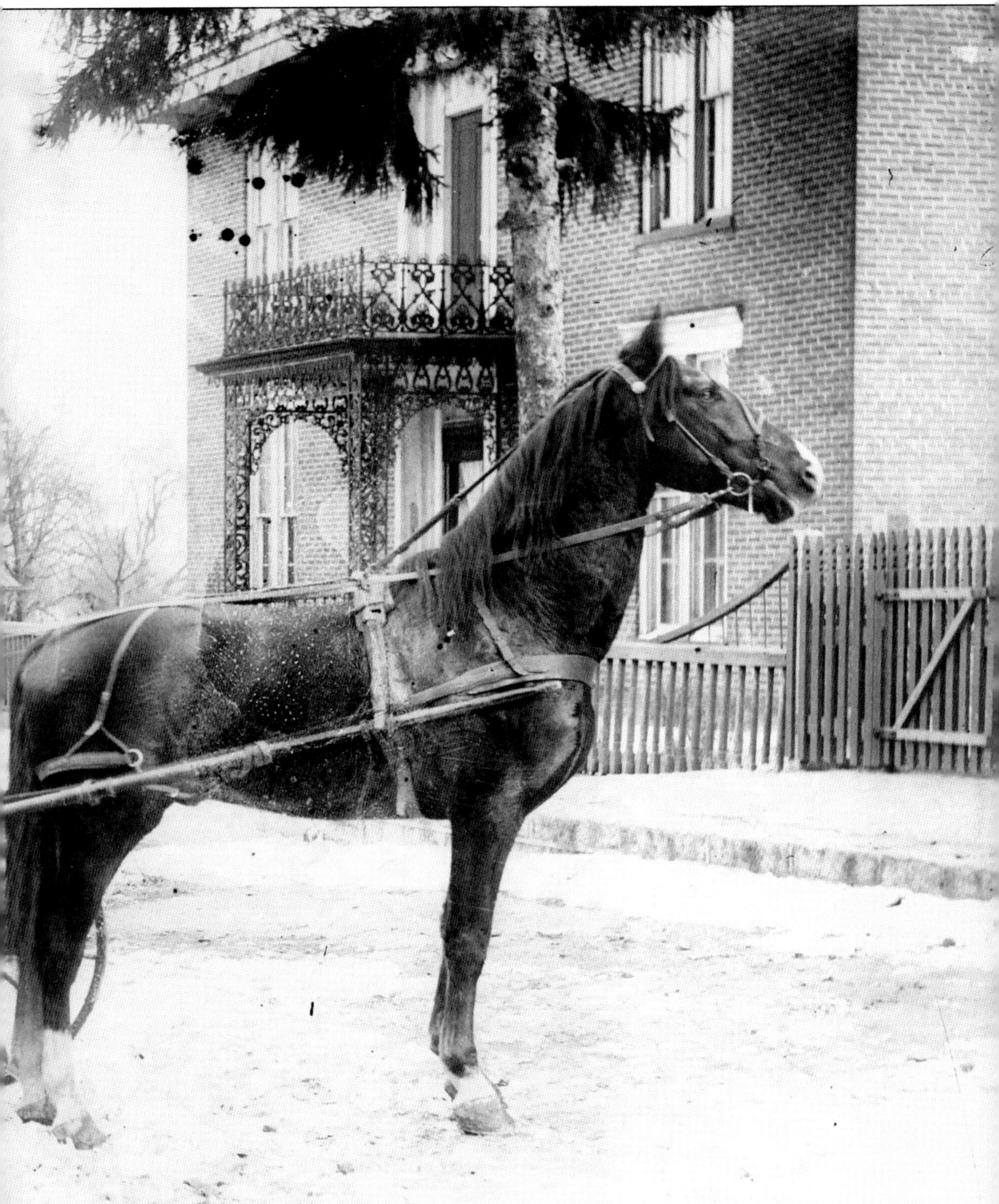

looked quiet during this time with only a few homes in sight. (Courtesy of the Mt. Washington Historical Society.)

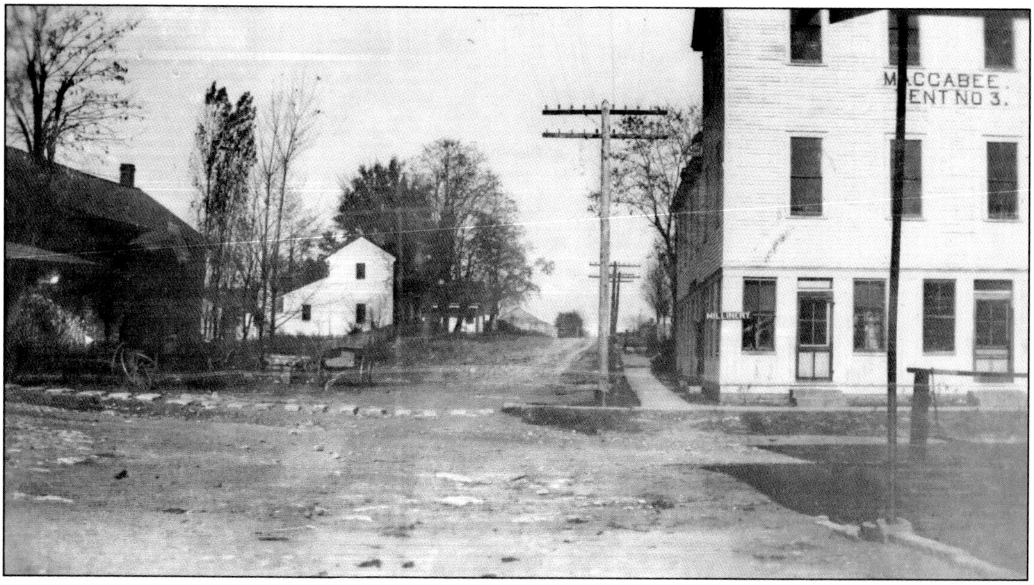

On the left in this c. 1915 street scene stands Parrish's blacksmith shop and German Branham's home. German owned and operated a restaurant at Maccabee Hall, pictured right. Just past the Branham home, facing Snapp Street, lived Maynard Jasper along with his wife, Nina, and family during the 1930s and 1940s. Maynard would one day own the property housing the blacksmith shop and Branham home and run a successful business called "Central Garage." (Courtesy of the Mt. Washington Historical Society.)

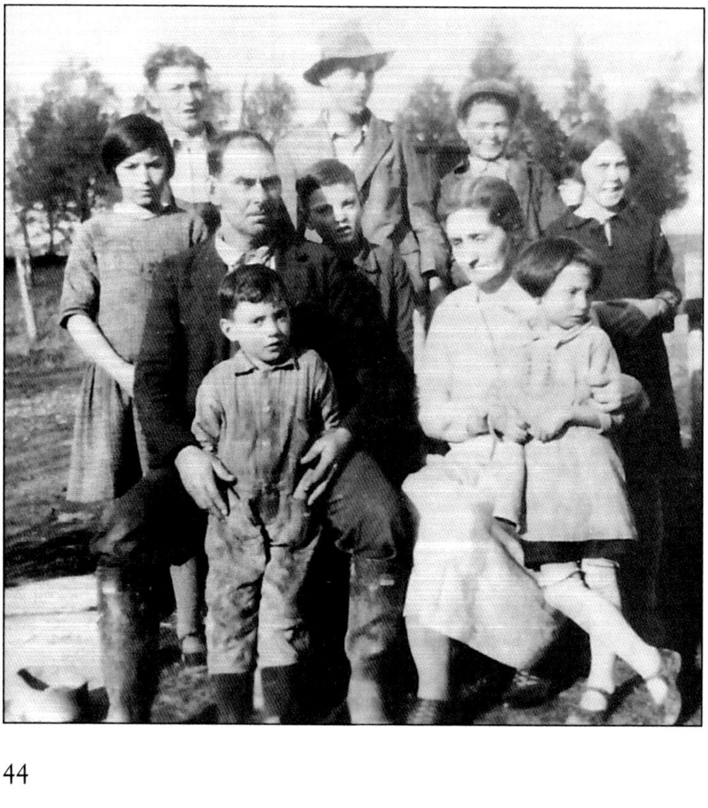

German Branham and his wife, Elizabeth, had 11 children and lived in the two-story house located at the corner of Highway 44 and Snapp Street. German owned and ran a diner in the old Maccabee Hall for several years but lost everything when it burned in November 1940. He later moved his family to Waterford Road, and his son William "Buck" Branham's family moved into the home with his wife Irma, twins Bernice and Beverly, and daughters Betty and Bonnie. A family of Allenders lived there following them. (Courtesy of the Branham family.)

Two

Movers, Shakers, Music Makers, and Bakers

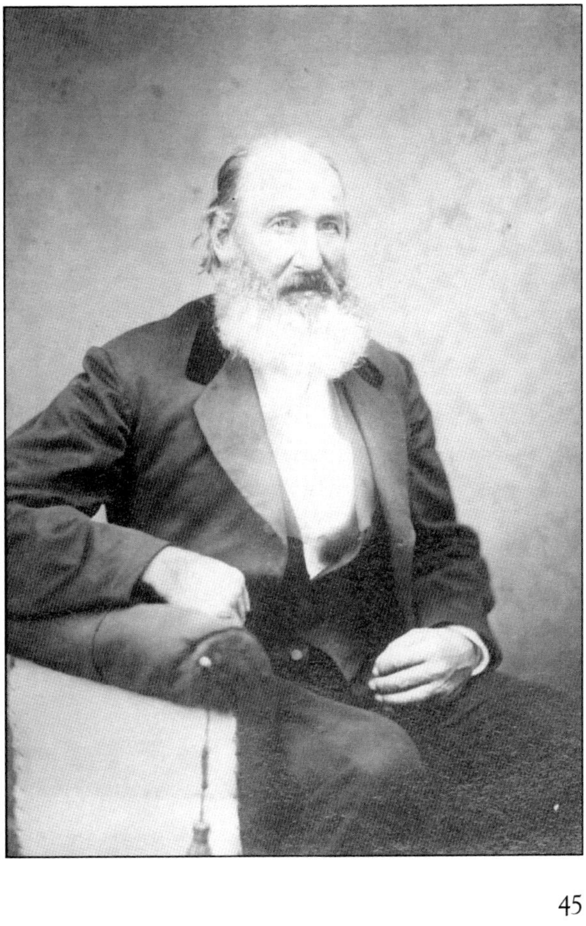

Samuel Carothers (1813–1882) was an entrepreneur; as a young man, he built covered bridges with his older brother James and accompanied Henry J. Barnes on another bridge in Western Kentucky. He later became a retail salesman in the 1860s and had a store near the Settle Hotel. He also dabbled in the distillery business during the 1870s. But Sam was mostly known for starting Mt. Washington's first funeral business. Sam became an embalmer, built an embalming shop across the street of his home on Main Street, and had a horse-drawn carriage built to carry the casket to the cemetery. (Courtesy of Gayle and Eleanor Troutman.)

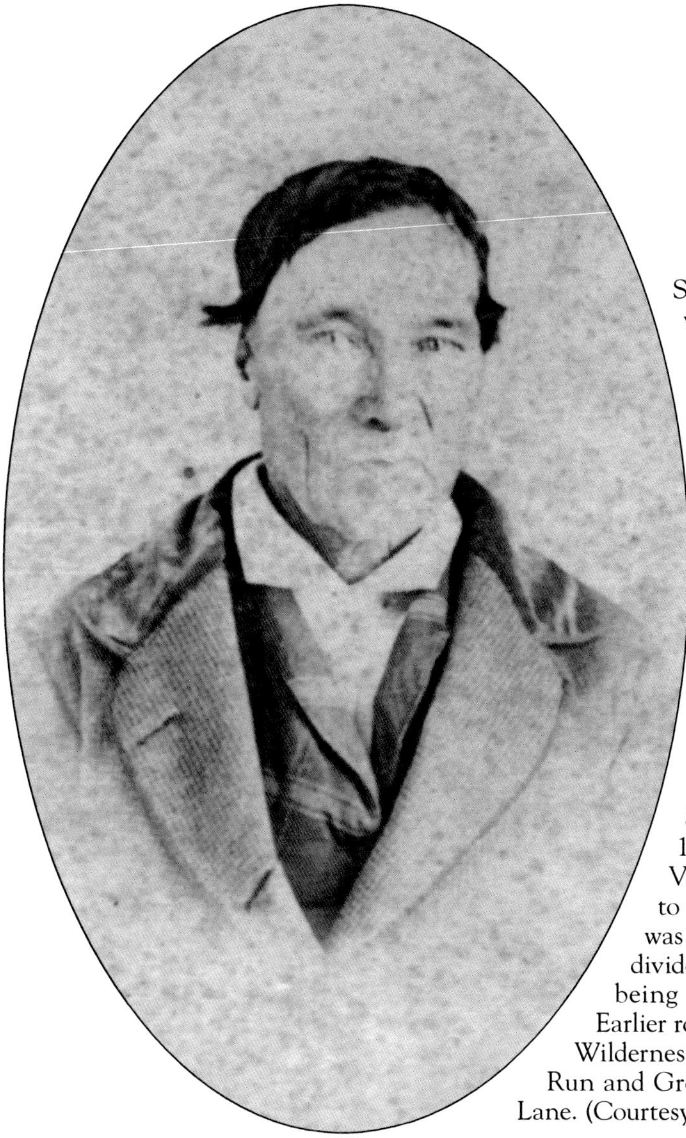

Simeon Harris (1780–1858) was a founding father of Mt. Washington. His parents, Thomas Harris and his second wife, Sarah (Hall), left Virginia in the late 1700s for Kentucky and settled near Salt River near McCullough's Run. Simeon and his older half-brother Zedekiah began buying land and farming along the Salt River bottoms near Stringer Lane. Simeon was an early property owner in town, along with his son Brinton. Simeon and his wife, Susanna (Owen), had at least 10 children together. Documented in the note below, Simeon was commissioned in 1819 to survey the road from Mt. Vernon (later Mt. Washington) to Clark's Ford at Salt River. This was just one year after the city was divided into lots and a new road was being forged through Sugar Valley. Earlier roads into town followed the old Wilderness Road trail near McCullough's Run and Greenwell Ford Road to Stringer Lane. (Courtesy of Brenda O'Brian.)

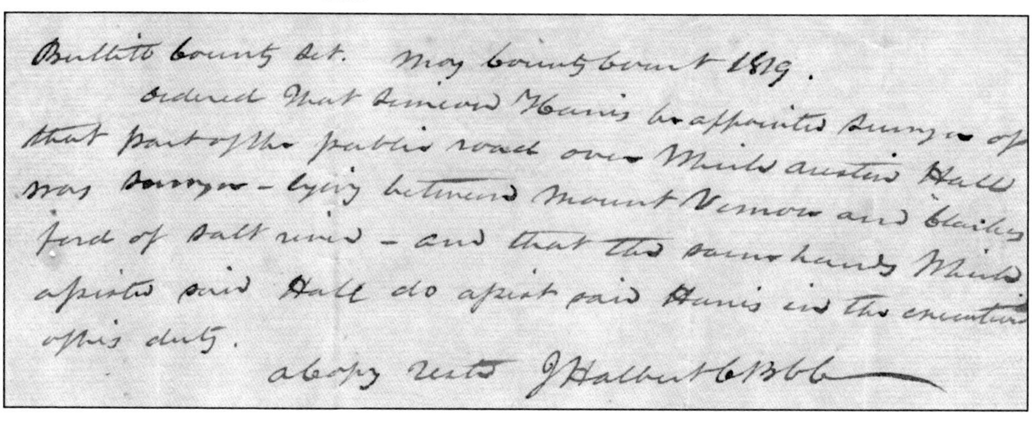

Bullitt County Sct. May County Court 1819.
Ordered that Simeon Harris be appointed Surveyor of that part of the public road over which Austin Hall was Surveyor – lying between Mount Vernon and Clarks ford of Salt river – and that the same hands which assisted said Hall do assist said Harris in the execution of his duty.
A copy Teste J Halbert [illegible]

Squire Fidler was born in Mt. Washington in 1809 to parents Martin and Judith (Jones) Fidler. Martin was a blacksmith by trade, and Squire followed suit and eventually learned the trade of a gunsmith. Squire and his family lived in one of the first homes built in the city, a humble two-story log cabin to the left of the original McFarland Funeral Home on Main Street. He specialized in making Kentucky long rifles that were works of art with beautiful inlays, carvings, and brass metalwork. Sometime after 1866, he and many of his family members moved to Orleans, Indiana, where he continued to make rifles. Squire died in 1866 at the age of 76 in Valeene, Indiana. (Courtesy of the Mt. Washington Historical Society.)

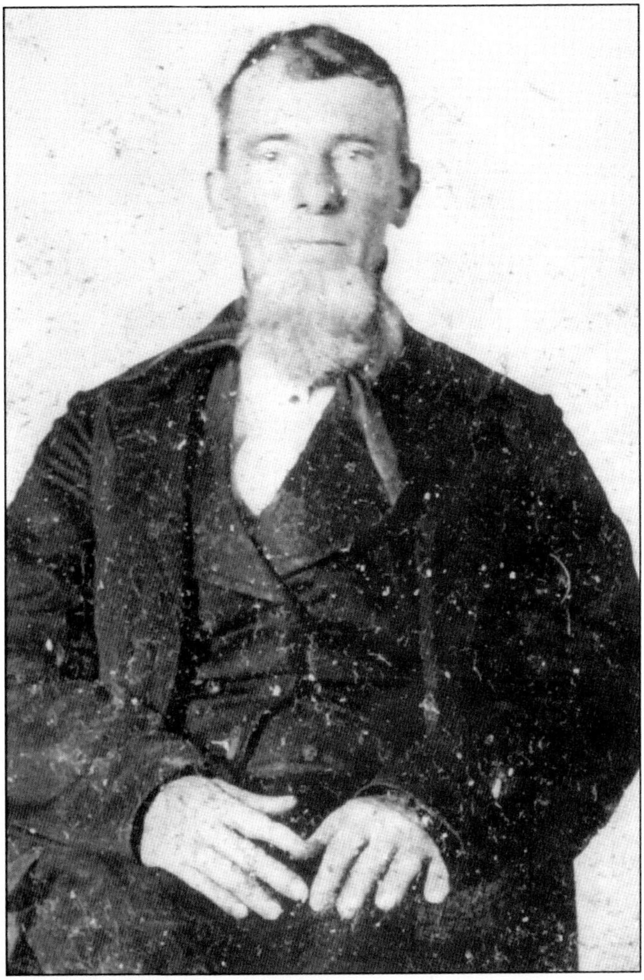

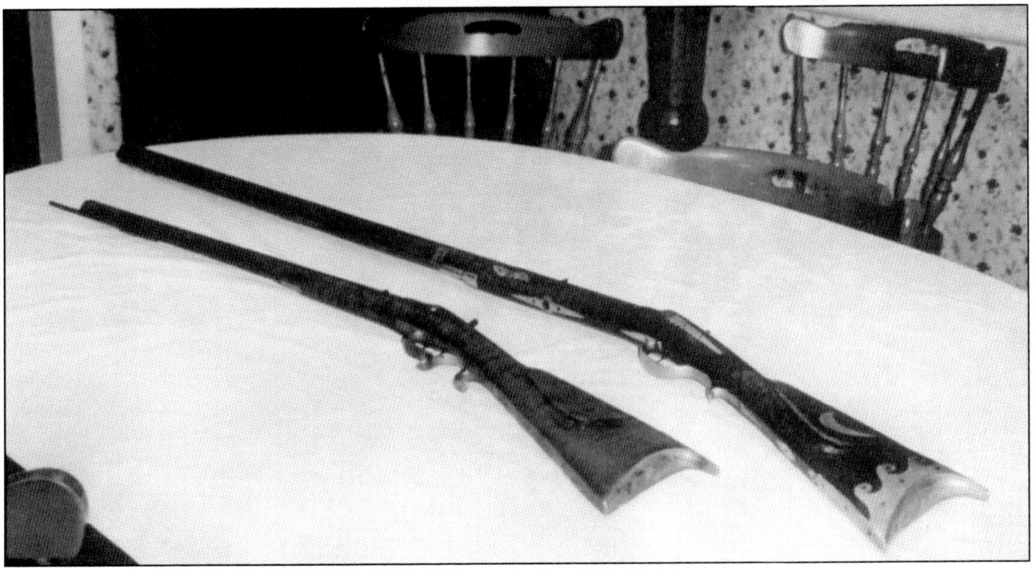

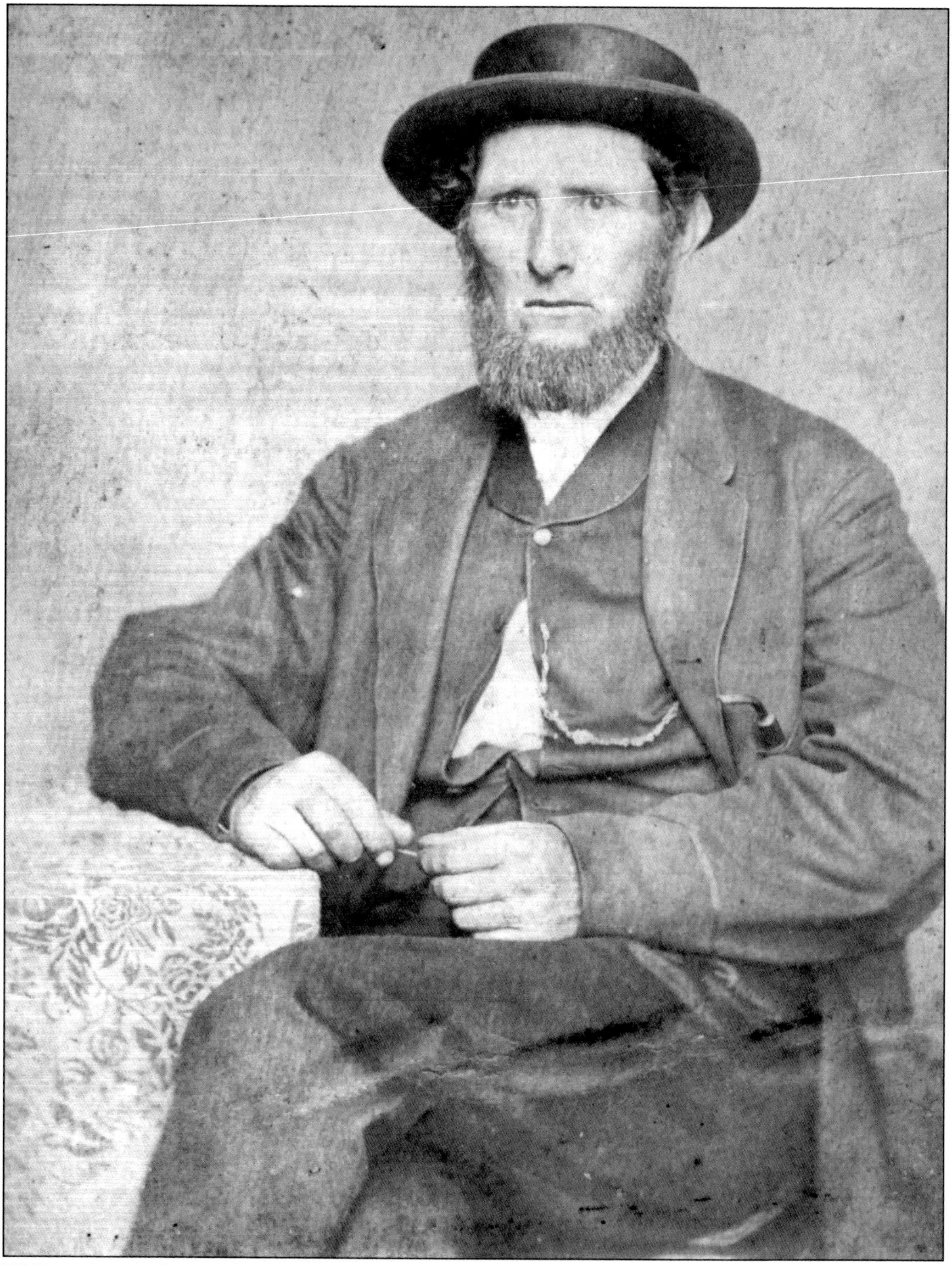

William Stanford McFarland (1839–1911) moved to Mt. Washington from Owensboro after finishing law school and married Samuel Carothers's daughter Mary. William took to the funeral business that his father-in-law began and continued it after Samuel's passing. He remodeled a lower room into a funeral parlor, and their home became the McFarland Funeral Home. Mary became an embalmer, the first woman to be licensed in the state of Kentucky. William also worked for the IRS and was highly regarded and respected by everyone. (Courtesy of Mark and Lisa Rouse.)

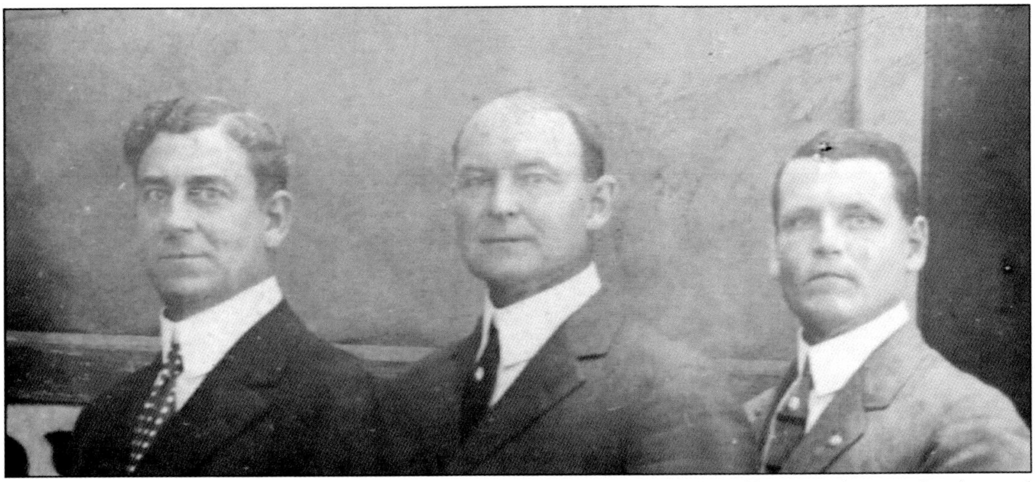

McFarland had three sons: Sam, William H., and John. Sam and William took over the funeral business from their father and also started a Dodge dealership across the street from the funeral home. John went a different direction and became postmaster of Lebanon Junction. He later left for a postmaster position in Kansas, where he lived out the rest of his life. (Courtesy of Gayle and Eleanor Troutman.)

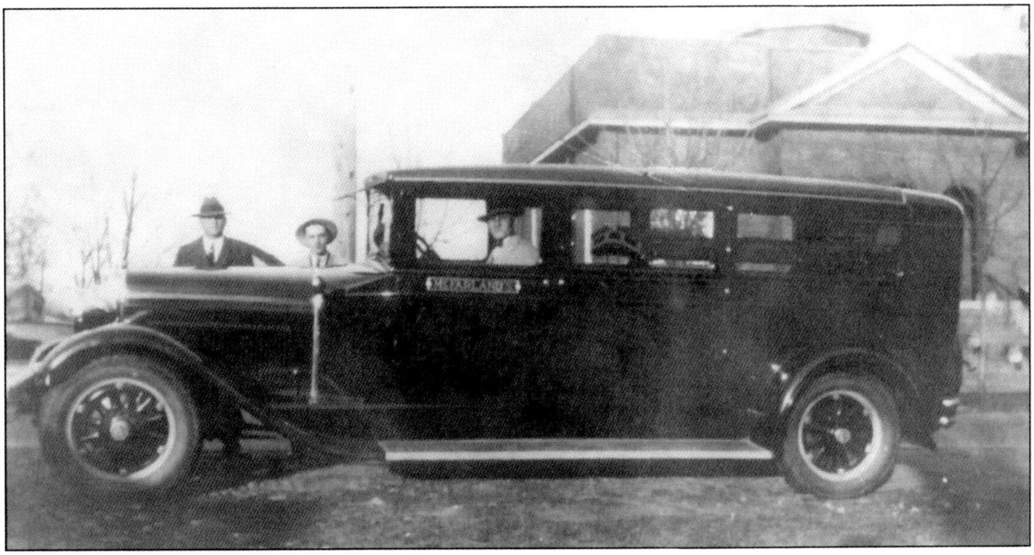

William H. McFarland's son Grigsby continued in their funeral business. He was the first to use an automobile for a hearse, which he nicknamed "Lorraine." Grigsby and his wife, Elizabeth, ran the funeral home until in he passed away in 1972. Their daughter Eleanor and her husband, Gayle, maintained the funeral business, which had been operating for over 100 years, until the 1990s. (Courtesy of Gayle and Eleanor Troutman.)

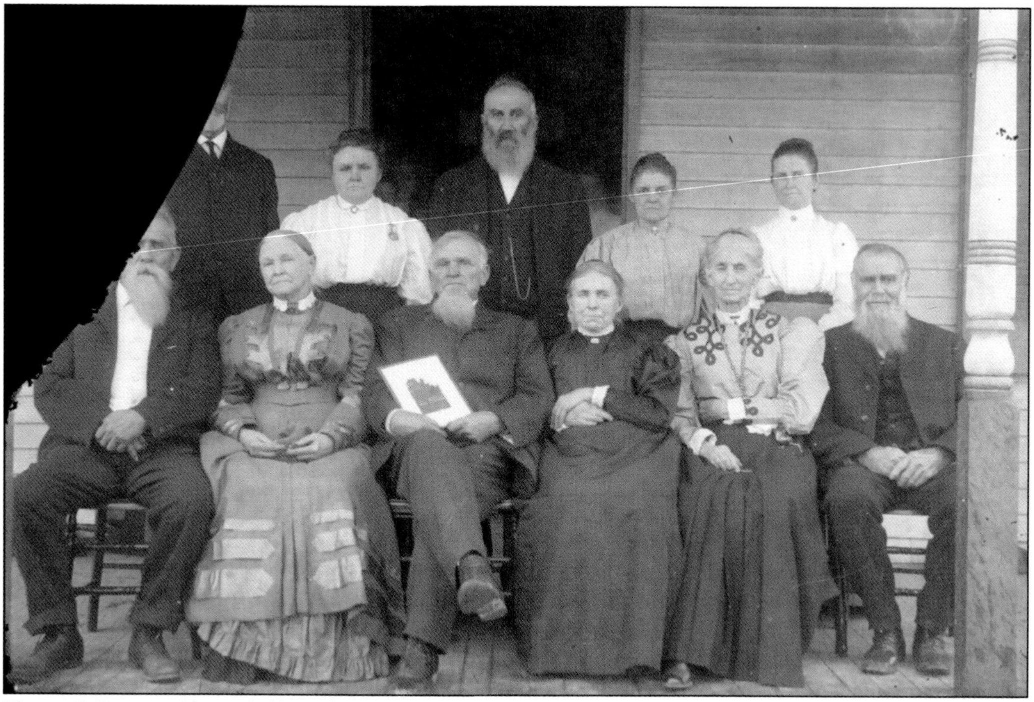

Henry J. Barnes (front left) and William Perry Barnes (front right) were extraordinary men who built several covered bridges across Kentucky between the 1830s and the turn of the century. One of their finest creations (below) still stands across the Beech Fork Creek in Washington County. Henry was a carpenter and furniture maker who built the home next to the Masonic lodge and the beautiful mansion that has been the McAfee Funeral Home and is currently the McFarland-Troutman-Proffitt Funeral Home. William was also a furniture maker and held the office of deputy clerk of the Bullitt County Court. (Courtesy of the Mt. Washington Historical Society.)

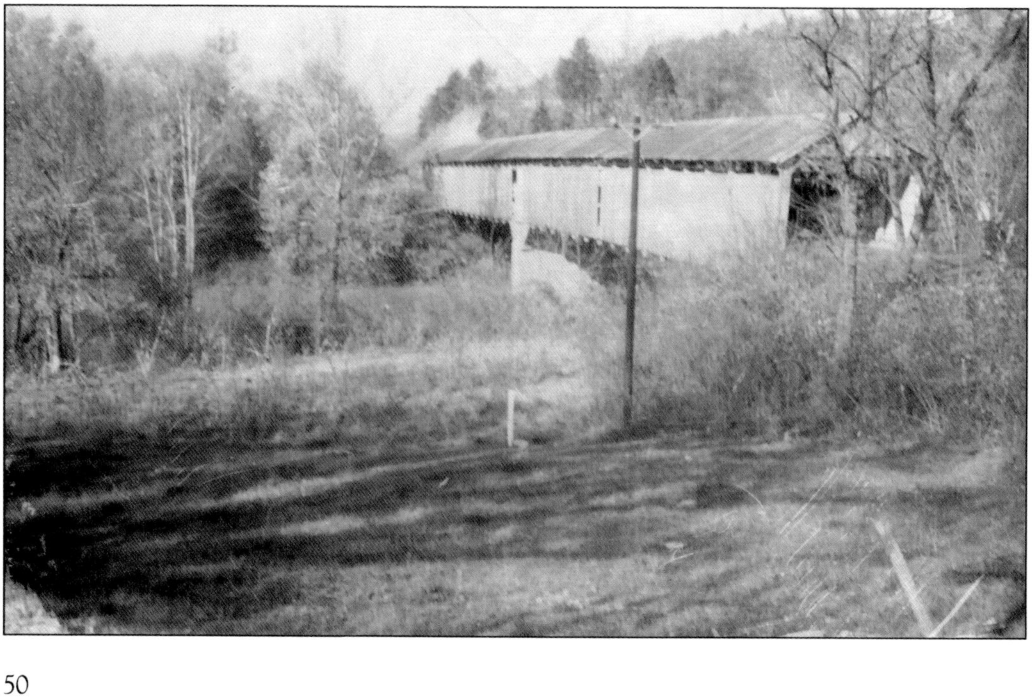

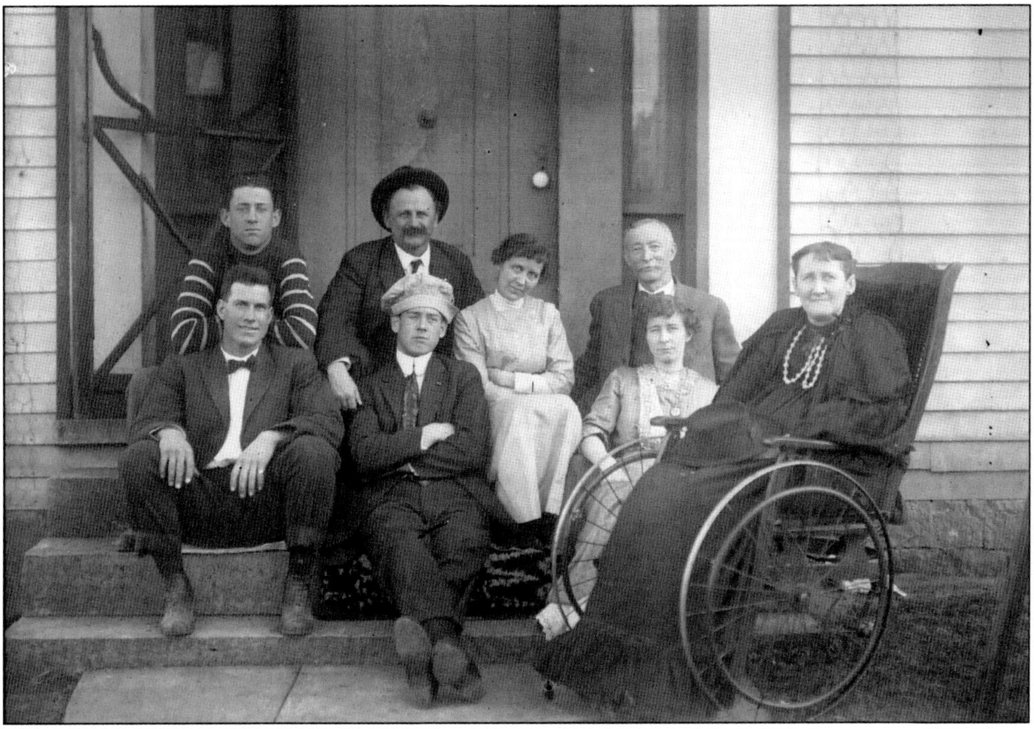

J. Edgar Fisher was instrumental in getting the Mt. Washington High School funding for accredited teachers. He was a charter member of the Mt. Washington Lion's Club and an active singing, teaching, and sometimes preaching member of the Methodist church. He is best known for running the Barnes Brothers' store with wife Bernice. Pictured here from left to right are (front row) J. Edgar Fisher, two unidentified people, Bernice (Barnes) Fisher, and unidentified; (second row) Jack Barnes, Maurice Harris (owner and proprietor of the Mt. Washington Hotel), and Almer Barnes. (Courtesy of the Mt. Washington Historical Society.)

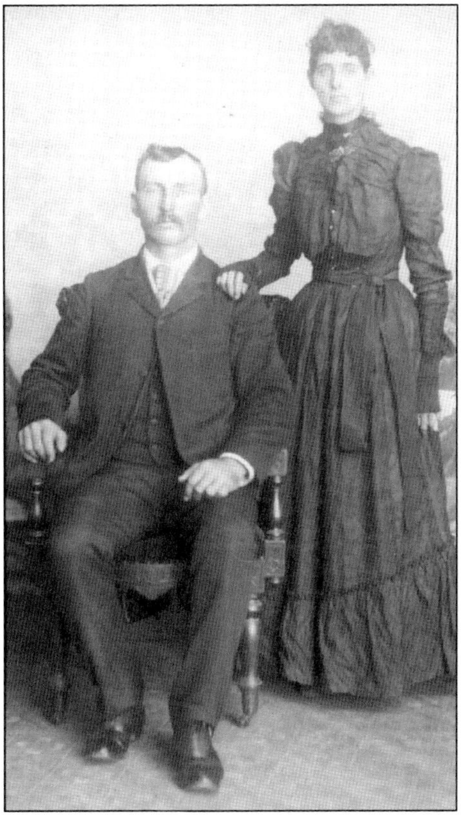

William A. King was certainly the most prolific builder in Mt. Washington, erecting innumerable houses, buildings, and churches. His grandest achievement was the Maccabee Hall, which was a three-story multipurpose building at the Crossroads. Many of his creations were ahead of their time, and many still stand as beautiful now as they were when first built. King was also responsible for the building of the Baptist church (Coakley Chapel), the Methodist church on Main Street, and the old Bethel church on Highway 44. (Courtesy of Lloyd and Arbidella Dooley.)

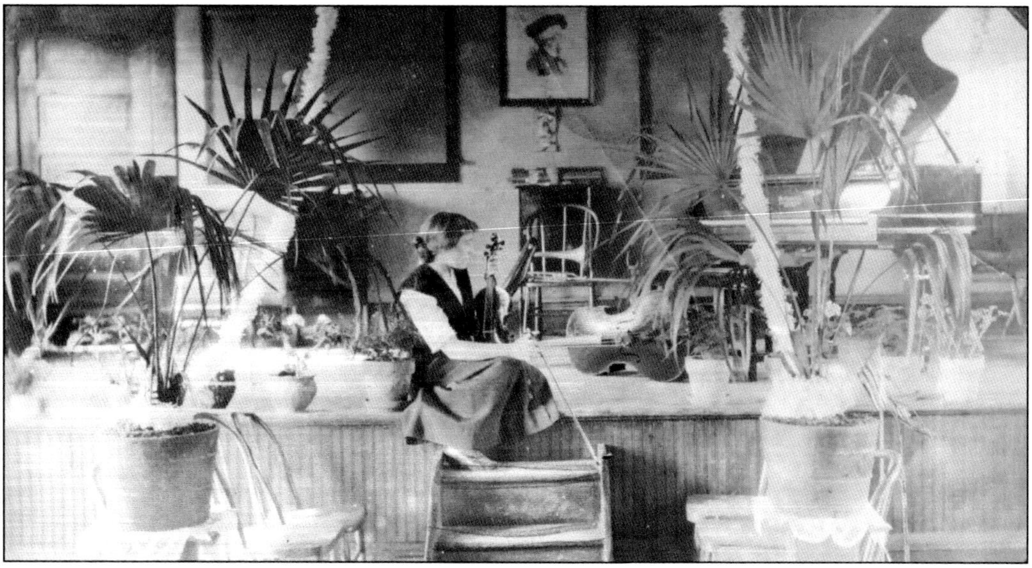

Edna Grotefendt (1895–1989) was the youngest child of Frederick and Maria Grotefendt, who settled in Illinois after emigrating from Germany. Almost all of the family members played instruments in their father's band. Edna excelled musically and attended the College of Music of Concordia, Missouri, and the Kansas City College of Music. She was capable of playing 18 different instruments. Horace McGee, a young widower from Mt. Washington was living and working in Fern Creek as a mechanic when he met Edna while she was visiting her sister. They were married April 10, 1929, and returned to Mt. Washington. Edna McGee organized a band that played at various venues and occasions, including Maccabee Hall and Memorial Day services. She continued teaching students for many years to come (including the author). In the 1930s, Horace was an expert mechanic and became the chief mechanic and driver for the hydroplane boat *Fern Creek II* (below) owned by Ewing Stout, which broke several records in its class. Horace and family members worked as the pit crew and traveled as far as California, Texas, and New York. (Courtesy of the Mt. Washington Historical Society.)

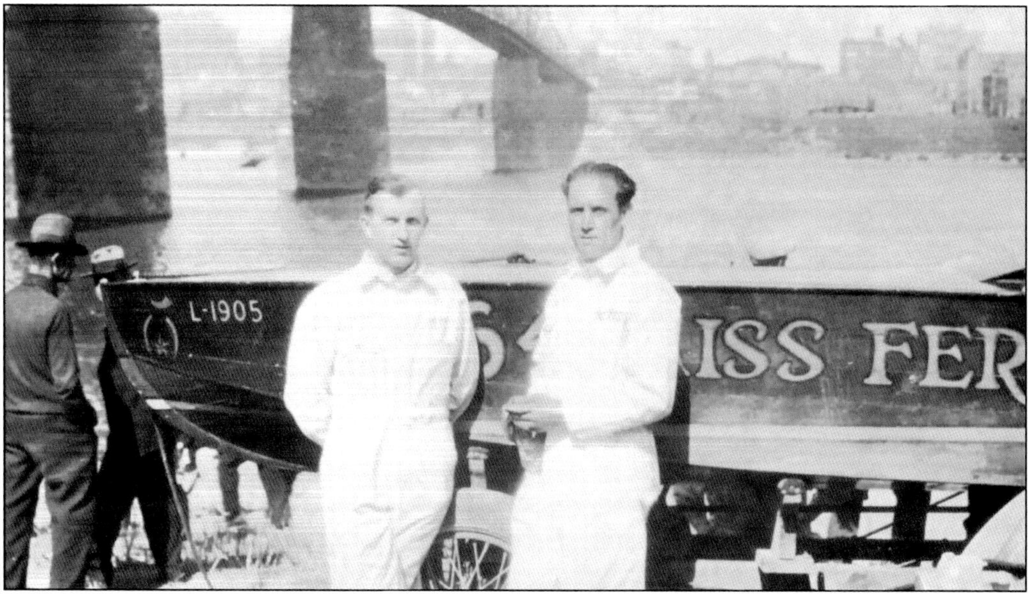

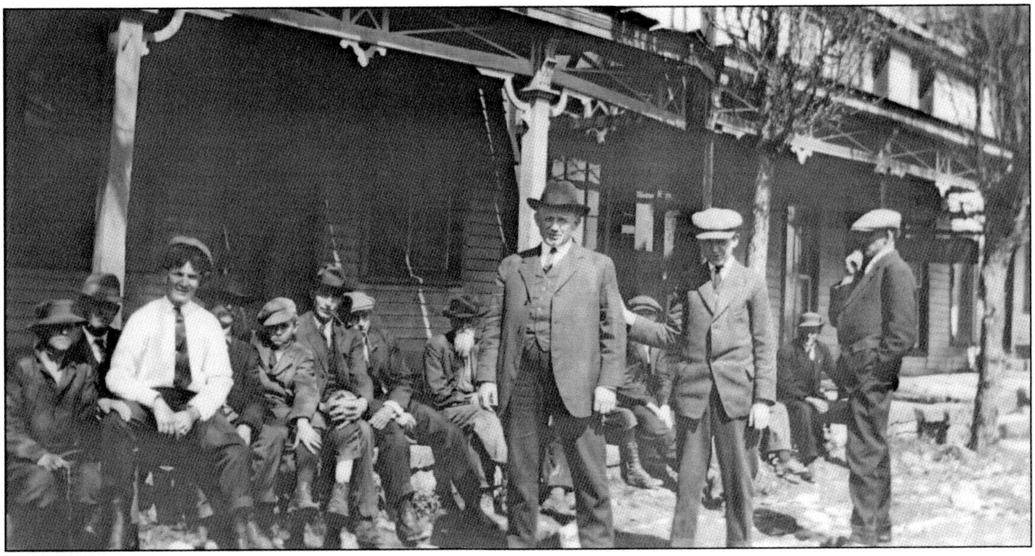

Bert Hall (center) was a skilled and versatile citizen of Mt. Washington. He was a man of great integrity and talents. Bert was elected Bullitt County sheriff between 1902 and 1905. When the Mt. Washington Peoples Bank became an independent, he was chosen as president and held that position from 1909 to 1947. He successfully ran for one term (1942–1944) for state representative of the 33rd District, including Bullitt and Spencer Counties. Bert was also a former master of the Masonic lodge and a licensed auctioneer. (Courtesy of Gayle and Eleanor Troutman.)

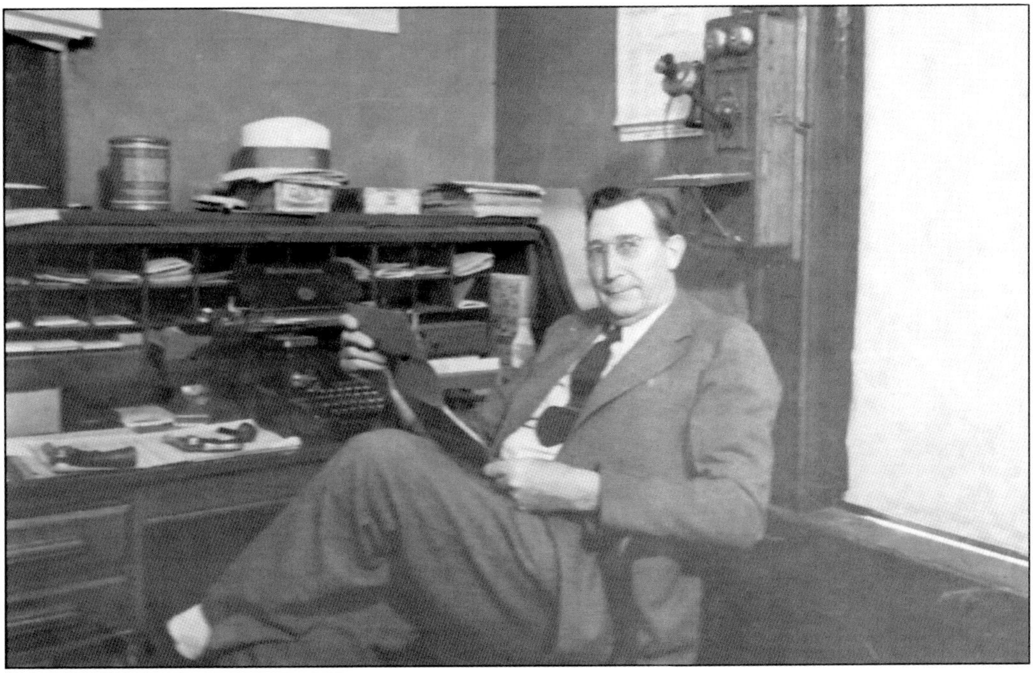

Robert "Bob" Emmett McAfee (1883–1951) was an important man not only in Mt. Washington, but also in Bullitt County. He had been a deputy sheriff before he was elected sheriff of Bullitt County in 1930 and served until 1938. He was then elected judge and served in that office until 1942. Bob was also a director of the Mt. Washington Peoples Bank for several years. He was married to the former Mabel Harris of Mt. Washington. (Courtesy of Maurice Wise.)

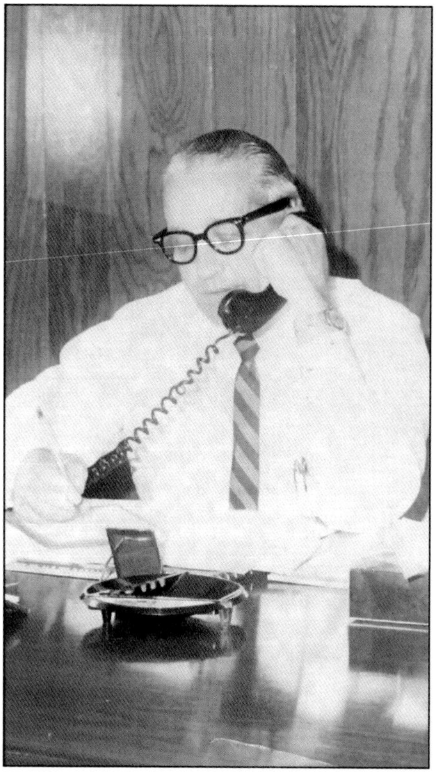

Leo Andrew Bleemel (1913–1971) was an elected member of the Kentucky House of Representatives (31st District) for nearly four terms (1954–1971). In February 1971, Leo died from injuries sustained from a single-car accident near the Floyds Fork Bridge on Bardstown Road. His wife, Virginia, carried out his remaining term. Before serving as a representative he had been a chairman for the House State Government Committee. He was also the founder and president of Services Erection & Machine Company, which was a large manufacturer of conveyors and equipment. (Courtesy of Billy Breeden.)

Sidney "Sid" Griffin moved to Mt. Washington in the late 1950s and opened a grocery in the old McFarland building on Main Street, which he renamed Mt. Washington Shopworth. It was colloquially known as "the Fruit Stand" and immensely popular due to its proximity to the high school. In 1961, Sid was selected as a trustee and ran in the city's first mayoral election (1967) but lost. Sid ran again and won, serving the people for three terms (1970–1981). He was instrumental in acquiring sewers, city water, sidewalks, and a new city hall. (Courtesy of Sidney Griffin.)

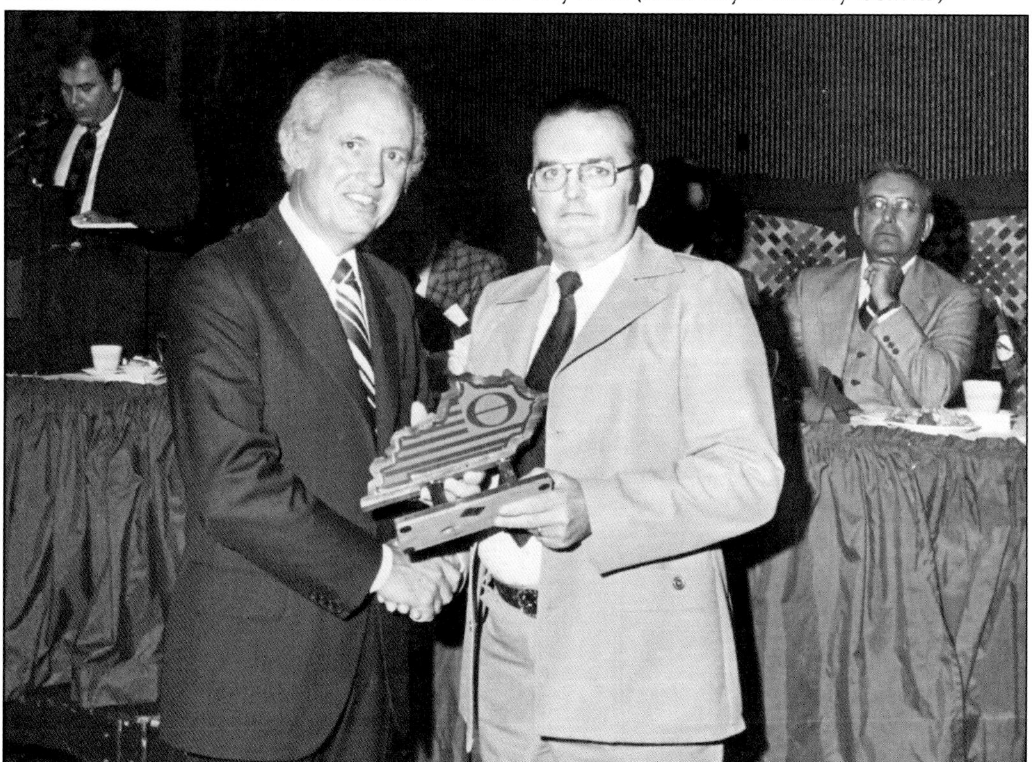

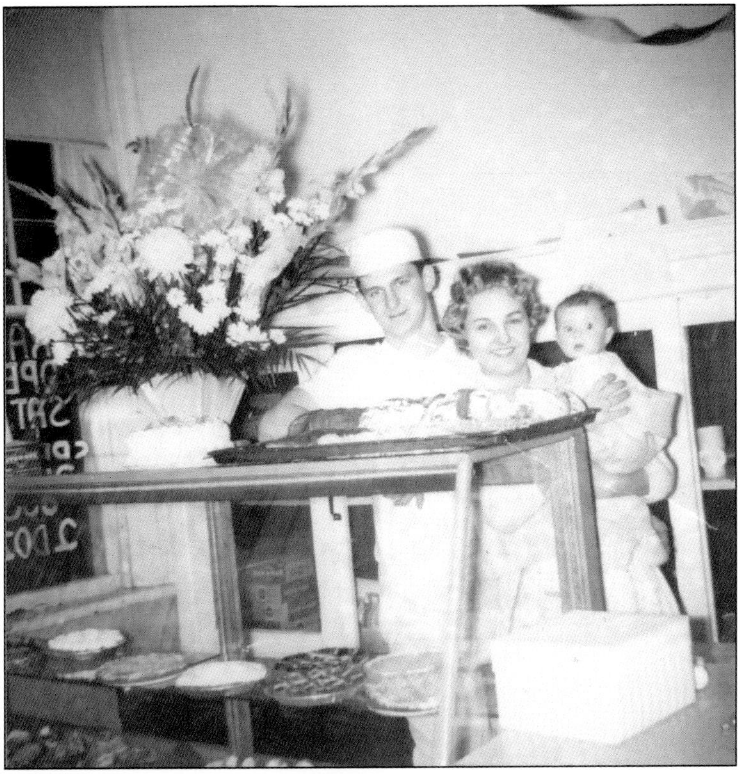

Frank Sullivan began his baking career at an early age at Heitzman's Bakery on Bank Street in Louisville. Frank, his wife, Beth, and newborn Robin came to Mt. Washington in 1958 when he found a struggling bakery for sale. His passion for quality confections made him well renowned and successful. Locals stopping in for breakfast, businesspeople going to work, and weddings kept Frank's business booming for years. After retiring, Frank successfully ran for mayor and served from 2003 to 2006. (Courtesy of Frank Sullivan.)

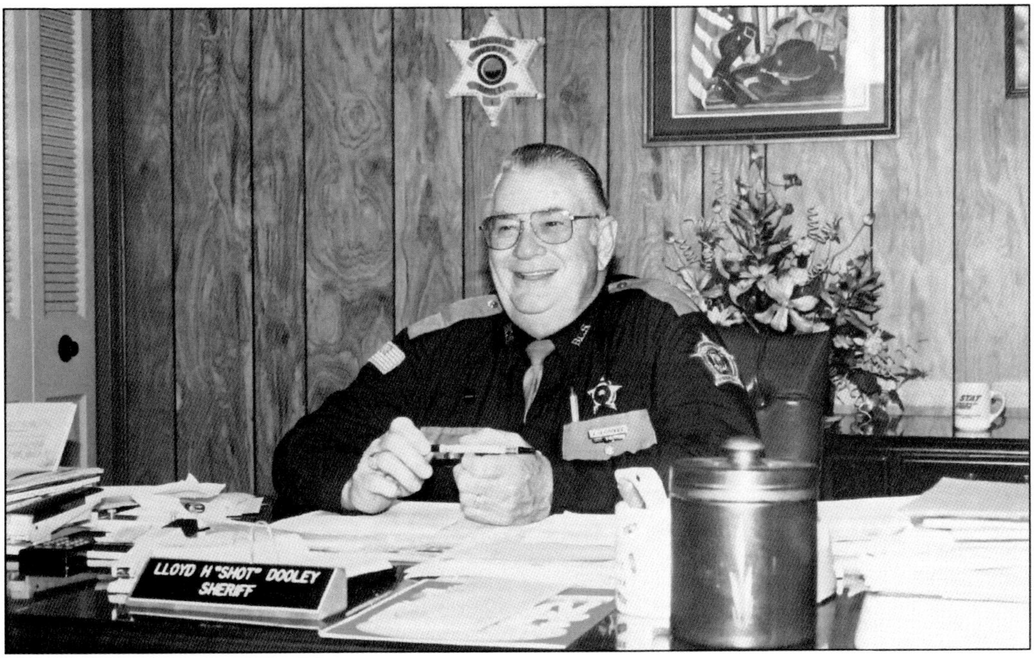

Lloyd "Shot" Dooley, a lifelong Mt. Washington resident, held the office of Bullitt County sheriff longer than any other sheriff in Bullitt County history from 1982 to 1998. Shot also served as deputy sheriff four years prior to that under Sheriff George Rummage. He also has served on the Mt. Washington city council for the last several years. (Courtesy of Lloyd Dooley.)

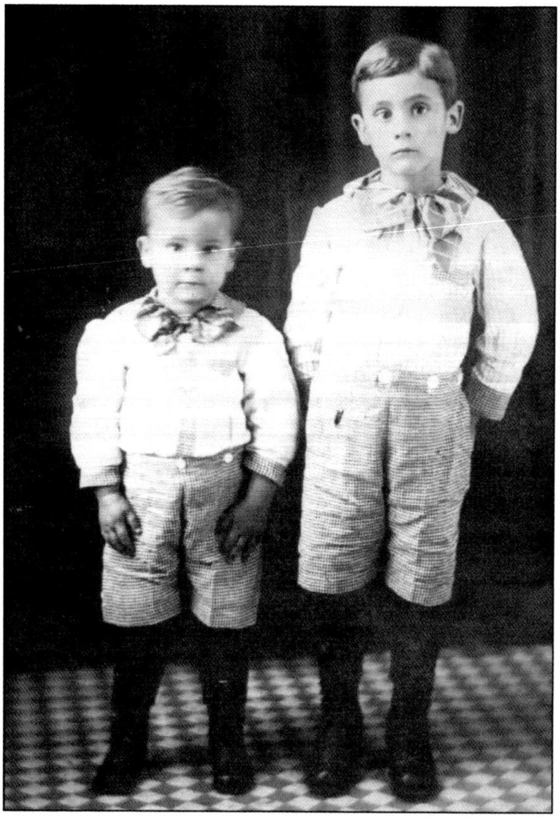

Arson Moore served as Bullitt County judge from 1970 to 1981. He was the last "true judge" to serve before the term of office was changed to "judge executive," and the office did not require any type of law background or education. Pictured here are Arson (left) and his older brother Dexter. He surely could not have envisioned he would one day become a judge. When he and his wife, Dona Meza (Harris), first married, they lived in a humble two-room shack on her father's property. (Courtesy of Paula Ashe.)

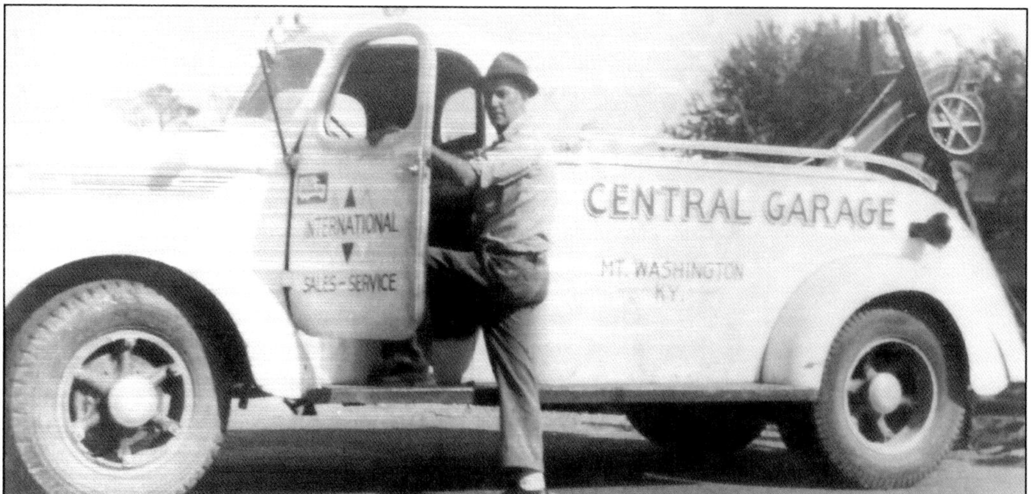

Maynard Jasper knew that the automobile was here to stay and there was a need for a dealership in the city. He named his business the "Central Garage." In the late 1920s, the Central Garage was housed in the old McFarland building then moved to the Standard Oil building at Main and West Streets in 1935. Outgrowing that quickly, Jasper bought the property at the Crossroads where Wilder Harris's Ford dealership had burned in 1937 and built a new building. He was also involved with local government as chairperson of trustees, the equivalent of mayor. (Courtesy of Tom Jasper.)

William Threlkeld built one of the most beautiful and grand homes of Mt. Washington in 1876. It was a two-story Italianate brick home, one of the very few brick houses in the city until the 1950s. For some unknown reason, he and his family traded homes with his in-laws George and Georgia Wigginton after living there for only two years. This switch set in motion amazing future circumstances. Several important men would come to live there in the years to come. (Courtesy of Leda Barnes.)

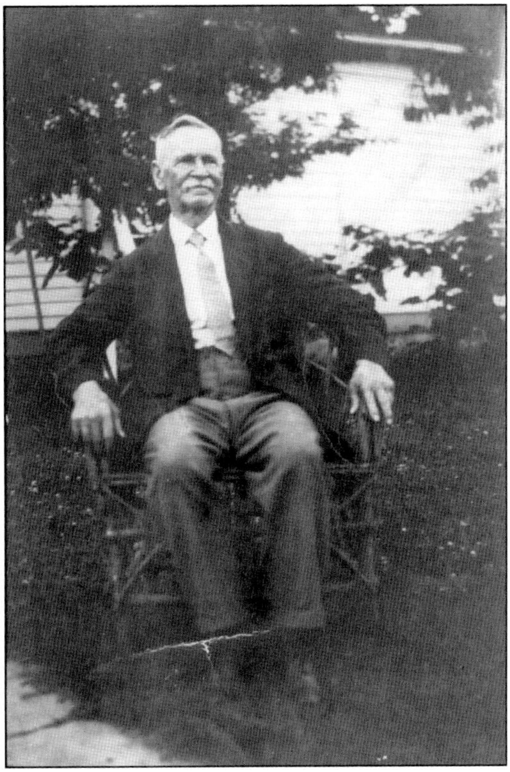

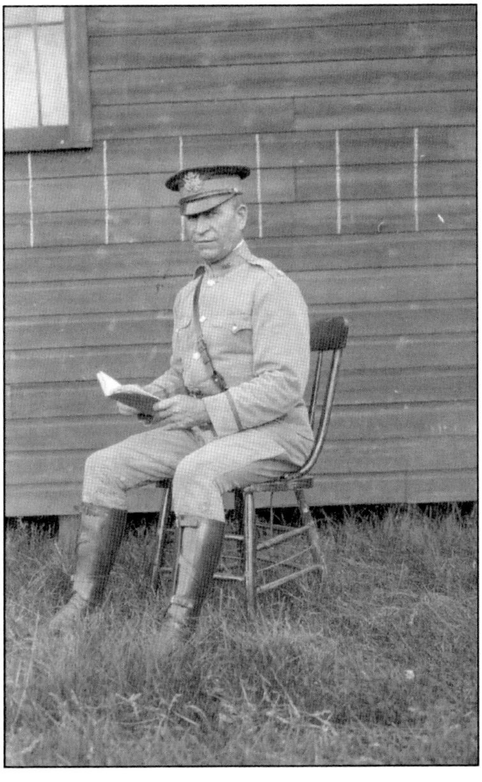

Dr. George W. Threlkeld was born in Mt. Washington and lived for two years in a mansion that his father, William, built in 1876 but then moved to Plum Creek and later Louisville. After high school, he worked at a drugstore and taught at Edgewood School on Waterford Road. He continued his education at the Hospital College of Medicine then left to be a physician during the construction of the Panama Canal. In 1913, he took a position at the Jefferson Reformatory. During World War I, George became a captain in the Medical Corps of the US Army. He served with the Veterans Administration and made major by 1921. After returning home, he acquired his childhood home. (Courtesy of Leda Barnes.)

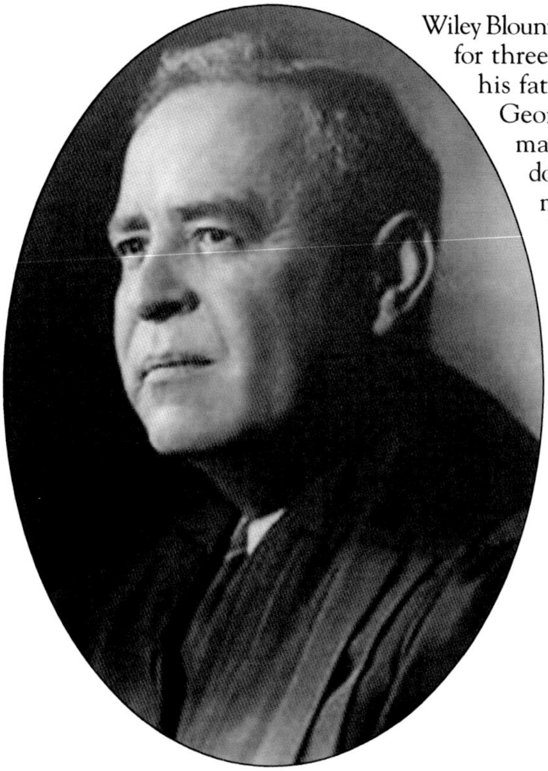

Wiley Blount Rutledge was only a resident of Mt. Washington for three years. After his mother, Mary, passed away, his father sent him to stay with his grandmother Georgia Wigginton, who lived in the Threlkeld mansion. He attended Sallie Reddish's school down the street. After returning home, his family moved continuously. Wiley graduated from the University of Colorado's School of Law and taught law for several years. In 1943, Pres. Franklin Delano Roosevelt appointed Wiley associate justice of the US Supreme Court, where he served from 1943 until his untimely death in 1949. (Author's collection.)

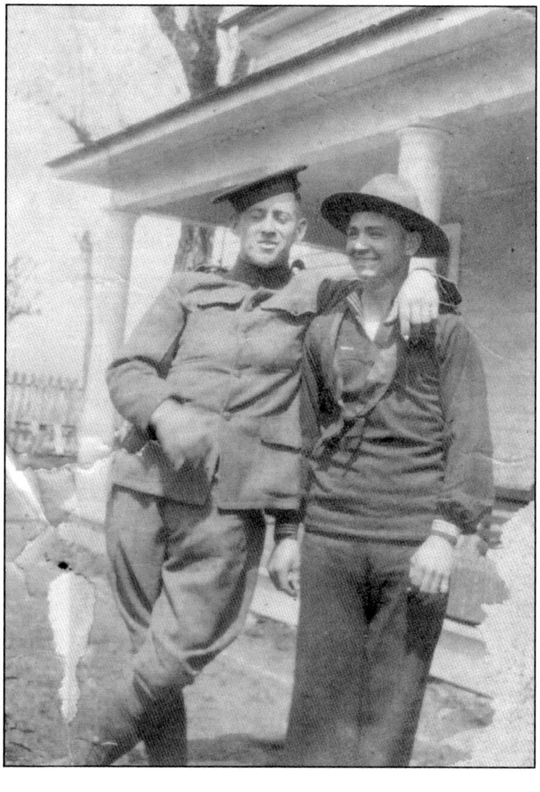

Harold "Jack" Barnes worked for his father, Almer, at the Barnes Brothers' store on Main Street. He enlisted in the Army during World War I, fought in the Hindenburg Line campaign, and received the Purple Heart. Jack's cousin Dr. George Threlkeld offered him the opportunity to take care of his home and farm, allowing his family to live in his beautiful mansion. He accepted. Jack ran for state representative and won, serving from 1934 to 1935 and 1946 to 1947. Jack also served as president of the Mt. Washington Peoples Bank from 1950 to 1954 and 1960 to 1968. (Courtesy of Leda Barnes.)

Athol Lee Taylor was born on August 27, 1917, to Athol Bailey and Leila (Swearingen) Taylor, Mt. Washington natives living in Louisville. He attended Male High School, the College of Liberal Arts, and law school at the University of Louisville. His first position was with Mahan & Mahan Law Firm. Soon afterward, he became a professor of law at the university. He married Carolyn Roederer in 1951, joined Burlyn Pikes Law Firm, and bought the Threlkeld mansion as their residence. In 1984, Athol became Bullitt County circuit judge and held that position until 1991. (Author's collection.)

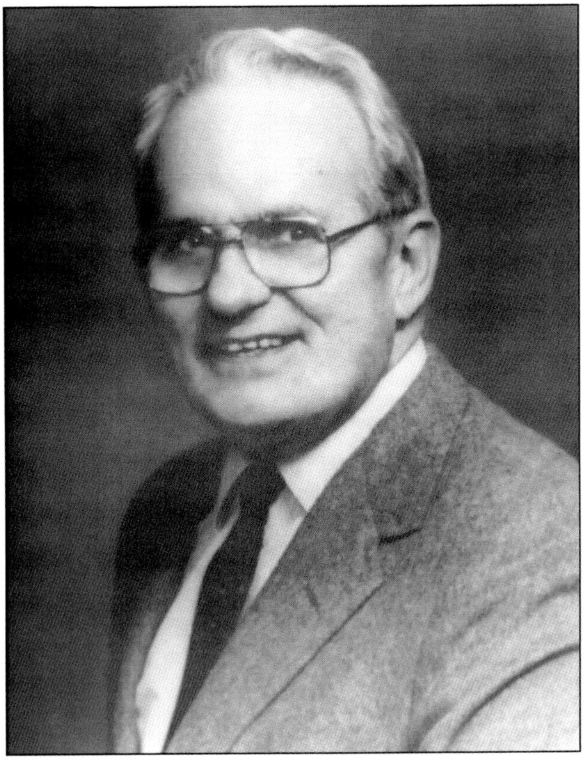

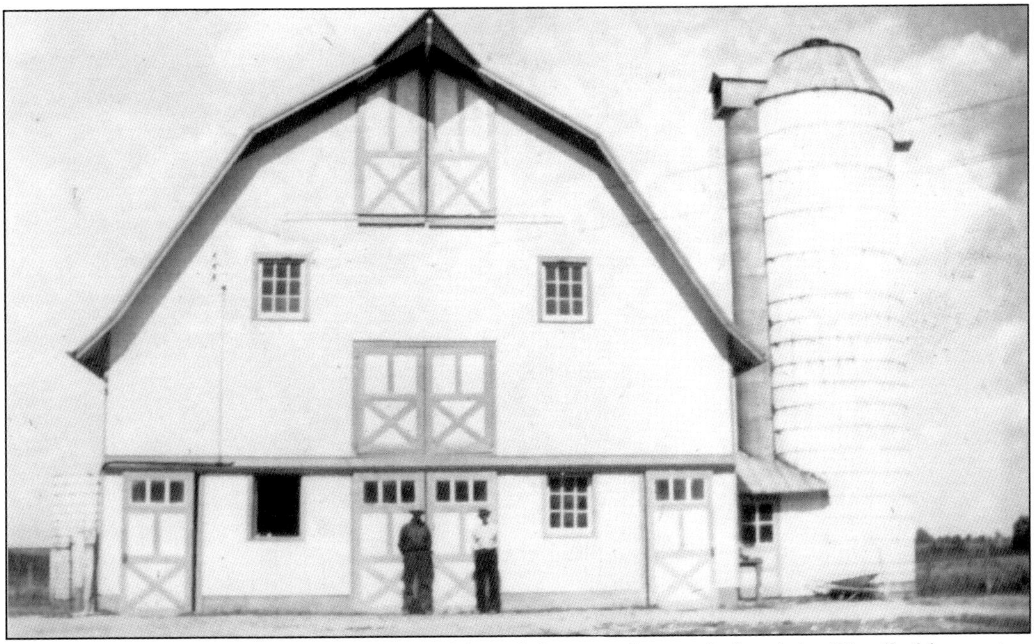

Some barns can be architecturally beautiful, and this one that sat behind the Threlkeld mansion certainly was. The massive dairy barn was built around 1935 and supervised by Jack Barnes. Many of the locals would walk or drive up to the barn and get their milk for the day. The author remembers sneaking over to the barn after it was no longer in use as a dairy and playing in the hayloft, which was like being in a large auditorium full of straw. (Courtesy of Leda Barnes.)

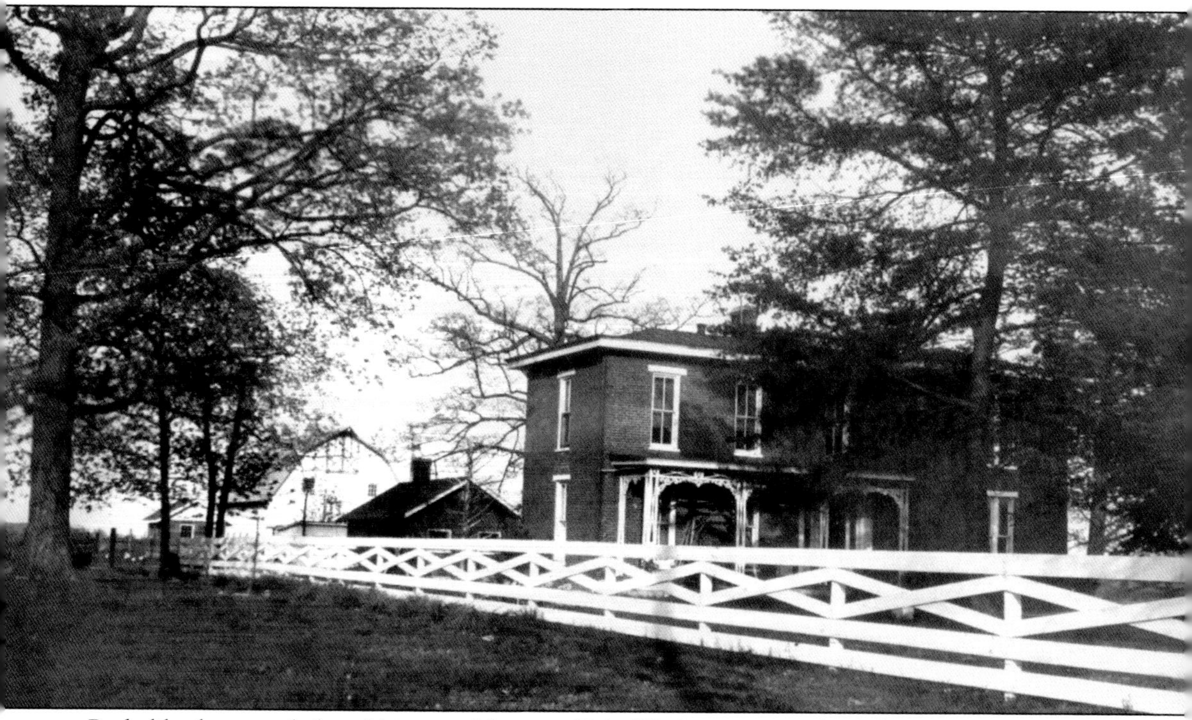

Probably the most beloved historical home of Mt. Washington was built by William Threlkeld in 1876. So many important people have lived in the home, and many interesting places on the property were visited frequently by the citizens of Mt. Washington. The senior class of 1969 had their superlative photographs taken at the mansion, showcasing the beautiful carpentry inside and intricate ironwork on the outside porch. (Courtesy of Lloyd and Arbidella Dooley.)

Three

Hell's Kitchen to Heaven's Gate

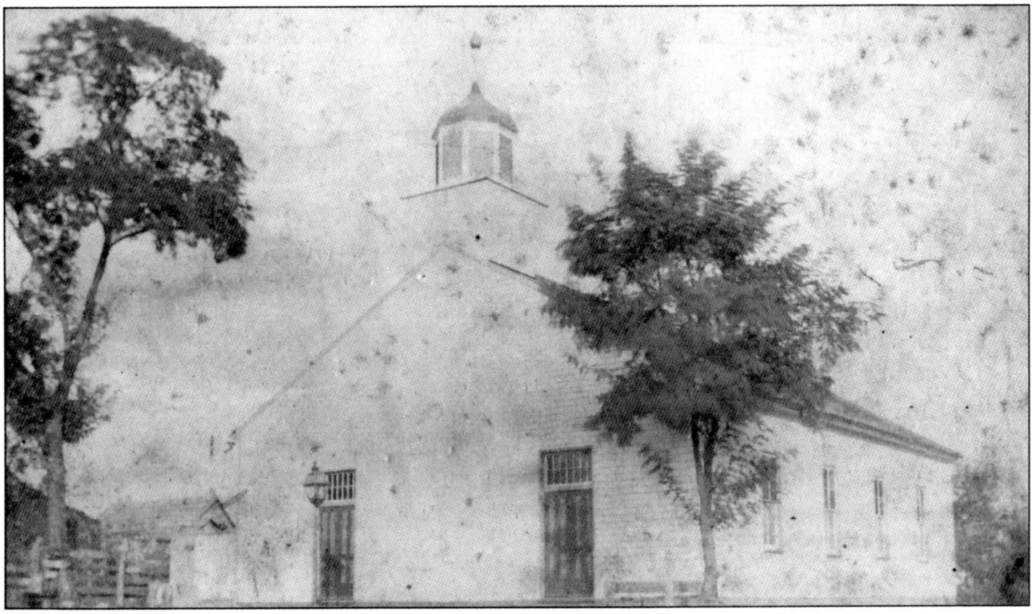

The first settlers in the area were God-fearing people who quickly established churches in the city. The first church in the area was Kings Church, established in 1805. The first known church inside Mt. Washington was Simeon Hall's church, which was located off of Half Moon Drive in the early 1800s. He started another that was located at the southeast corner of the Mt. Washington Cemetery, which was affiliated with the Methodist Church. This Methodist church was built in 1843 and located just east of the Crossroads on Highway 44 just behind the Maccabee Hall. (Courtesy of Anna Joyce Hall.)

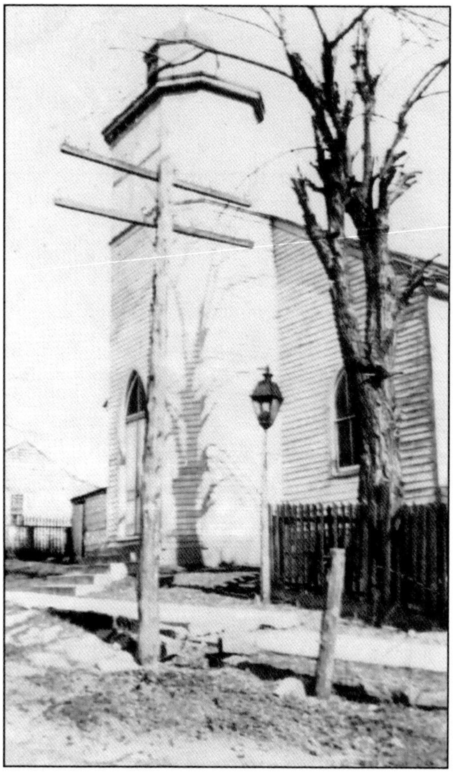

Around 1910, a front foyer was added along with a new cupola, using the top portion of the old one, a practical addition when people had to walk in from a muddy road and needed a place to clean or maybe even remove their shoes and hang their coats before entering into the sanctuary. (Courtesy of the Mt. Washington Historical Society.)

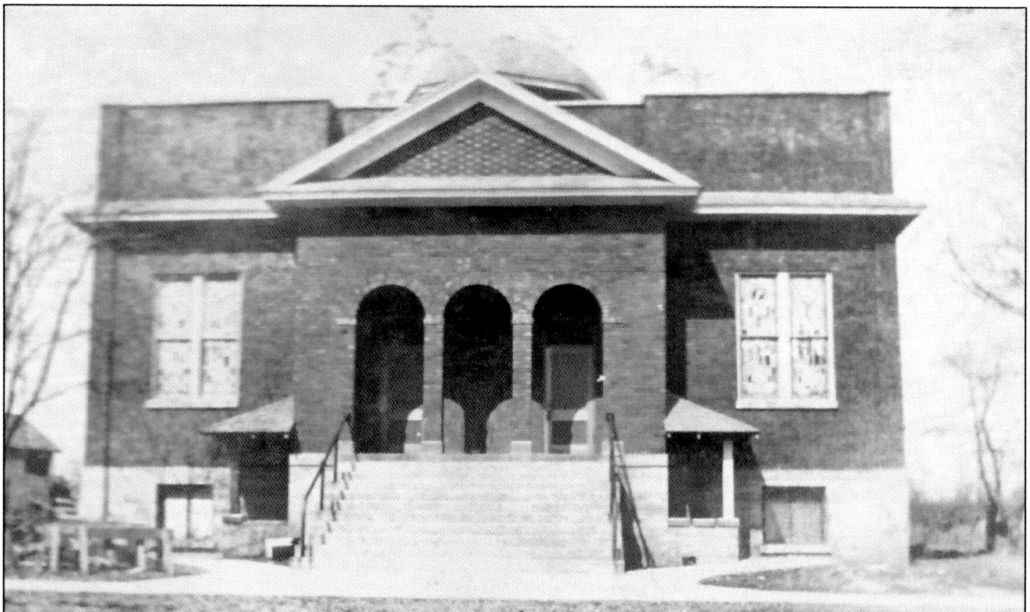

The second Methodist church was built in 1919 next to the preexisting Methodist parsonage on North Main Street. It served until 2010, when a new church building was erected on Flatlick Road. The original building featured a domed roof. A bell tower and a large addition with schoolrooms and a kitchen were added in later years. (Courtesy of Stuart Tichenor.)

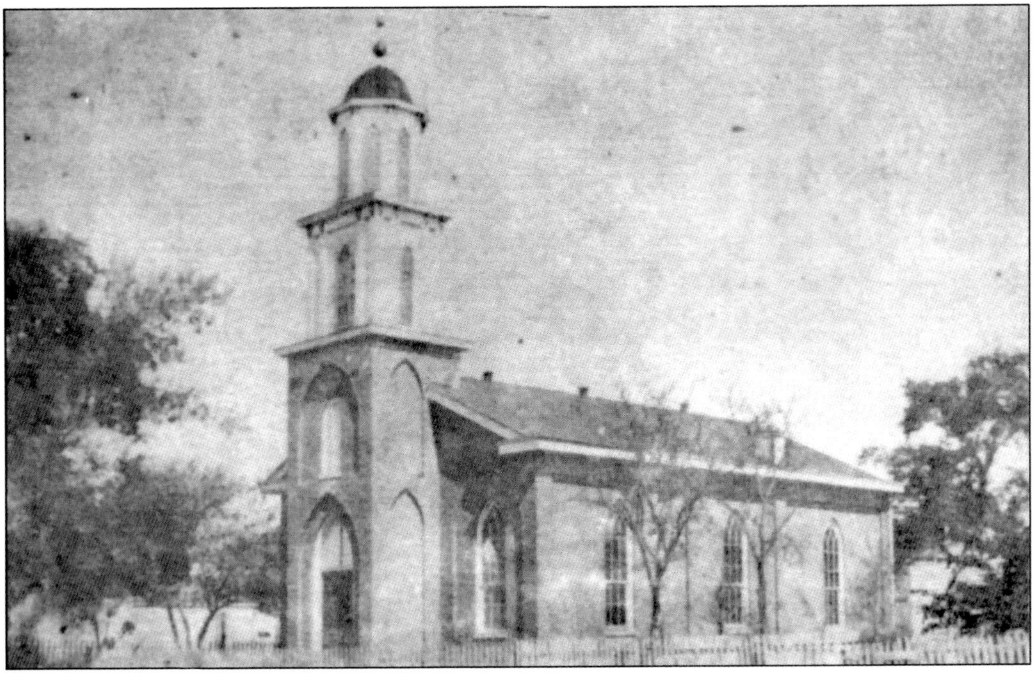

The first Baptist church building was erected in 1838 on property owned by Samuel Evans. It burned sometime in the early 1870s, and a new church building (pictured above) was erected in 1874 on the same lot. It served until 1922 when it was torn down and much of the brick and lumber was used for a new building (pictured below). Construction began in 1922 and finished in 1926. The building was eventually named after Brother W.S. Coakley, who spearheaded the campaign. W.A. King was in charge of the building's construction, and R.H. Hunt was the architect. Many members of the congregation lent their labor and skills to the project; women cleaned mortar off of the brick from the previous building to be used for Coakley Chapel. Many of the men helped with construction, plastering, and painting. (Courtesy of Stuart Tichenor.)

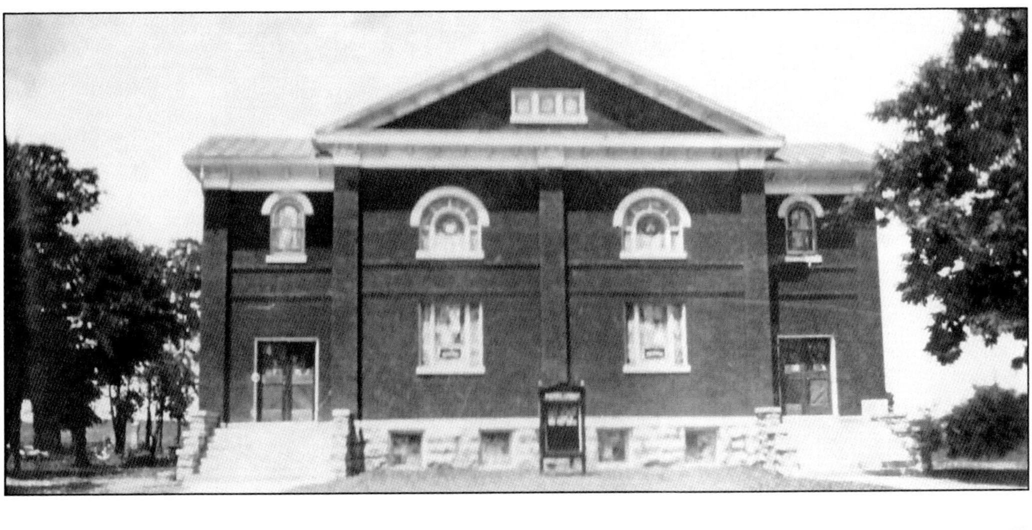

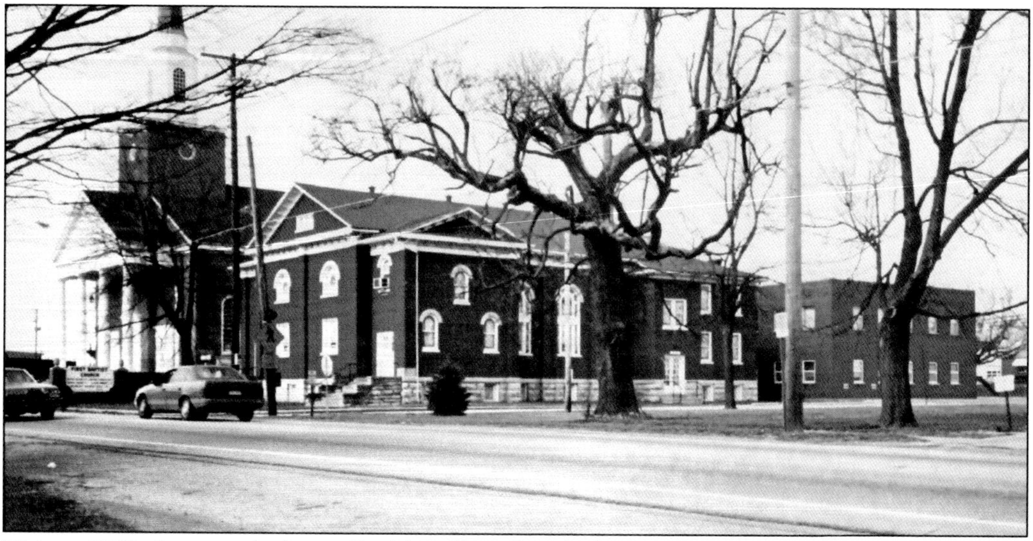

This c. 1980 photograph shows Coakley Chapel with the newer sanctuary built in 1969 beside it. The education building behind Coakley was added in 1955. A Christian Life Center has been added since, making it quite a large complex. (Courtesy of Lloyd and Arbidella Dooley.)

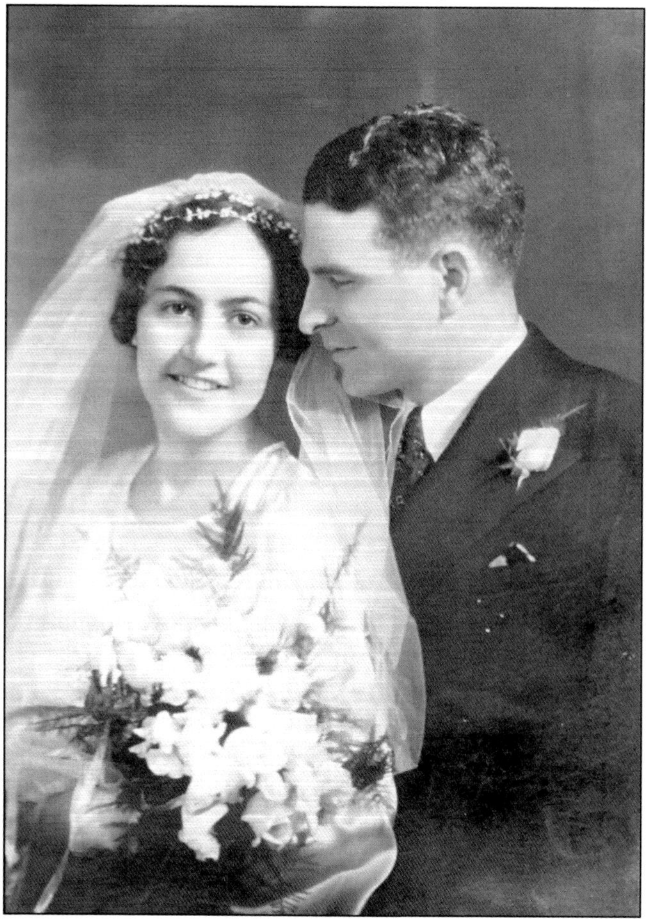

Rev. W.A. Criswell led the Baptist church in Mt. Washington from 1932 to 1935. An Oklahoma native, Criswell attended the Southern Baptist Seminary in Louisville. He married the church's pianist, Betty Harris, and was suddenly called to another church. In 1944, he replaced evangelist George Truett at the First Baptist Church of Dallas, Texas. By the 1960s, the church had grown immensely and was at one time the largest church in the United States. Reverend Criswell was the author of several religious books, twice president of the Southern Baptist Convention, and founder of Criswell College. (Courtesy of Mildred Brown.)

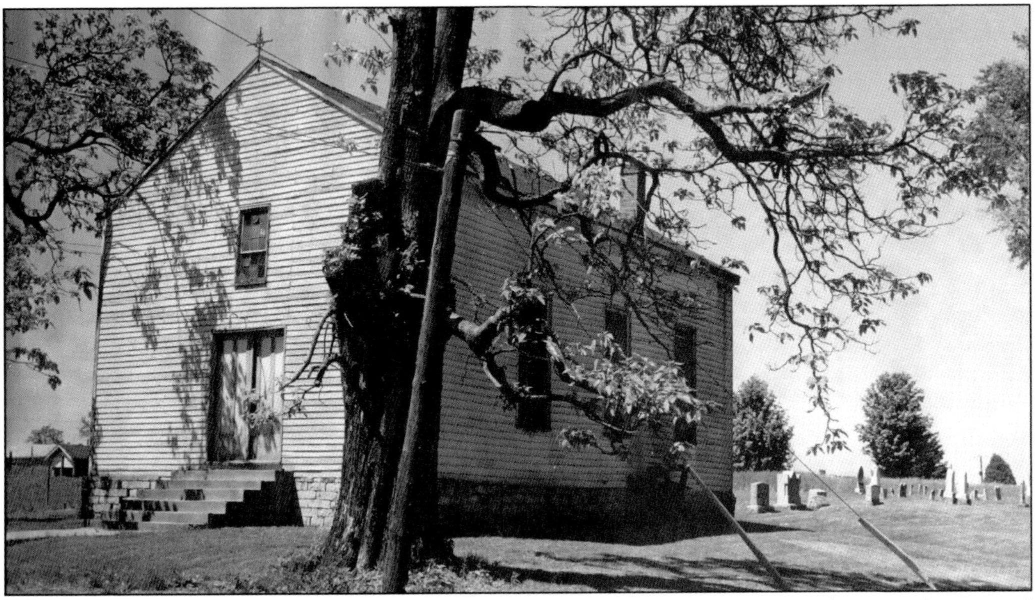

The first Catholic church in Mt. Washington was located at the corner of Snapp Street and East Street (now Dooley Drive). Land was donated by J.C. and Ellen Dent, and the building was constructed in 1848. Father Callahan, a priest from Fairfield, Kentucky, would come and have services once or twice a month. The Catholic cemetery remains on the property where the church was located. Property was acquired at Highway 44 and Stringer Lane in 1961 for a new church that was built shortly thereafter. (Courtesy of the Bullitt County History Museum.)

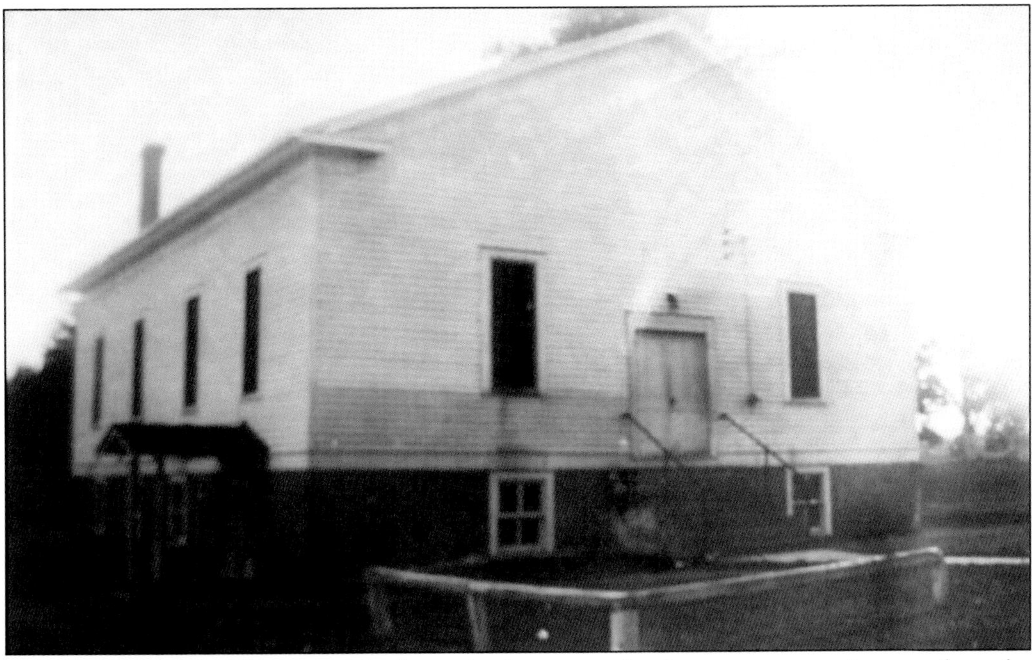

Pleasant Grove Church is located a few miles from town but has a strong contingency from the city. This building was replaced with a more modern one in the 1960s and one of the first in the area to feature a gymnasium and multipurpose building. The old church building was converted into a basketball gym in which the author remembers playing. (Courtesy of Adelyn Proctor.)

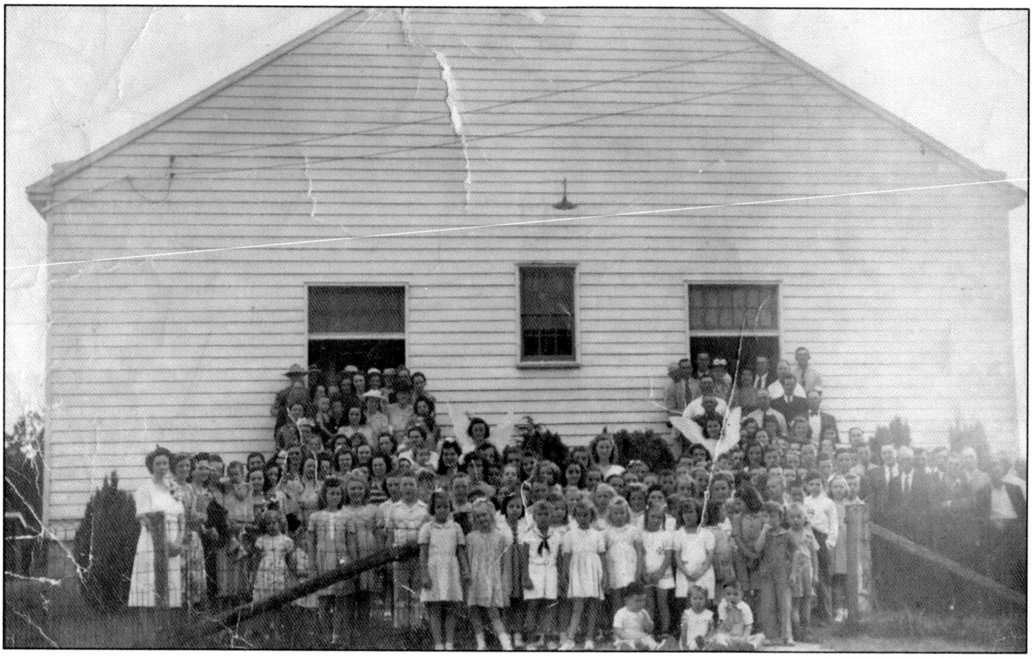

Kings Baptist Church began as Cane and Back Run Baptist Church around the Back Run Road area in 1800. In 1805, Alexander King donated land for a new church building on what was then known as Shelbyville Road, now King's Church Road. That building was used until 1831, and the next building burned to the ground in 1843. The third building (top) lasted until 1958. In 1940, Garner Dooley raised the building and dug a basement without one crack in the plastered walls. In 1958, a more modern building (bottom) replaced the aging, 115-year-old church. One unique feature of the older building was a partition in the middle of the sanctuary that divided the men from the women. Between 1833 and 1876, William Barnett served there as pastor for 43 straight years. (Courtesy of Carolyn Quebbeman.)

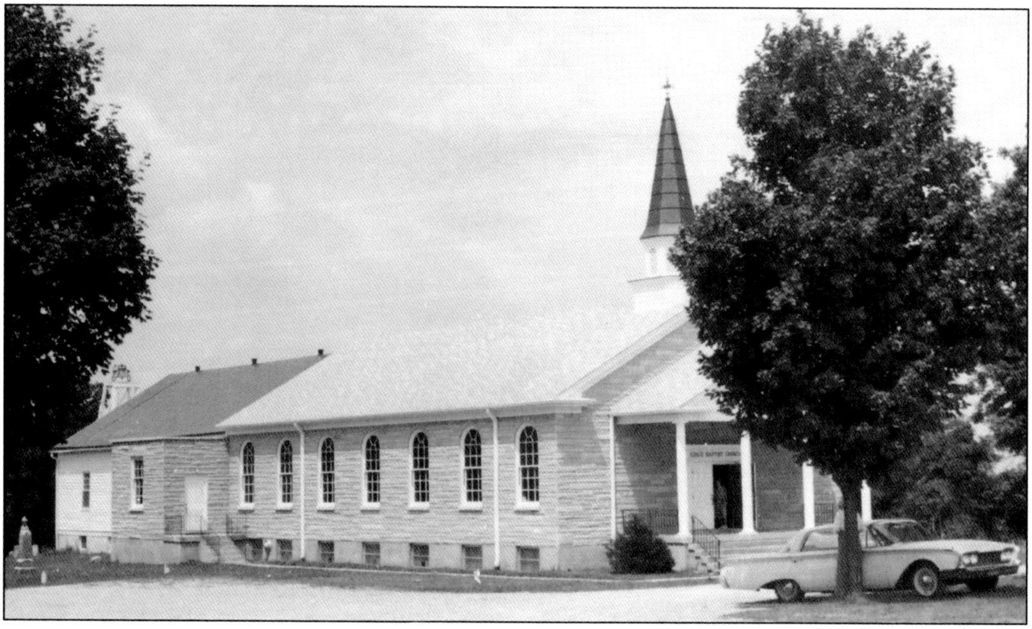

Four

Motoring through Mt. Washington

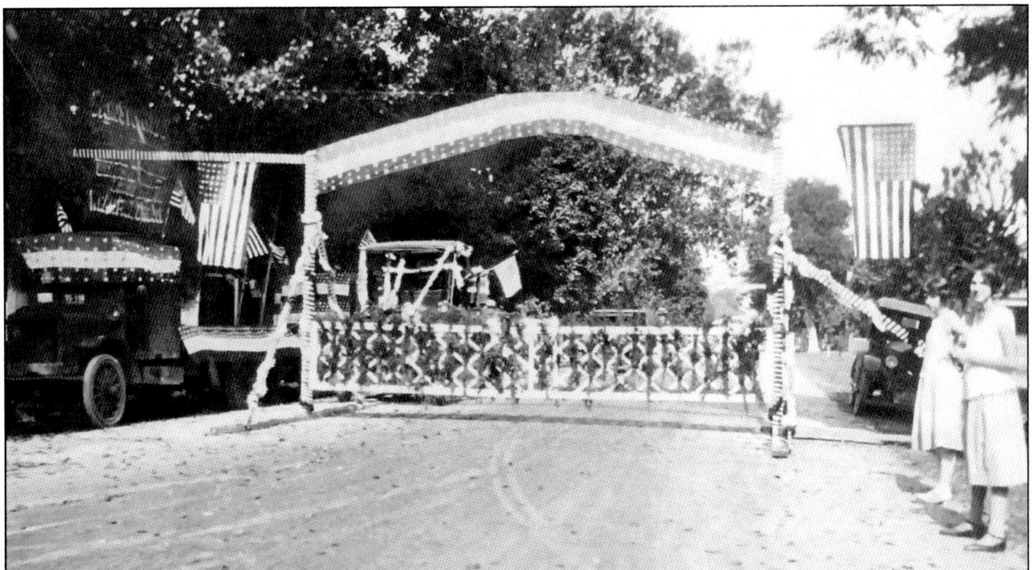

In the early 1920s, Bardstown Road, or the Jackson Highway as it was called, was finally being paved from Louisville to Bardstown. It was a massive undertaking and virtually shut the city's businesses down during construction on Main Street. In the end, it was a great boon to the city and allowed it to grow. On August 29, 1925, the new highway was dedicated in a celebration on Main Street. Gov. William J. Fields gave a speech, as did local resident and state representative Bert Hall. (Courtesy of Gayle and Eleanor Troutman.)

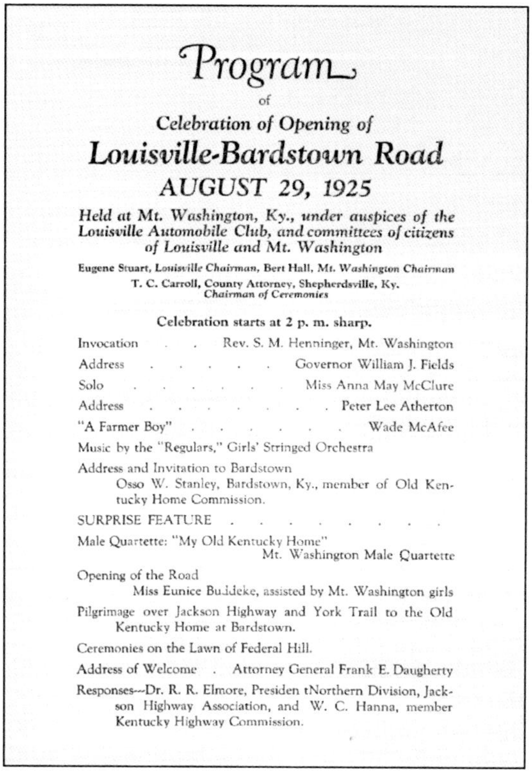

Program

of

Celebration of Opening of

Louisville-Bardstown Road

AUGUST 29, 1925

Held at Mt. Washington, Ky., under auspices of the Louisville Automobile Club, and committees of citizens of Louisville and Mt. Washington

Eugene Stuart, *Louisville Chairman*, Bert Hall, *Mt. Washington Chairman*
T. C. Carroll, County Attorney, Shepherdsville, Ky.
Chairman of Ceremonies

Celebration starts at 2 p. m. sharp.

Invocation . . Rev. S. M. Henninger, Mt. Washington
Address . . . . . . Governor William J. Fields
Solo . . . . Miss Anna May McClure
Address . . . . Peter Lee Atherton
"A Farmer Boy" . . . . Wade McAfee
Music by the "Regulars," Girls' Stringed Orchestra
Address and Invitation to Bardstown
Osso W. Stanley, Bardstown, Ky., member of Old Kentucky Home Commission.
SURPRISE FEATURE . . . .
Male Quartette: "My Old Kentucky Home"
Mt. Washington Male Quartette
Opening of the Road
Miss Eunice Buddeke, assisted by Mt. Washington girls
Pilgrimage over Jackson Highway and York Trail to the Old Kentucky Home at Bardstown.
Ceremonies on the Lawn of Federal Hill.
Address of Welcome . Attorney General Frank E. Daugherty
Responses—Dr. R. R. Elmore, Presiden tNorthern Division, Jackson Highway Association, and W. C. Hanna, member Kentucky Highway Commission.

Programs were distributed for the opening celebration, and many dignitaries of that time showed up to shake hands or give speeches. Bert Hall, a state representative at that time, was one of them. A local group of young women who called themselves the Regulars played their ukuleles for the crowd. It may have been the largest crowd that ever converged on the city of Mt. Washington for an event, estimated at 8,000 visitors. (Courtesy of the Mt. Washington Historical Society.)

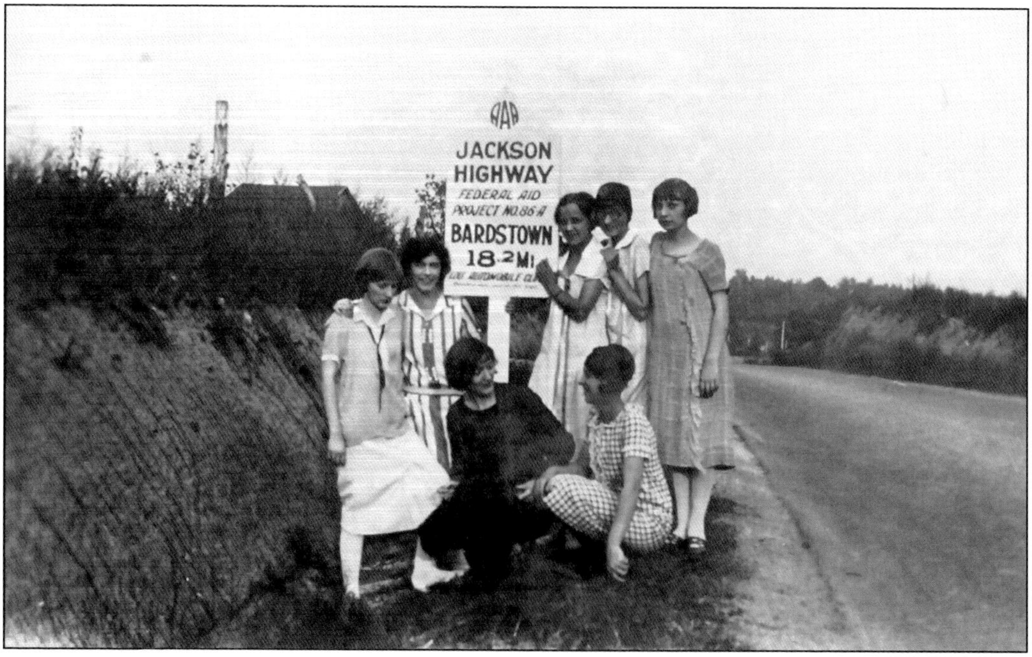

Here are the Regulars proudly displaying the new sign for the Jackson Highway. It would have been located just south of town on Bardstown Road. The days of difficult travel were over. The Regulars were a popular group of women that formed a club that stayed together for several years and traveled the area extensively, mostly on foot. (Courtesy of Gayle and Eleanor Troutman.)

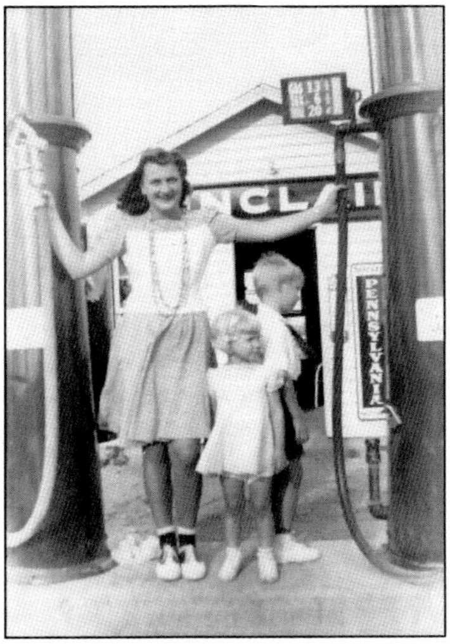

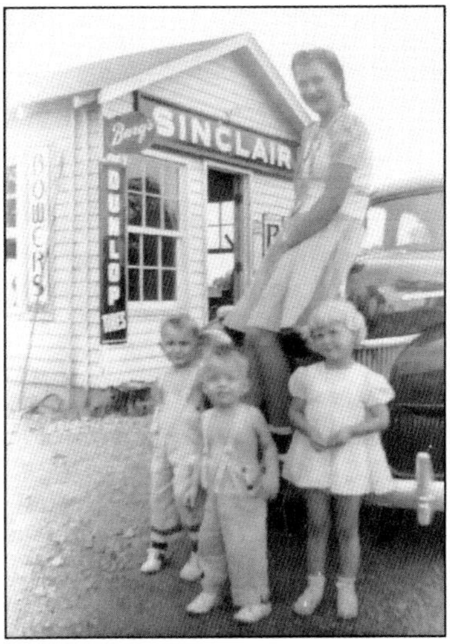

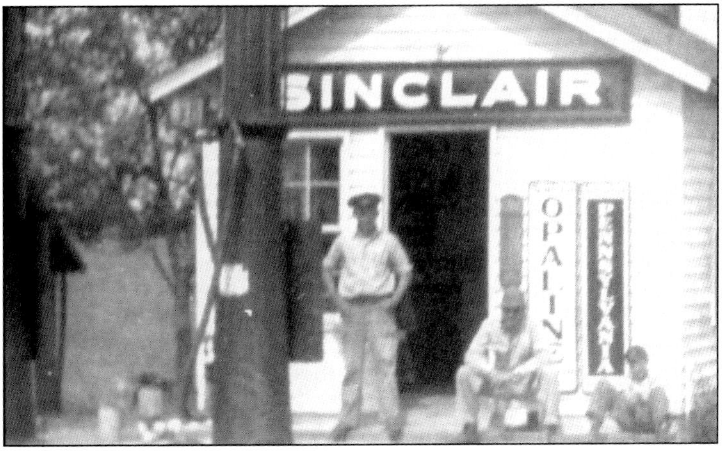

There were very few homes nearby when James Clark operated his Sinclair Station near Clark's Lane in the 1940s, but he was at the north end of town and caught everyone going to and coming in from Louisville. He offered items such as motor oil but did not have a garage to do repairs. However, he did have an oil pit where he could pull a vehicle over and drain the oil. The pit was still visible years later, long after the station was gone. James retired and moved to Gulfport, Florida where he lived to the impressive age of 104. (Courtesy of Jimmy Breeden.)

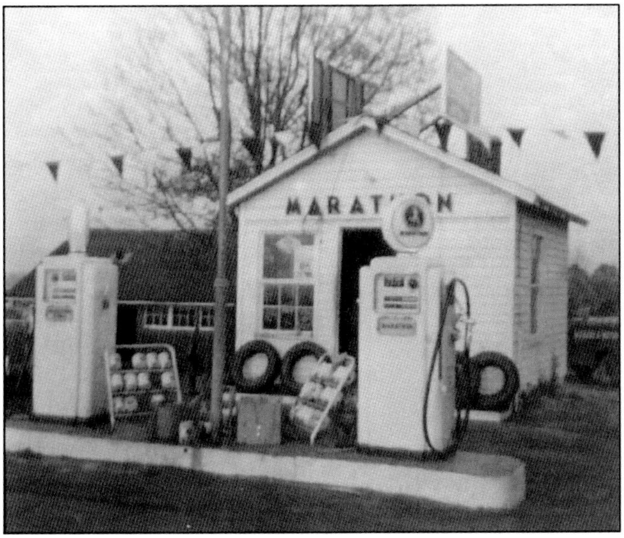

When James Clark moved to Florida, Glenn Armstrong continued to run the station but changed to the Marathon brand. Glenn would later run his own natural gas company called Thermogas. He would also successfully run for county judge executive and serve from 1990 to 1993. (Courtesy of Jimmy Breeden.)

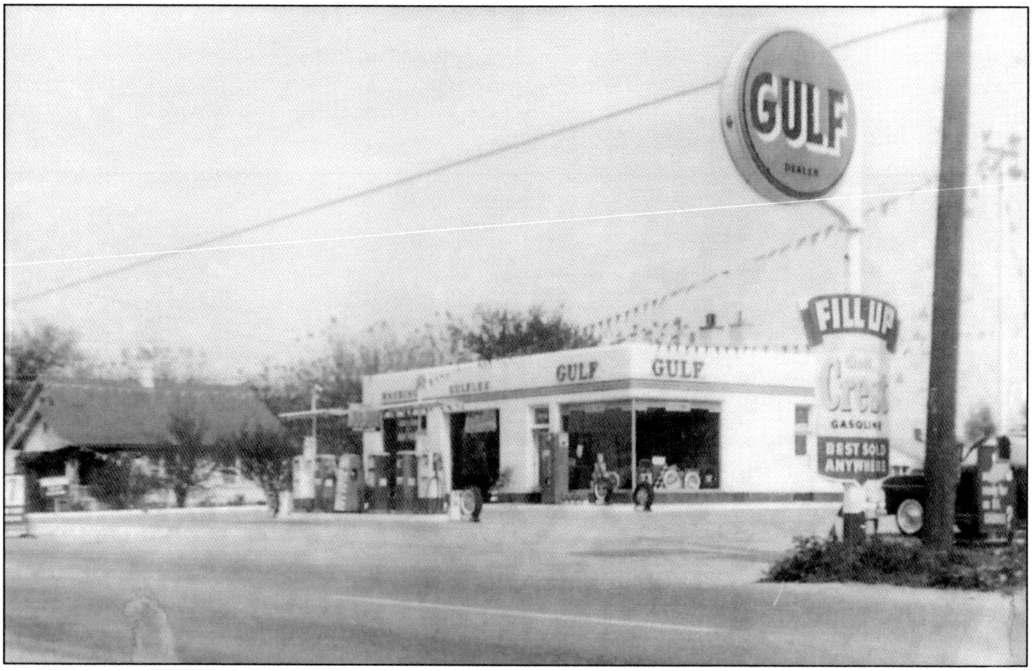

Tom Breeden ran this full-service Gulf Station owned by Newcome Oil Co. on North Bardstown Road from when it was newly built in 1955 until 1965. Skip Richardson, Bobby Dean Cornell, and Dennis Caudill ran it afterwards, and Elmer Newkirk converted it to a Chevron quick stop in the early 1970s. The station was built on a lot that once featured a large pond and the croaking of frogs at night earned the nickname "Frogtown." At the left is Carl Wigginton's home. During Christmastime, Tom got in a jovial mood and decorated the station with garland (below). (Courtesy of Jimmy Breeden.)

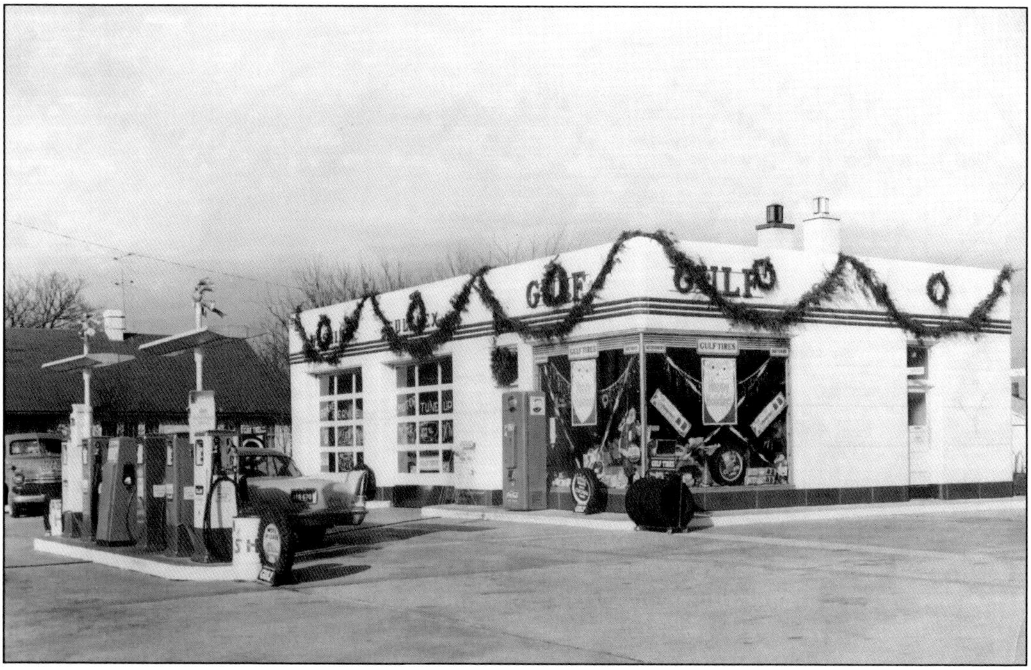

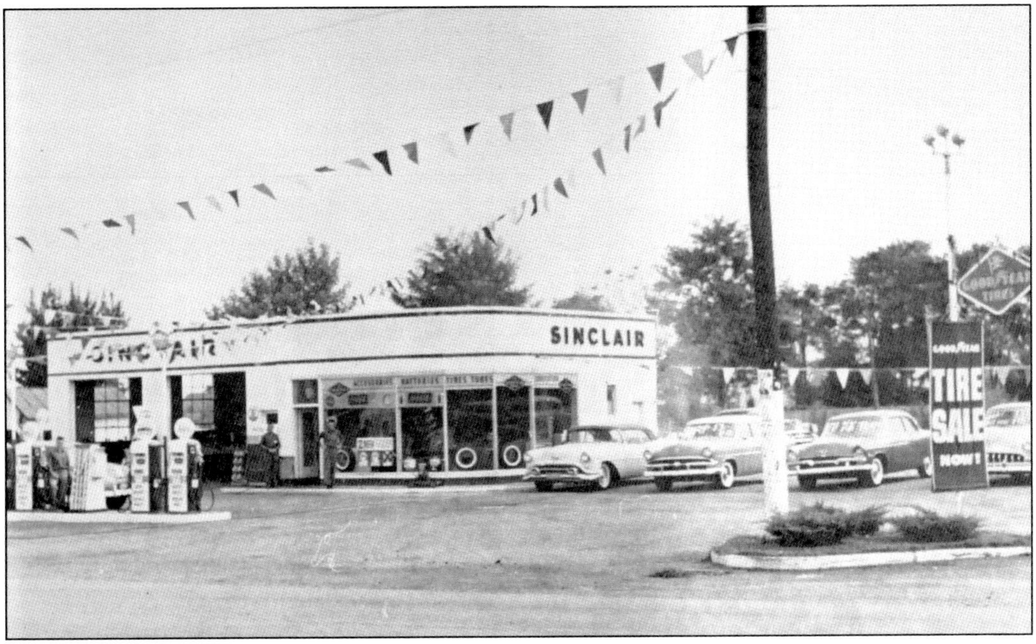

Oliver "Gator" Harris and Lindsay Wigginton celebrated the grand opening of their full-service Sinclair Station at the corner of North Main and Snapp Streets on December 19, 1953. Gator's father, Wilder, had previously owned and operated the Mt. Washington Motor Company Ford dealership on Main Street. Lindsay sold out his part to Gator, and for a while the business was leased to Roy Tinsley. Gator returned and had a booming business, thanks to great service and promotions. (Author's collection.)

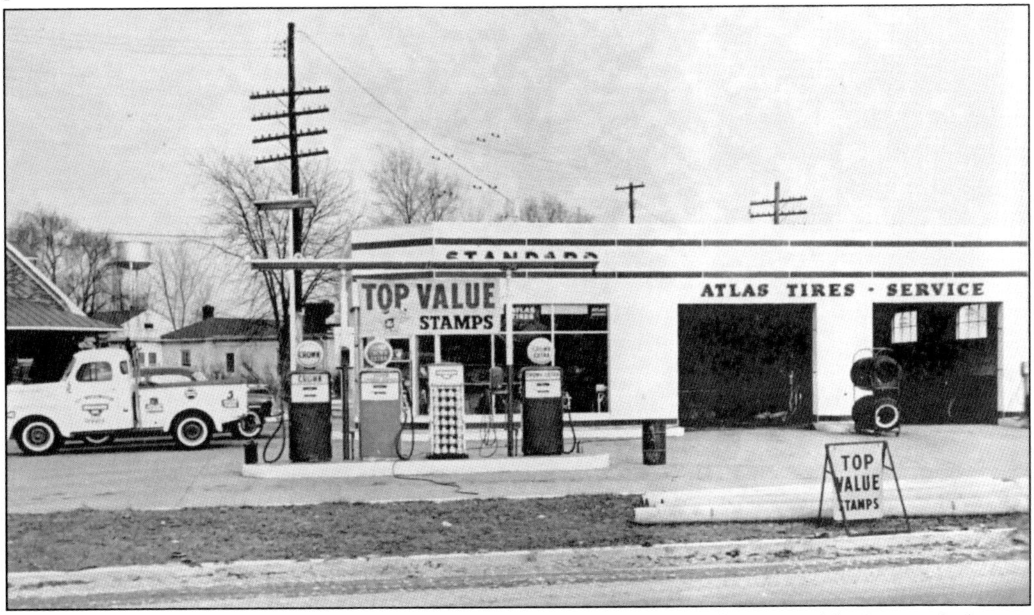

This full-service Standard Station was built in the early 1960s and operated by James Coleman and Jack Lloyd. It was located on North Bardstown Road near Flatlick Road, on the same property where James had spent his youth. Other operators were Charlie Long and Don Morgan. It was most recently Jo-Mar Automotive. (Author's collection.)

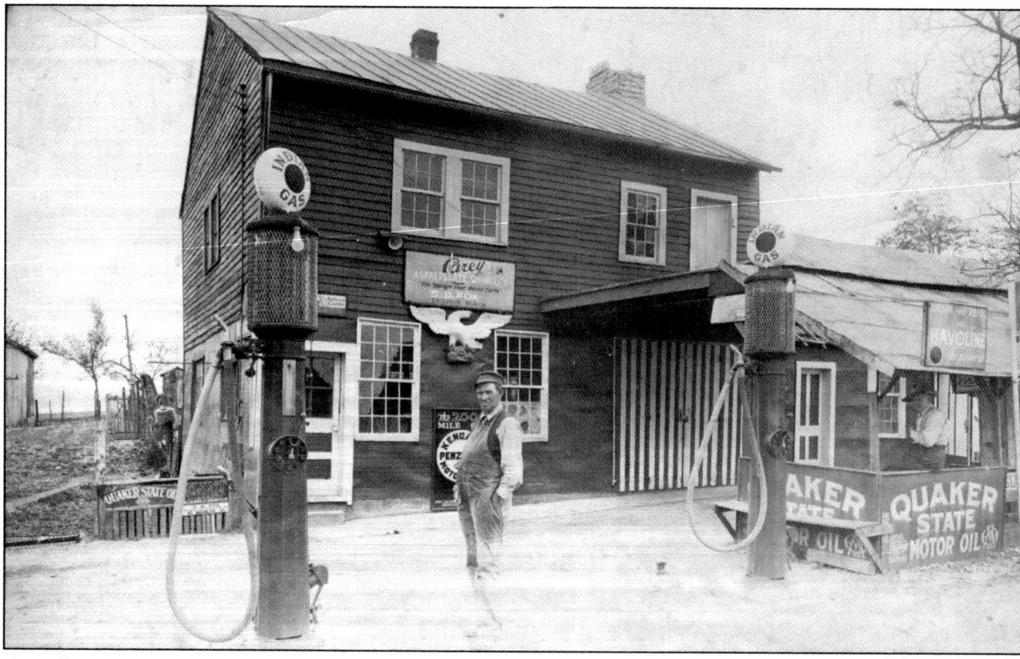

Sam Fox converted the property that was once his father's blacksmith shop into a grocery and gas station. He was one of the most well-liked men in town, and his store was a popular place for locals to spend time. He had a tendency to have his photograph taken in profile for some unknown reason. (Author's collection.)

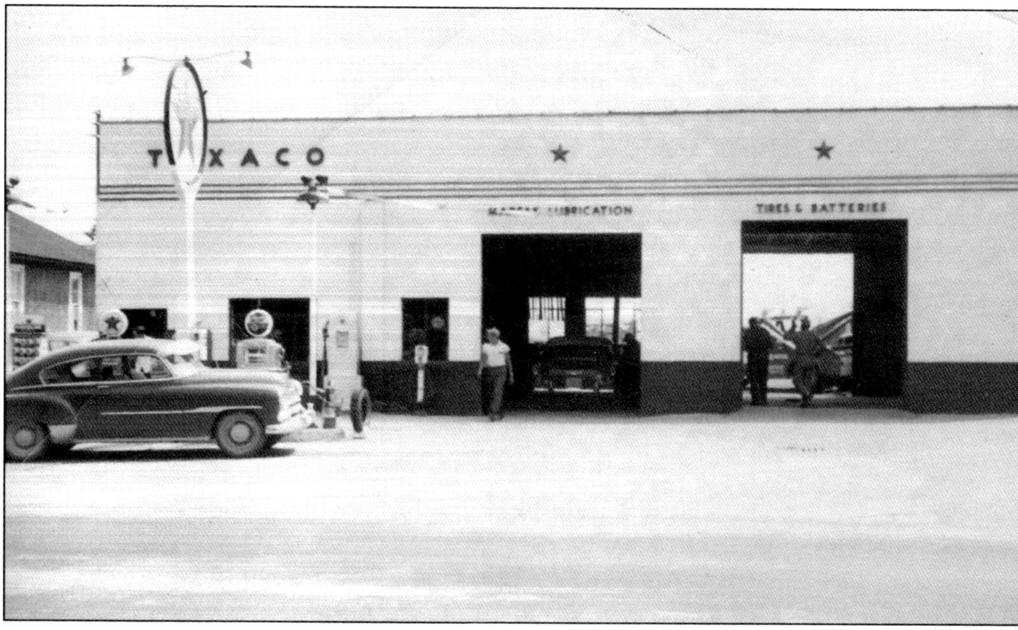

Marion "Unc" Jasper bought the property that Sam Fox's grocery and gas station had occupied for many years and built a modern concrete-block, full-service gas station in 1950. W.A. Lutes, Bob Gordon, and Gary Laswell also ran it but as a Marathon affiliate. The eagle on the front originated on Sam's building and stayed until the building was sold by the Jasper family. (Author's collection.)

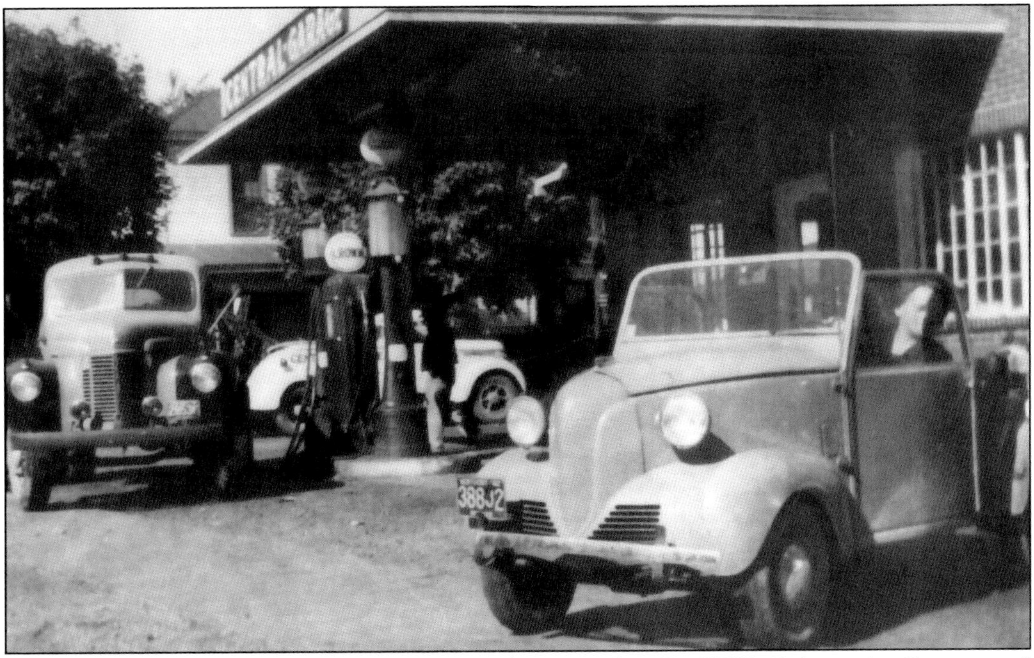

Standard Oil Company bought the property that served as Dr. W.W. Coleman's office around 1925 and built a new brick service station. Maynard Jasper moved his auto dealership there in 1935, shown in this image. Numerous other businesses have occupied the building, including another gas station run by Ed "Eck" Bleemel, Sandy Melton's diner, and Melvin Porter's Western Auto Store. Tom Breeden bought the building and ran a Remington Tire and auto maintenance business. His son Jimmy still owns it and leases it to various businesses. Maynard's wife, Nina, is pictured here in the car on the right. (Courtesy of Tommy Jasper.)

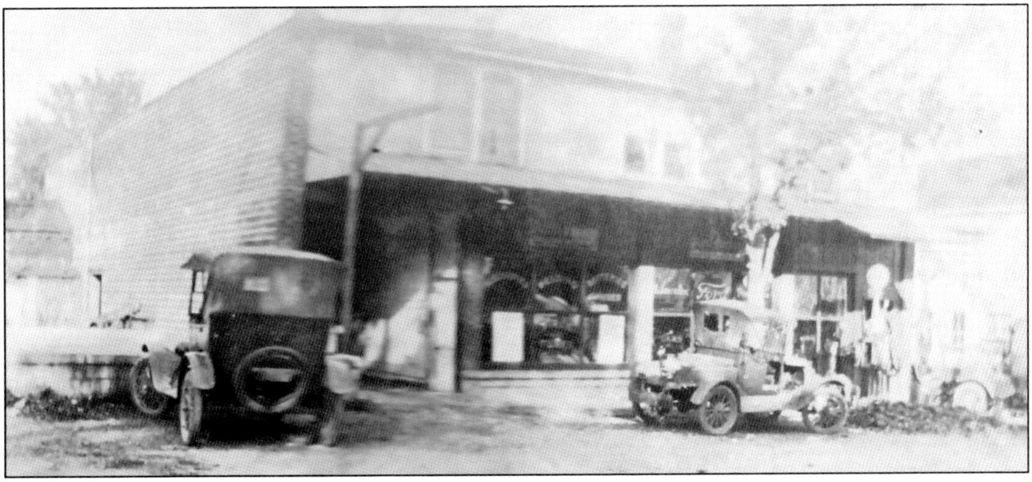

In the early 1920s, Wilder Harris bought the property on which the Parrish blacksmith shop was located at the corner of the Crossroads. He built a large, two-story brick building which housed his Ford Dealership that he called the Mt. Washington Motor Company. The dealership was a great success and a popular hangout where people would congregate to talk and play music. Maurice McAfee was an employee. On June 2, 1933, it caught fire and burned to the ground. The cars were spared, but almost all else was lost. His son Oliver "Gator" Harris would follow in his father's footsteps and own a Sinclair service station. (Courtesy of Stuart Tichenor.)

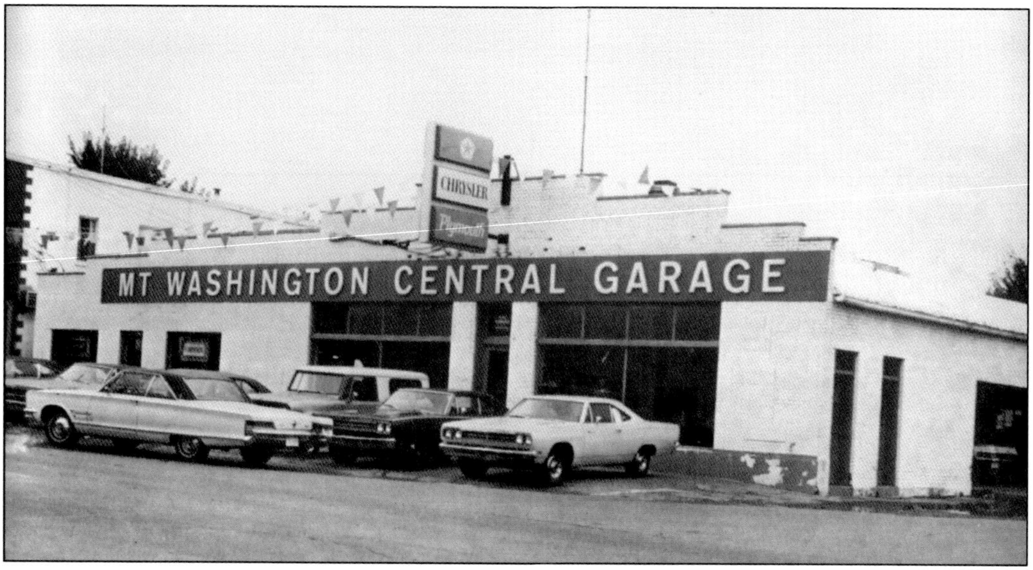

Maynard Jasper bought the property that Wilder Harris's Ford dealership was on around 1942 and constructed a building reminiscent of an airplane hangar. It was his third move in fewer than 15 years. The Chrysler-Plymouth-Dodge and International farm equipment dealership was well known and prospered throughout the years. His sons J.R. and Tommy were also involved in the business. Ultimately, Tommy ran the business and eventually moved it a few miles west on Highway 44. (Author's collection.)

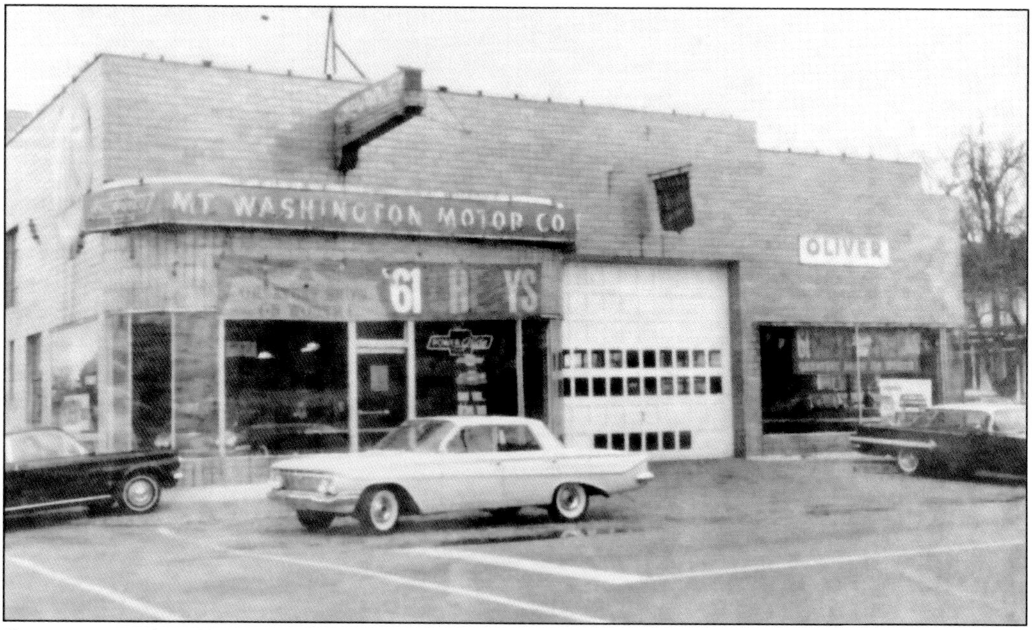

Sometime in the 1930s, Marvin Porter started a Chevrolet dealership in Mt. Washington, possibly in the rear of the Cyclone store. Marvin resurrected the name "Mt. Washington Motor Company" from Wilder Harris's Ford dealership. He bought the empty lot where Maccabee Hall had been in addition to several adjoining lots, and in 1947 built a beautiful new garage and showroom on the property. There was also a large lot to display new and used vehicles. Tommy Jasper bought the building and business when Marvin retired. (Author's collection.)

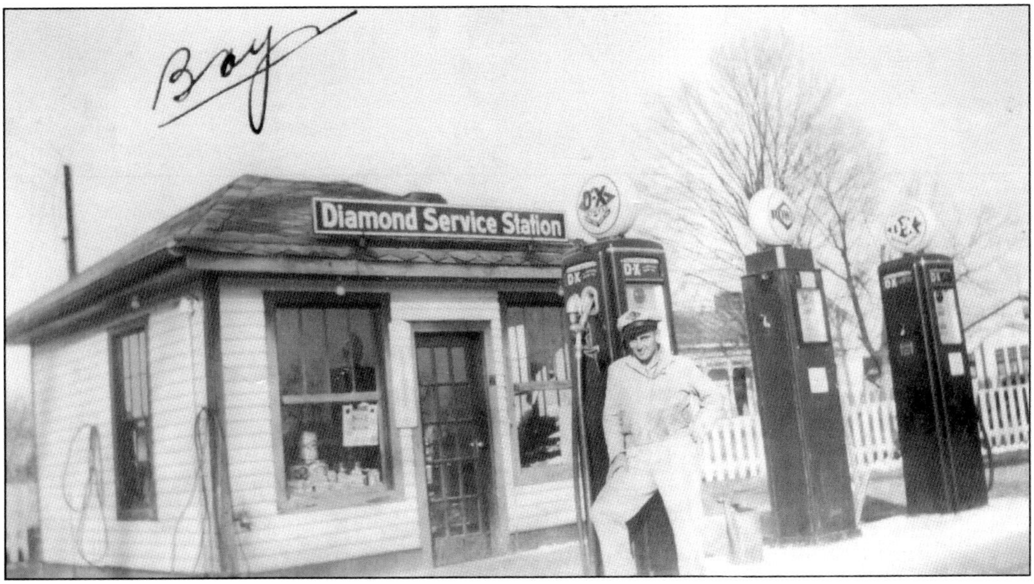

The DX Station at the south end of town near Morning Glory Drive was operated by numerous people, including Kenneth Lutes, W.A. Lutes, Ed Moore, and Raymond "Red" Calvert. A larger full-service station (below) was built to the left of it and operated by Billy Couch, Ed Moore, Roy Tinsley, and Roy Hall. The building later was home of Tireland, operated by Bernie Stevenson. (Courtesy of Jimmy Breeden and Trulaverne Couch.)

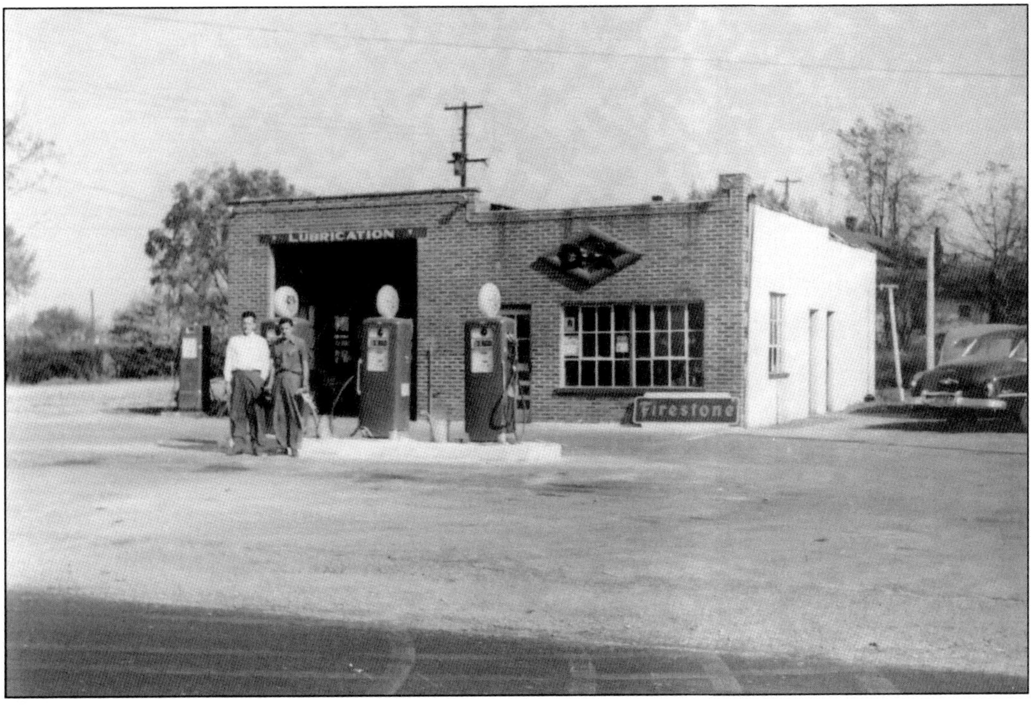

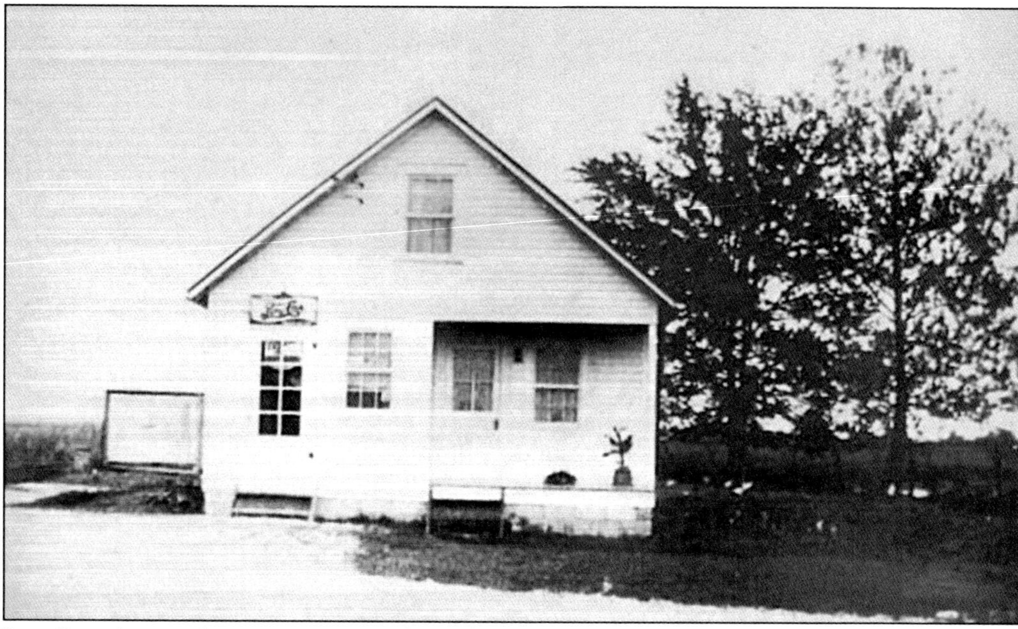

Jesse Brumley ran this grocery on North Bardstown Road during the 1940s when that part of town began to expand. Before then, there were only a few houses in the area. The store was turned into a residence in the 1950s and had the distinction of remaining standing while the Towne and Country NAPA store was built around it to avoid zoning violations. It was torn down after the building around it had been completed. (Courtesy of Louise Cornell.)

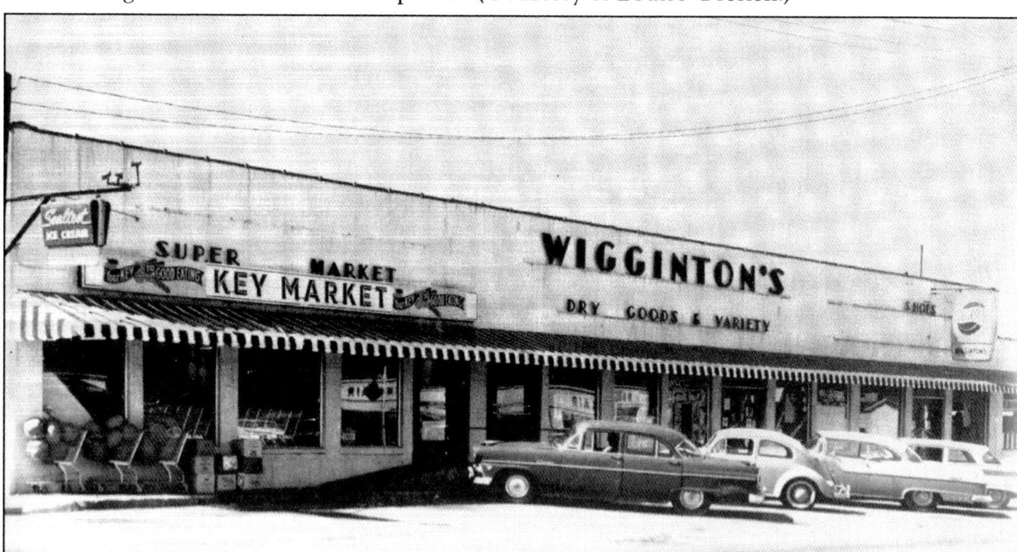

Hubert Wigginton started in the grocery and retail business in 1911 when he partnered with Clarence Porter and bought the Cyclone store from James Gentry. That partnership dissolved, and Hubert and his brother Carl leased the old Methodist church behind Maccabee Hall, turning it into the Union store. Carl left, and in 1927 Hubert built a new modern block building on the property to the right of his childhood home on Main Street near Flatlick Road. In the following years, the business expanded to include home furnishings and clothing, and other businesses leased space from the Wiggintons. (Author's collection.)

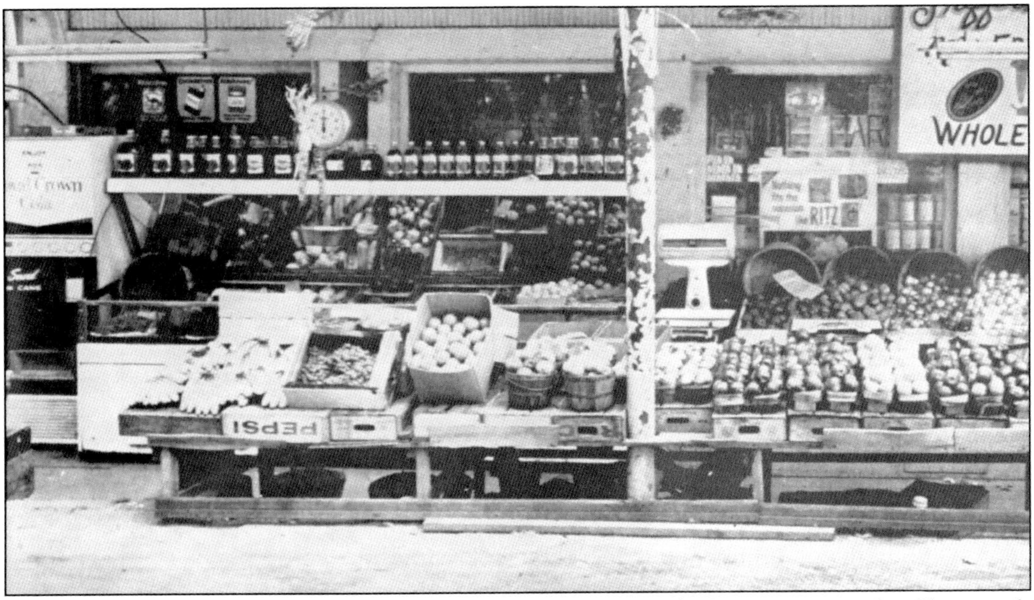

Sidney Griffin had been in the produce business for some time before opening up his Shopworth grocery store on Main Street in 1959. Sid would have tables set up outside to display an array of fruit and vegetables that entice the passersby to stop in. Inside, he had a variety of groceries and common needs. He also had a large glass-enclosed case of candies that were a delight to anyone with a sweet tooth. Its proximity to the high school was a boon to business when students would venture over after school or basketball games. (Author's collection.)

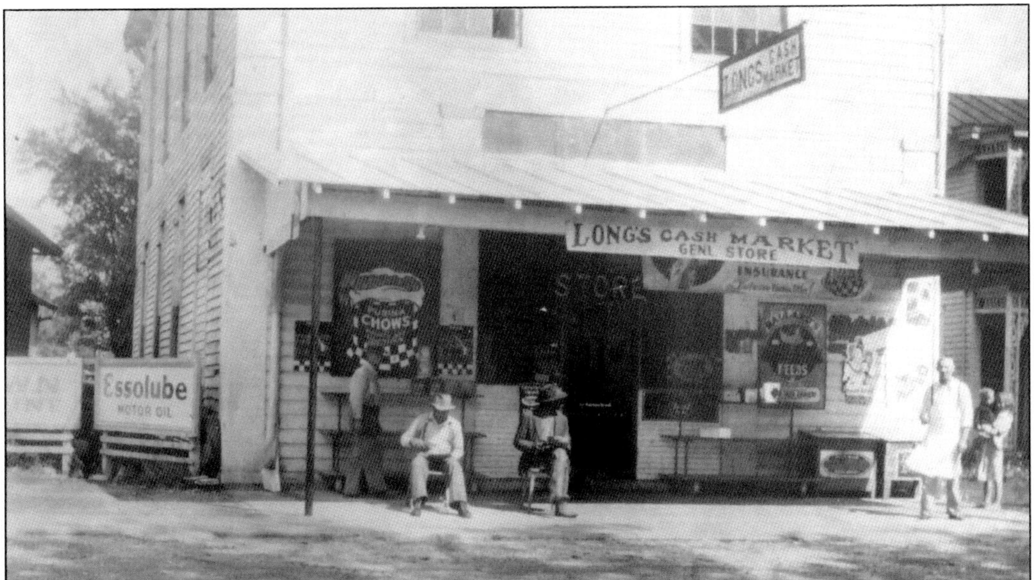

Charles Long and his son Thurston leased the lower floor of the Masonic lodge building and started Long's Cash Market during the late 1930s through the 1940s. Charlie was a former Bullitt County deputy sheriff. There was friendly competition between them and the Barnes Brothers' store across the street. Photographed here from left to right are Virgil Lewis, Eddie Lee Weaver, Ed Weaver, Charles Long, and Anita (Dooley) Lutes holding Thurston's son Charles Abel. (Courtesy of the Mt. Washington Historical Society.)

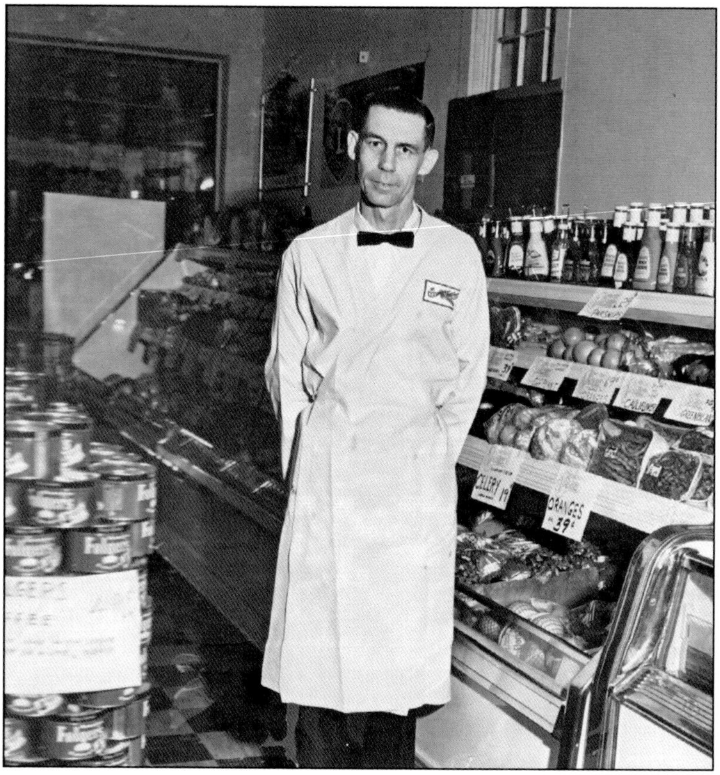

In 1969, Amos and Mildred Brown opened up their IGA grocery store in the old Cyclone building. They later moved into a more modern building and ran it until they retired in the early 1980s. They were a hands-on couple who were always there welcoming and helping their customers. They were also very generous and sponsored several athletic teams. (Courtesy of Mildred Brown.)

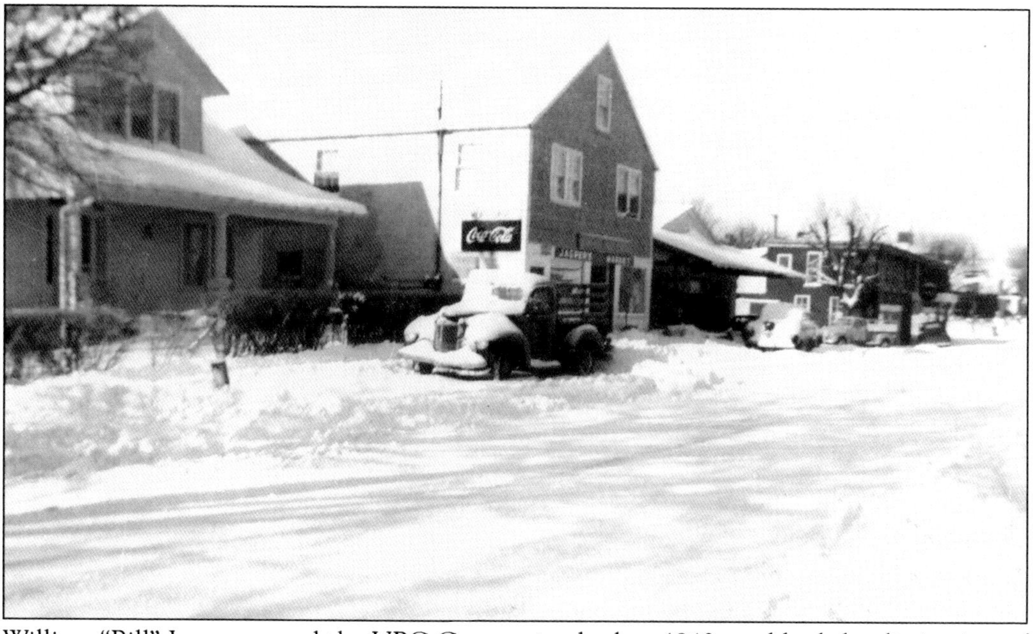

William "Bill" Jasper opened the UBC Grocery in the late 1940s and had the distinction of being the first grocery in town to use grocery carts. The spacious building was perfect for its next business, a retail furniture and appliance store called McAfee Brothers run by R. Lee and Maurice "Maury" McAfee. Weber and Hiron bought them out, and the building eventually became the home of Salmon Plumbing Supplies. (Courtesy of Chris Rothman.)

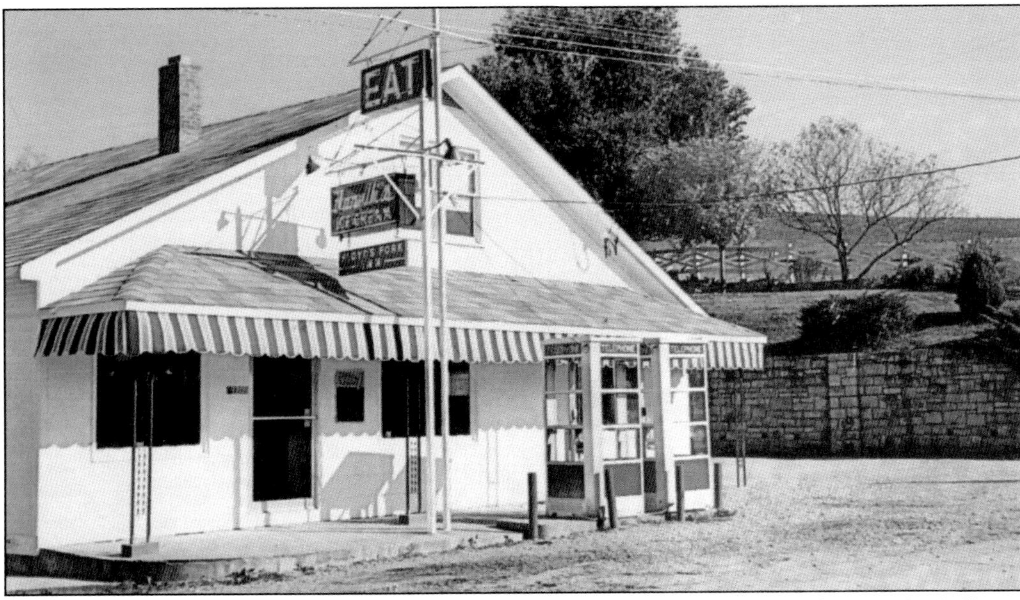

In the early 1940s, John Sollberger opened a restaurant next to Floyd's Fork near the Jefferson County line and appropriately named it Floyd's Fork Inn. It was a popular place for residents of Mt. Washington to eat and get gas while traveling to Louisville or just to get a good home cooked meal after church. Bennett Hunter owned it for a short while in the 1950s before H.H. Farmer bought the business and renamed it the Farmer's Restaurant. Farmer operated the restaurant until 1968 and then sold it to Stanley Perkins. The gas pumps were replaced with phone booths at a later date. (Author's collection.)

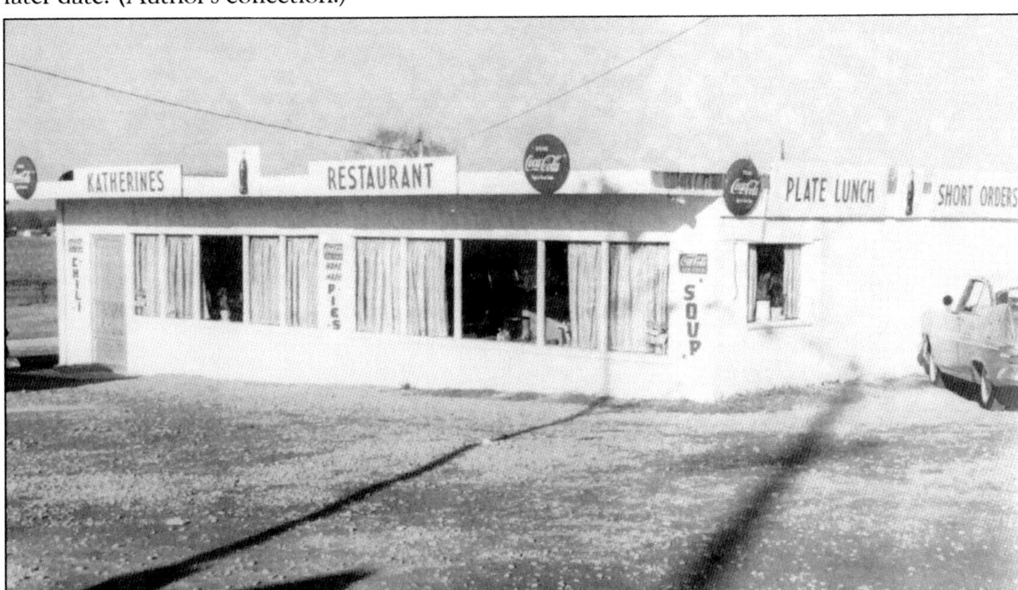

Kathleen's Restaurant was opened in the late 1950s by Mt. Washington High School coach Lloyd Mullin's wife, Kathleen. It was close to their home and a popular place for teens and adults alike to eat. Coach Mullin's popularity surely helped increase business. The Elzy family took over operations by the mid-1960s, and numerous restaurants and businesses have been there since. (Courtesy of Jimmy Breeden.)

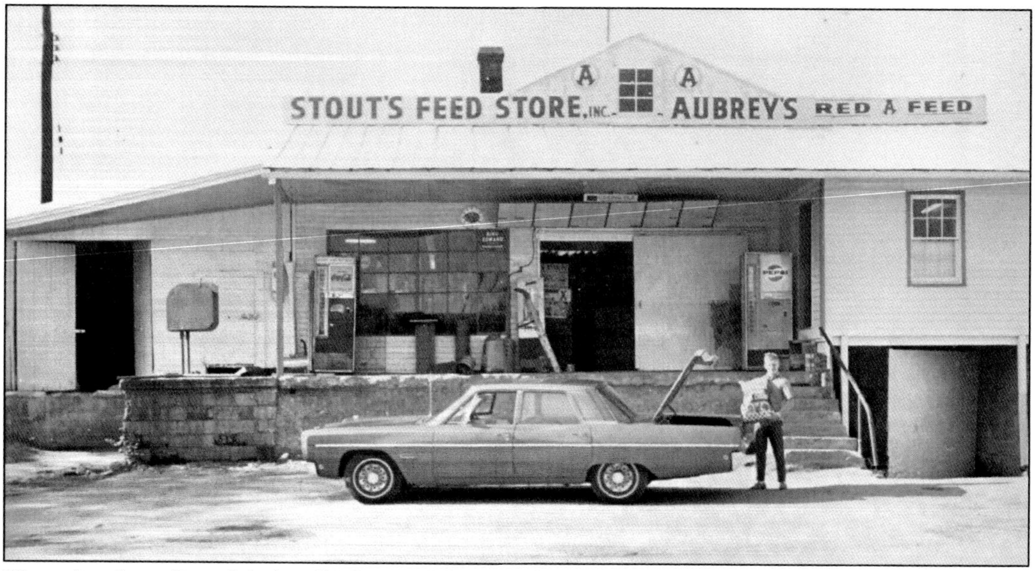

Three brothers, Jesse Markwell "Coonie" Stout, John Stout, and G.H. Stout, started a business in the late 1920s selling grains, seeds, farm needs, lumber, and water near the intersection of Main Street and Flatlick Road. When Mt. Washington expanded, they did too. The brothers erected a new building to the left of the original. The new business sold hardware, paints, household needs, garden items, and much more. A sensational fire in 1974 completely destroyed the building, but a new building, built farther off the road for easier parking, replaced it and remains standing to this day. (Author's collection.)

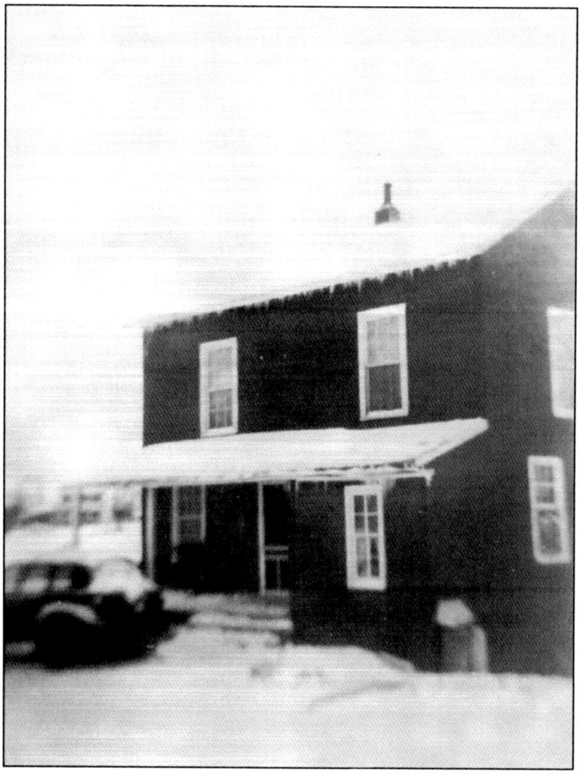

In 1919, H.T. Hall, his brother Rufus K. Hall, and Rufus's son Earl built a flourmill run by gasoline engines on College Street near Highway 44. Most of the flour and meal at that time had been ground at the mill on Salt River. James C. Dickey was a partner with them for a short time, and Robert "Bob" McAfee traded land for the mill in 1922. The mill was abandoned, and the property was sold to Jack Barnes who renovated it into apartments in 1968. (Courtesy of Leda Barnes.)

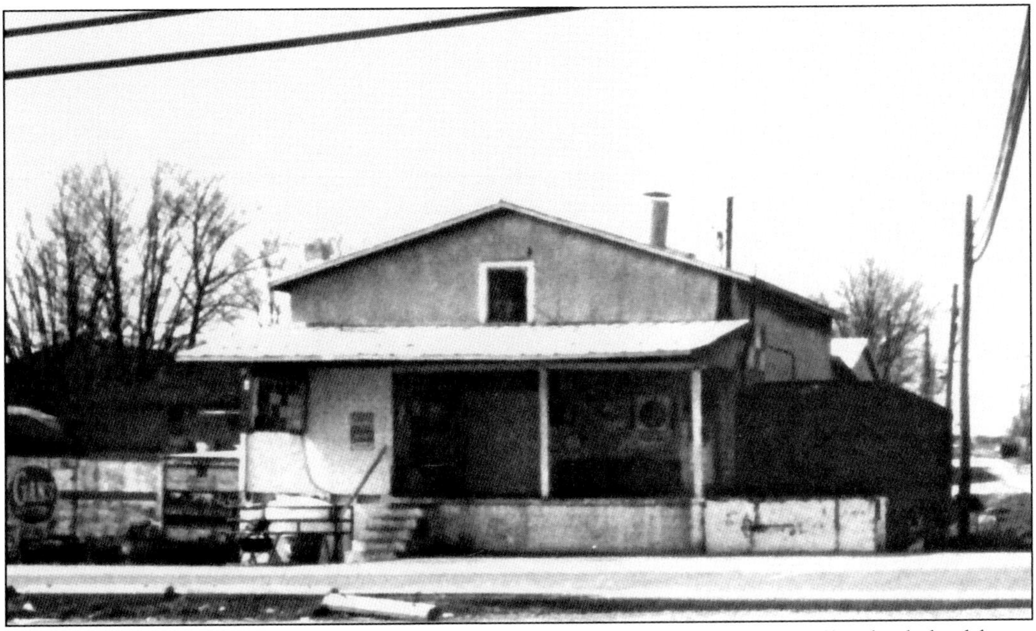

In 1946, Robert "Eggy" Bridwell bought the old Marshall Collier sawmill, which had been converted to a feed mill offering custom grain grinding and selling feed for livestock and small farm implements. At the time, Mt. Washington was largely still a farming community. Eggy ran the mill for about 30 years until he retired and sold it to Roy Kelien, who in turn sold it to Thad Cheatham. (Courtesy of Lloyd Dooley.)

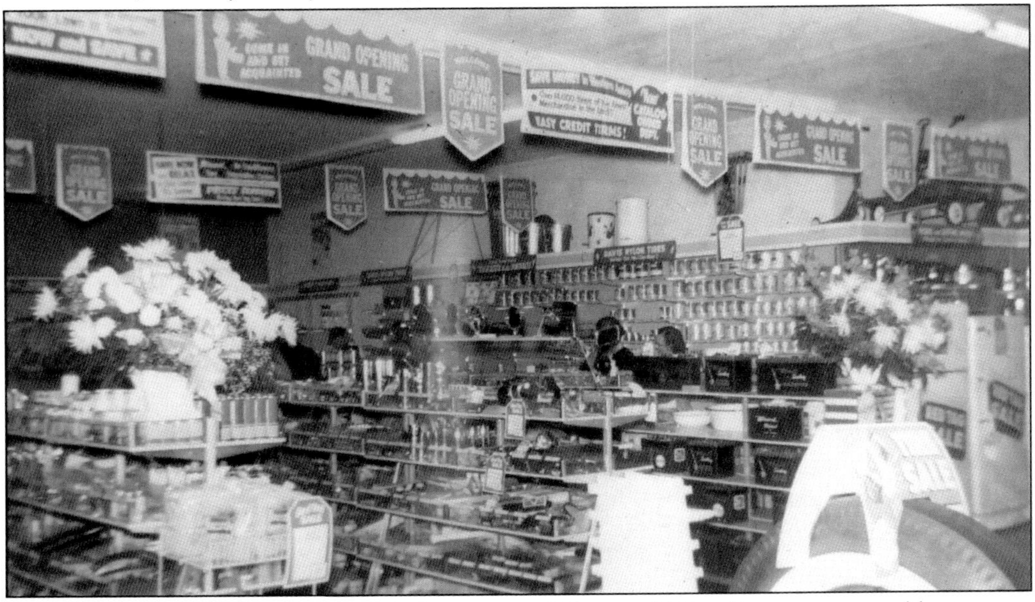

Standard Oil leased their building at the corner of Main and West Streets to several businesses, one of which was Melvin Porter's Western Auto Store. Its grand opening was on June 19, 1958, and this photograph of the inside shows the vast array of items for the home, garden, and auto. There was also a section for toys such as sleds and bicycles. Bob Benford took it over before moving the business to the corner of North Bardstown Road and Lakeview Drive. (Courtesy of Dorothy Dean Porter.)

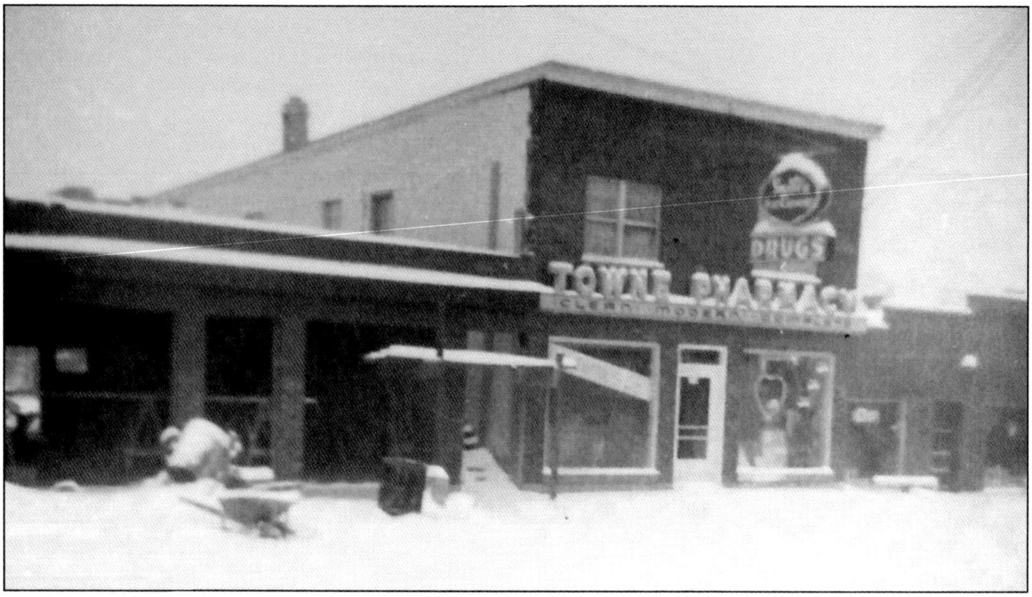

The Towne Pharmacy was started in 1950 by three men who owned three other pharmacies in Louisville. They hired a young pharmacist by the name of Winston Routt who later agreed to buy the pharmacy outright around 1954 and moved his family to Mt. Washington. The pharmacy was a tempting place to while the time away, browsing the aisles or sitting at the soda fountain drinking a cherry cola and eating what was described as the "best tuna fish sandwich ever." (Courtesy of Leda Barnes.)

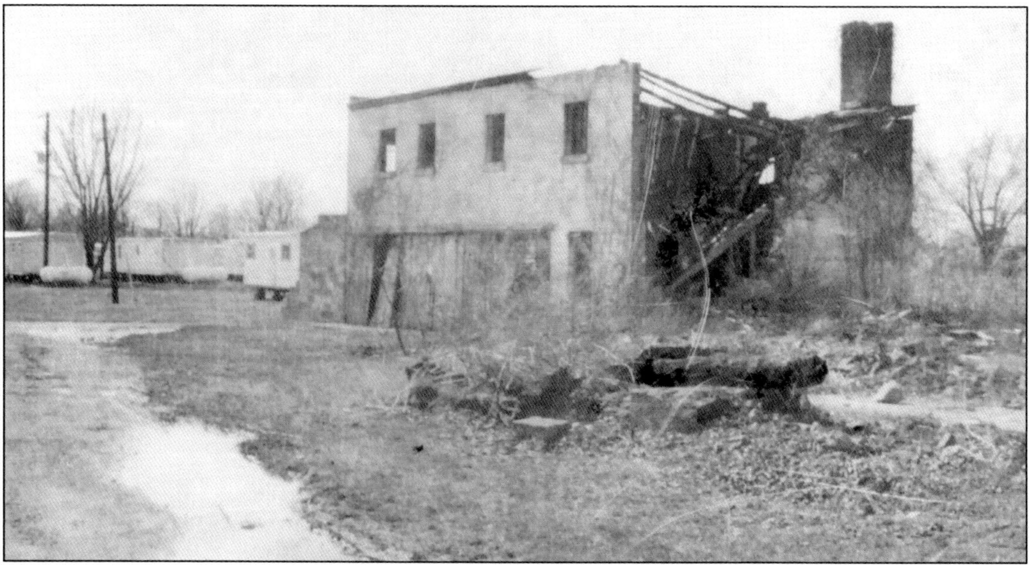

The Airport Skating Rink opened sometime in the late 1940s and was owned by Billy Couch and Lindsay Wigginton. It was on the same property as Billy's later rink, called the Whirlaway, on Highway 44. On September 12, 1959, it burned to the ground along with the Mt. Washington Airport, which was a complex connected to the Airport Skating Rink that was certified for small aircraft. The airstrip, complete with a lookout and air controller and airstrip operated in the 1940s and 1950s. Locals Billy Couch, Sterling Fisher, and others enjoyed flying their own planes. (Courtesy of Trulaverne Couch.)

Five

Home Sweet Home

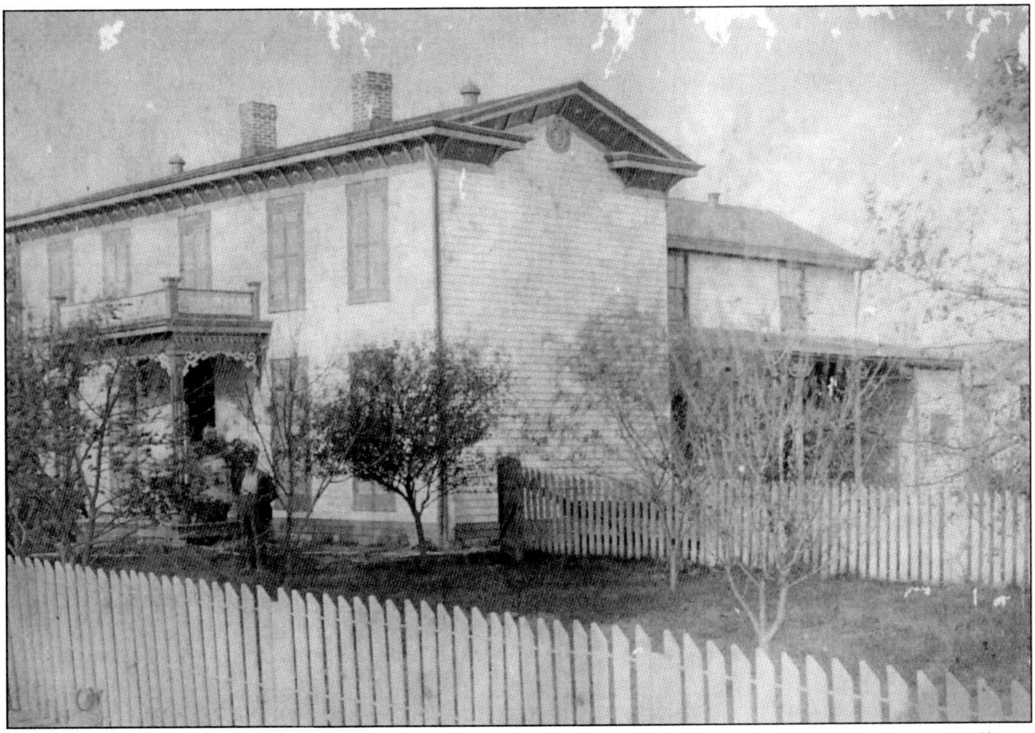

John Harris built this house near Stringer Lane high above Salt River in 1859. John's son William Levi, a Confederate soldier, made it his home and added a two-story addition, which was necessary, considering he had over 10 children. William Levi's son Wayne acquired the home when his father moved into town after remarrying. The house was passed down to his son Darrell, then to his son Darrell Dean. The residence has been in the family for 155 years to date. (Courtesy of Anita Harris.)

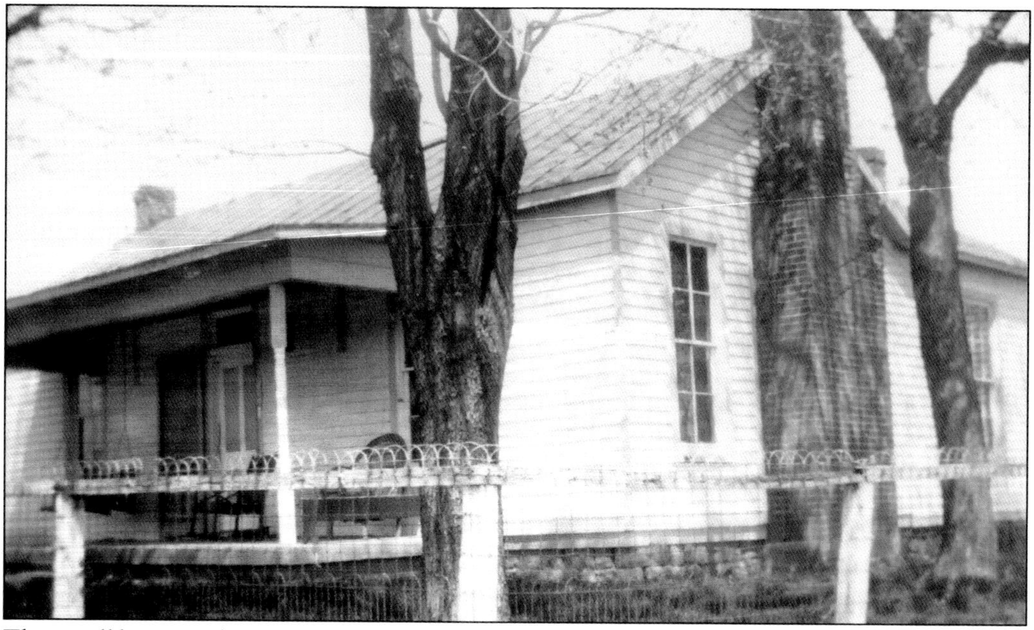

This small home at the corner of Snapp and West Streets had humble beginnings. In 1905, it had neither a porch nor windows. Those were added years later along with a rear addition. Garner and Bertha Dooley were living there when their son Lloyd "Shot" Dooley was born. Shot served as sheriff of Bullitt County from 1982 to 1998 and was deputy sheriff four years prior to that. The house is well over 100 years old. (Courtesy of Lloyd and Arbidella Dooley.)

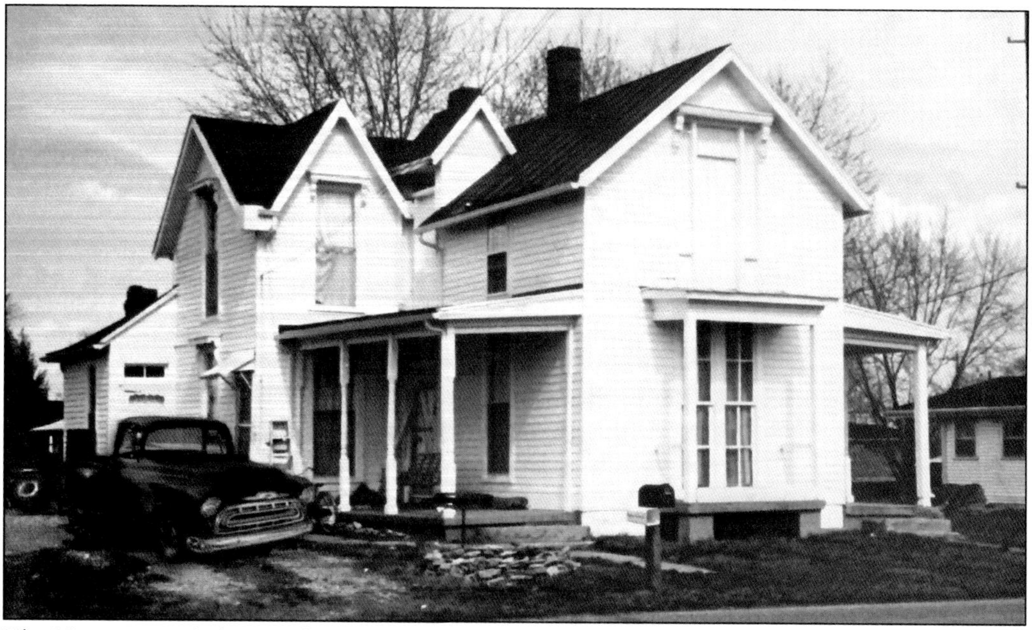

The Victorian-style home of Tom and Lillian Parrish on Snapp Street was labeled "The House of Seven Gables" due to its many gables and roofs. Many say the house was just as beautiful and impressive inside. Tom was a well-known blacksmith with his brother Charlie. Around 1920, their shop on Main Street either burned or was torn down, and Tom built another blacksmith shop nearer to his home on Snapp Street. (Courtesy of Lloyd and Arbidella Dooley.)

School traffic cop Virgil Lewis is pictured making sure all the children pass safely across Main Street. But note what appears in the background. Behind Lewis is the home of Walter "Fatty" Mathis and his wife, Statira. Walter was a farmer and had a farm just beside Mt. Washington High School. Statira (McFarland) was a great genealogist and historian. The house was previously occupied by the Herin family. (Courtesy of John Settles.)

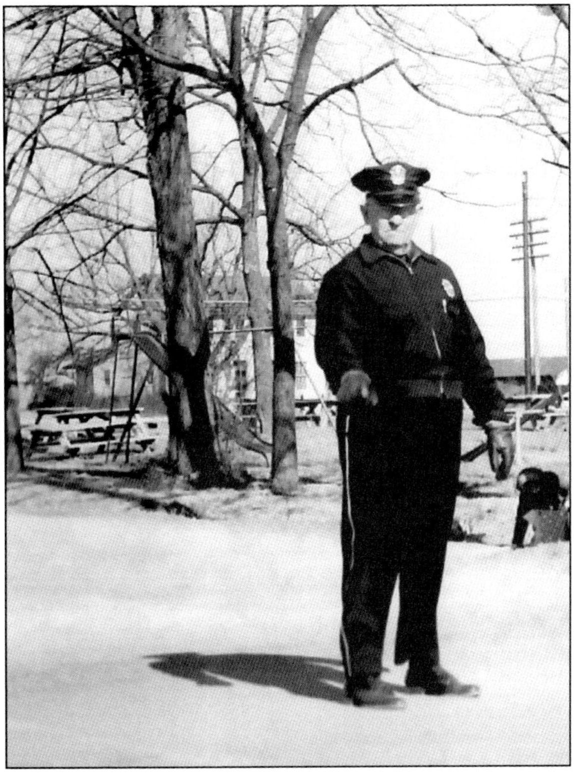

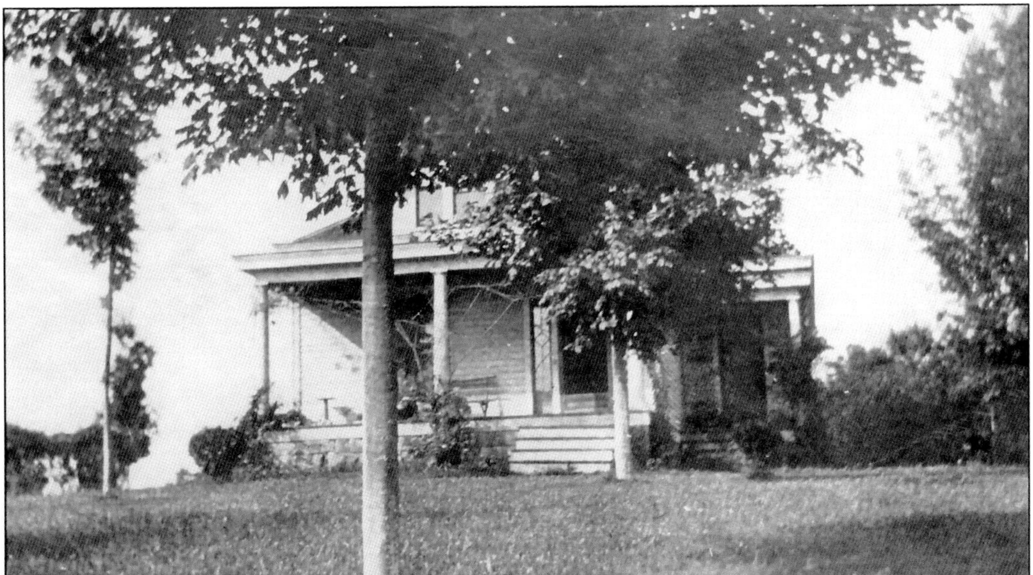

Pictured here is the home of W.T. McAlister, built by Hugh Calvert around 1926, partially with timbers salvaged from the covered bridge at Floyd's Fork on Bardstown Road. Located across from Clark's Lane on North Bardstown Road, it replaced the original homestead of James and Mary Clark where the old Bardstown Pike is still visible. William and Louise Cornell lived in the home during the 1930s. McAlister operated a business called Mac's Truck Sales for many years. (Courtesy of Louise Cornell.)

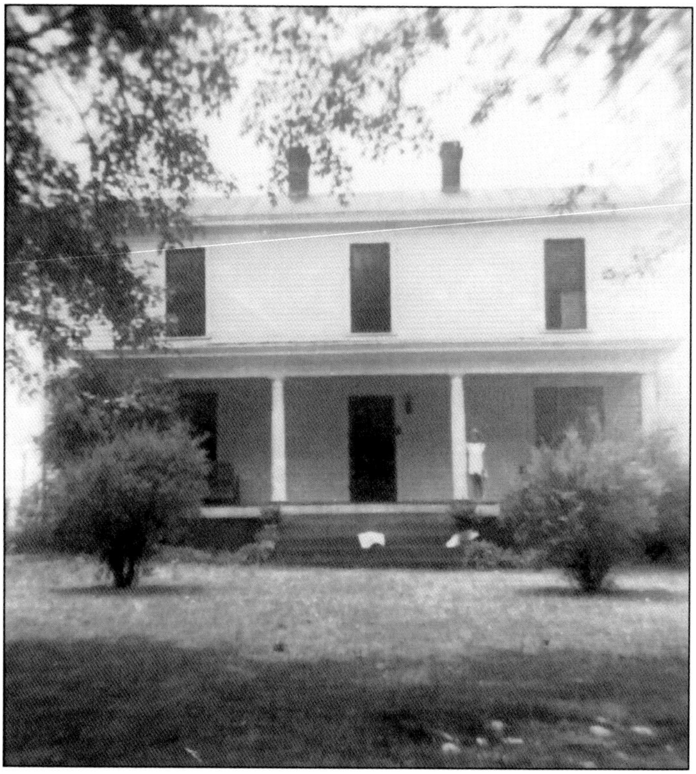

The home of John Franklin and Sarah "Sallie" McClure was a well-hidden residence for many years. Their farmhouse was located between the James Clark home off of Bardstown Road and Landis Lane. Their property was part of the Greenfield Circle apartment complex and the house was located approximately where the Mt. Washington police department is now. (Courtesy of Emma Mae Armstrong.)

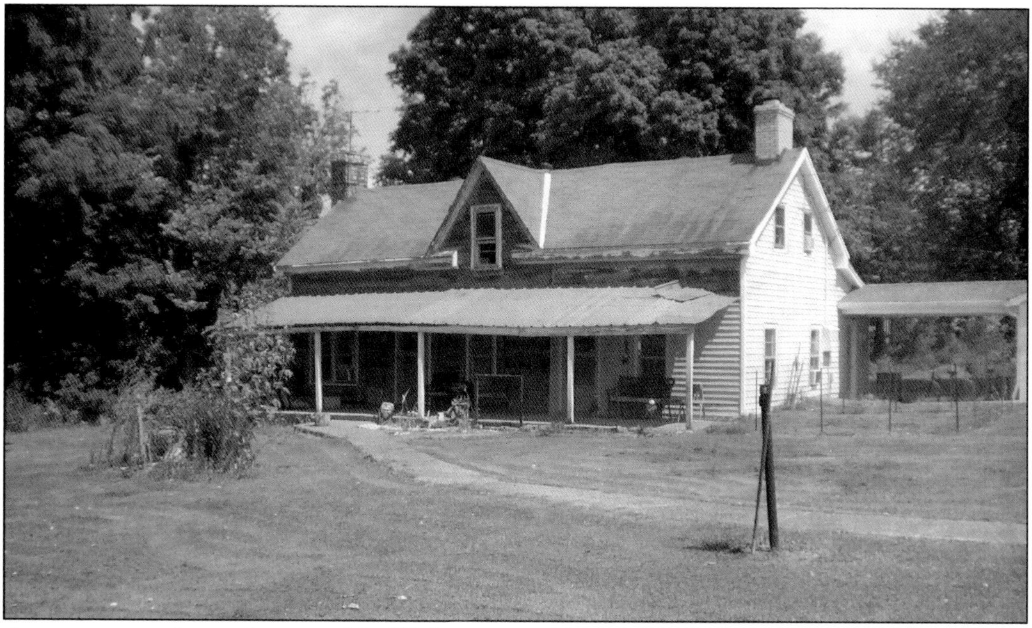

An even more obscure home in Mt. Washington is where Lounette Landis lived for many of her years. Landis Lane was named after her family, and she lived on a one-lane drive that was once a road that forded Floyd's Fork and connected to Manslick Road in Jefferson County. Surprisingly, when the clapboard siding was removed, it revealed the home was made of logs, which suggests it was built in the early-to-mid-1800s. (Author's collection.)

One of the most unassuming older homes in the city stands a short way down Flatlick Road next to the Methodist church. Built in the 1800s, it has a rock foundation and has had quite a few renovations. It was once the home of Marshall Porter and was the homestead for a large farm stretching all the way to Highway 44. Several members of the Harold Owens family have lived there. (Courtesy of the Mt. Washington Historical Society.)

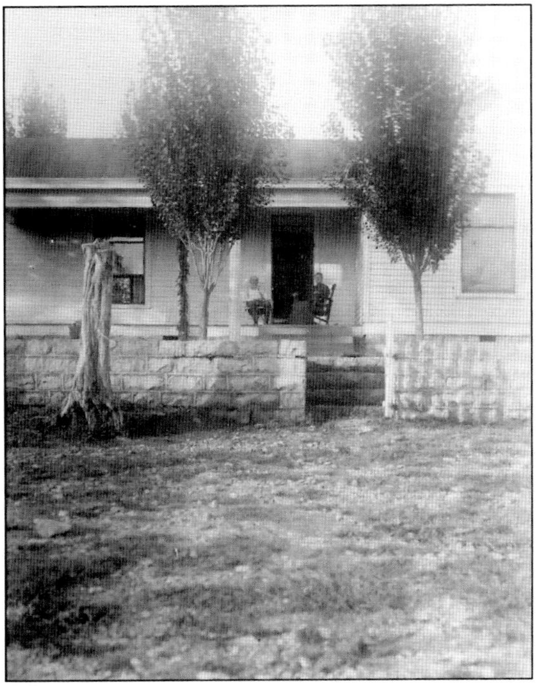

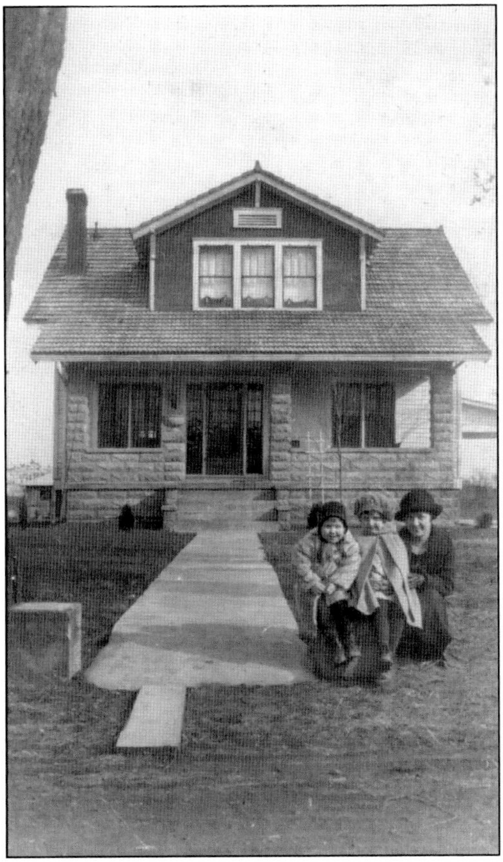

The Tyler family lived in this elegant house on West Street near the McGee farm from the 1920s to the 1940s. A.R Dorsey lived there from the 1950s until the 1970s, and the house looks much the same today as it did when this photograph was taken in 1925. (Courtesy of Stuart Tichenor.)

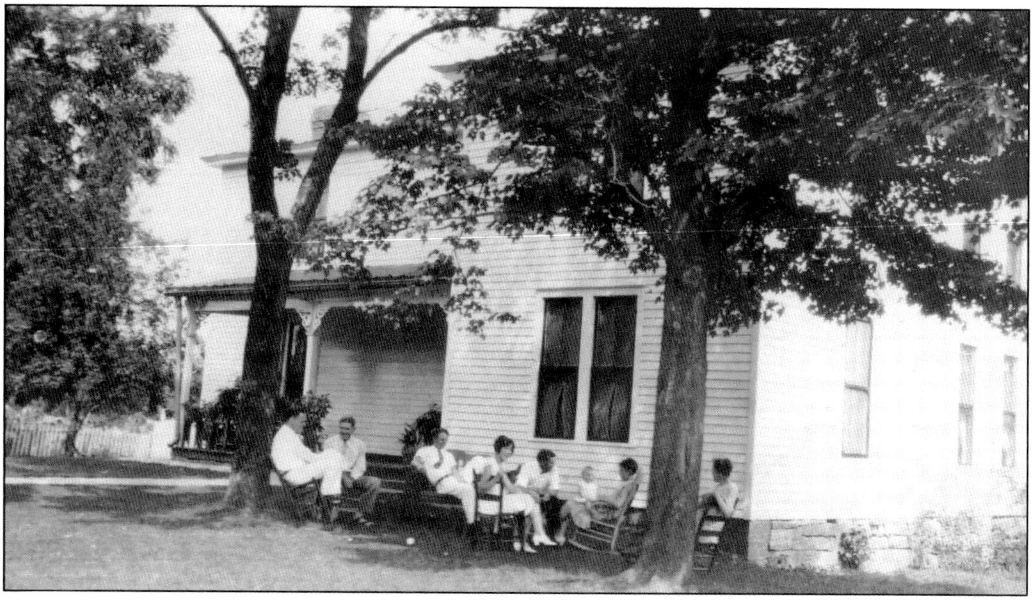

William McGee, his wife, Lizzie, and a large contingent of children lived in this home on a farm at the end of West Street off of Water Street. It was quite a complex of buildings and barns and even had a guesthouse. Large trees surrounded the farm and hid it well from other homes and even a school, which was built next to his farm in 1916. McGee was the first cashier for the Peoples Bank of Mt. Washington, making $15 a month. In the photograph below, McGee sits near his barns. He would grow the full beard each year to play Santa Claus for children during the Christmas season. (Courtesy of Stuart Tichenor.)

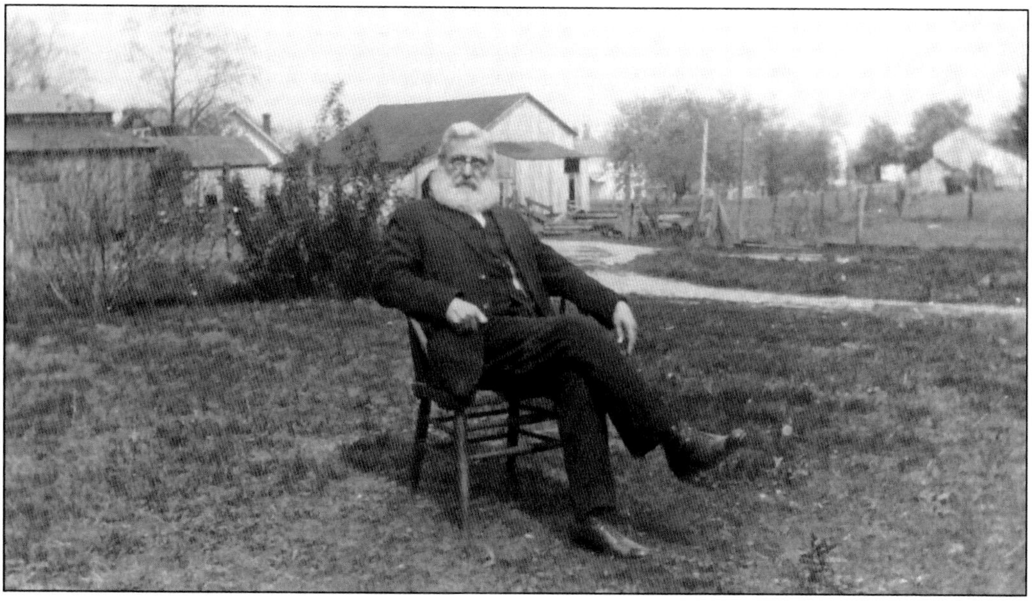

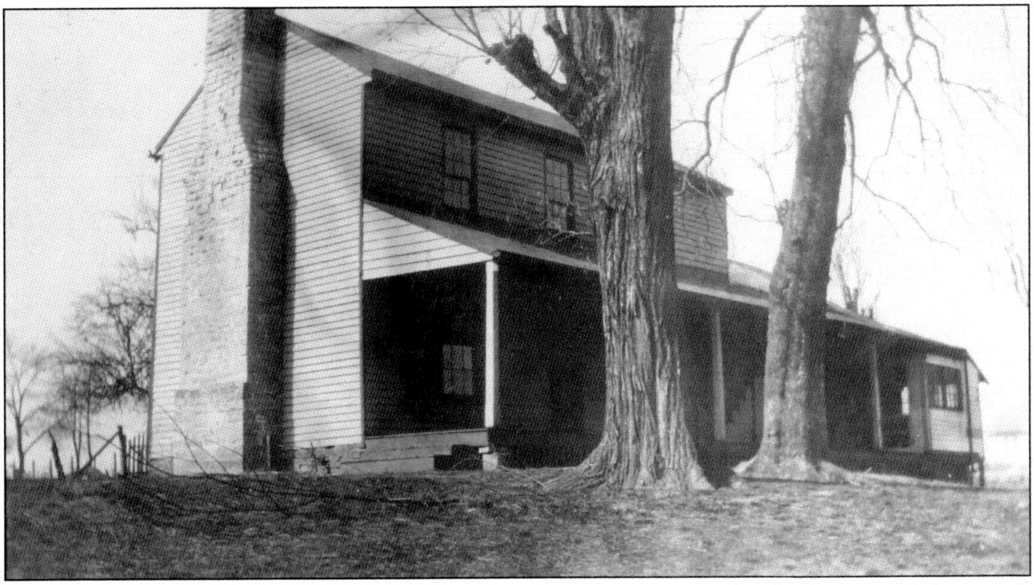

This was the home of Thomas McGee, who came from a prominent family that owned thousands of acres on the Salt River. He settled in Mt. Washington in the mid-1800s and lived in this unique home on Water Street that was pegged together. Thomas's sister Belle married Warren Troutman, and their son Vernon and wife Alberta (Snyder) lived in the home for several years. It was later divided and turned into apartments. (Courtesy of Stuart Tichenor.)

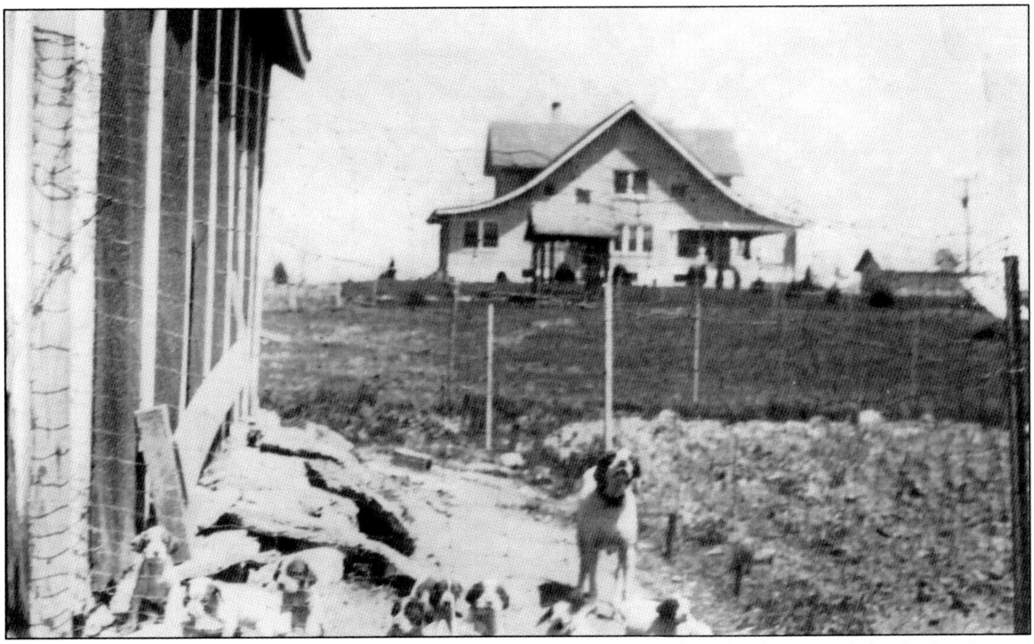

Clarence Porter, who owned the Cyclone store from 1913 until his death in 1937, built this house in 1923. With its ceramic-tiled roof, it was a one-of-a-kind in the city. In the left adjacent lot, they had a flower garden with stone walls and a gazebo where many of the locals would love to come and have their photograph taken. Clarence's widow, Marion (McGee), continued to live there until she passed away at the incredible age of 107. (Author's collection.)

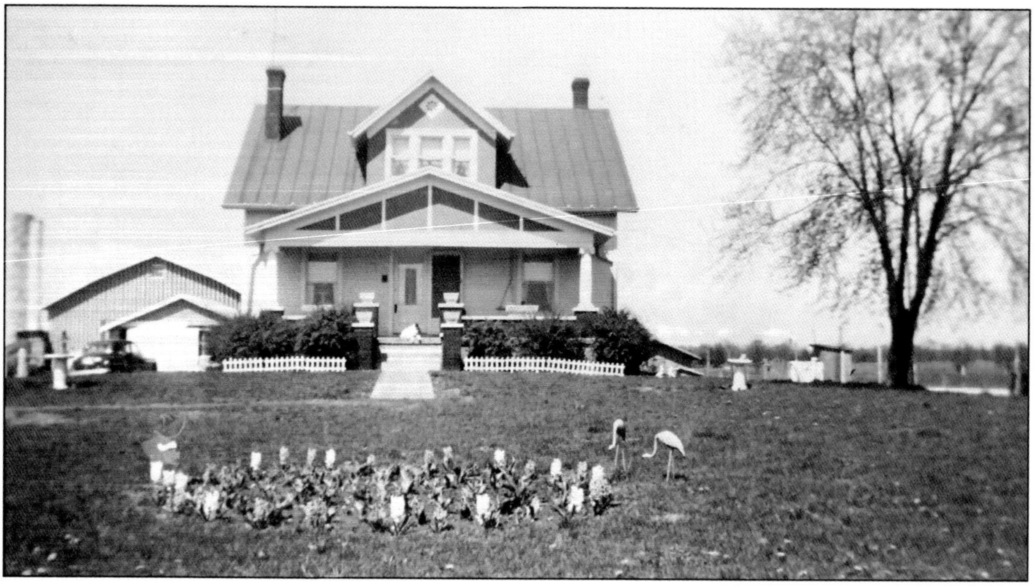

When Royce and Geneva (Overall) Swearingen married in 1922, they moved into this home near Bullitt East High School on the original Swearingen property. They later moved down to the old homestead just east of there. Herman and Effie Owen lived in the home during the 1940s, but Royce and Geneva moved back in during the 1970s. Royce lived to the grand age of 100. (Courtesy of Mildred Brown.)

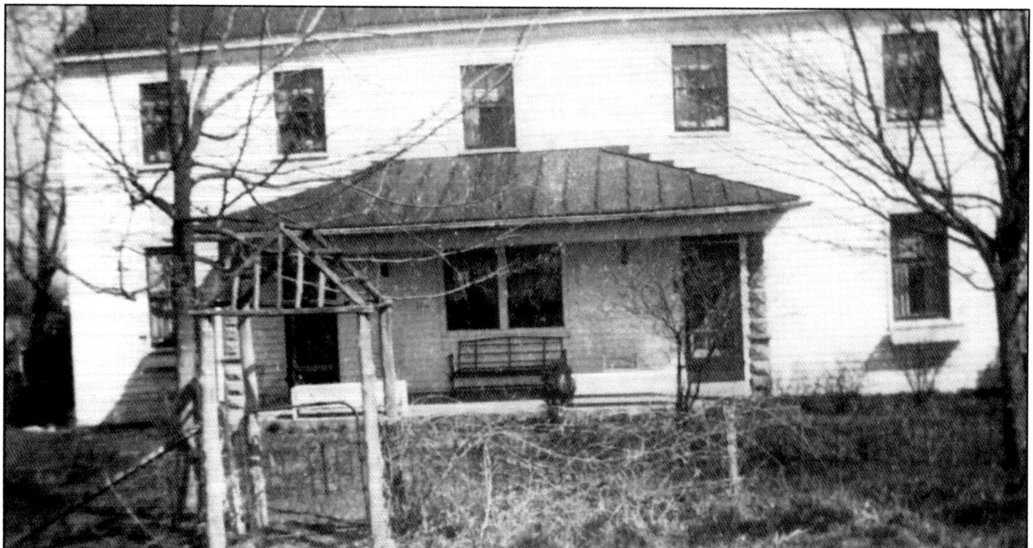

Rachel Swearingen traveled to Mt. Washington with children in tow sometime between 1807 and 1809 after her husband Obed had passed away. Two of Obed's brothers were already in the area. They arrived in 1805, and the families quickly began buying property. Rachel's son Joseph bought property east of Mt. Washington on Highway 44. Joseph built a large, two-story farmhouse in the 1830s just north of where Bullitt East High School is located. At least four generations lived there over a span of 150 years, including Joseph, William Thomas, Henry "Scammie," and Royce Swearingen. (Courtesy of Dorothy Dean Porter.)

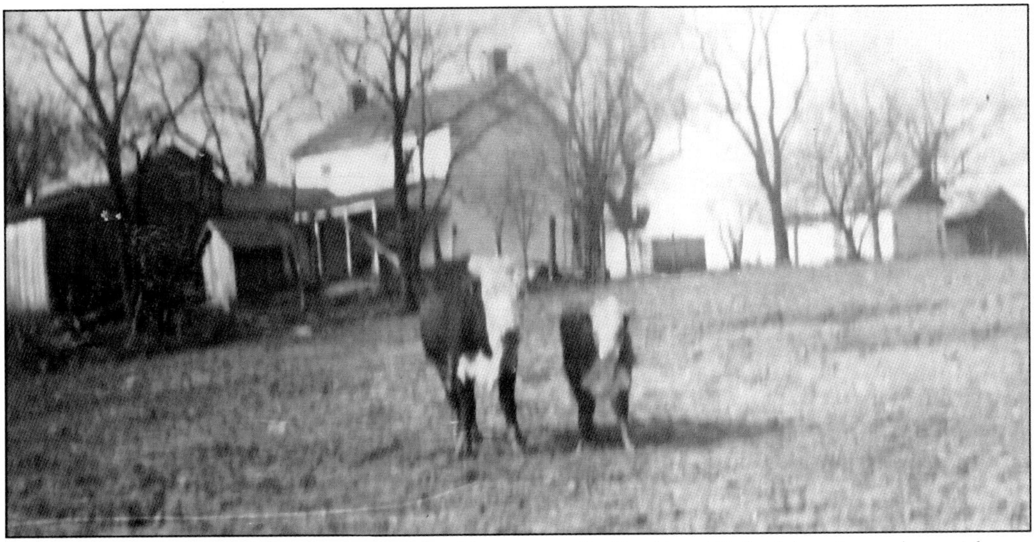

This old homestead hidden back off of Joy Drive near Bullitt East High School was the residence of Jess Swearingen. At least three or four generations of Swearingens lived there until the farm was sold, but it continues to be one of the few working farms in the city. The age of the home is not known but could be well over 150-years-old. (Courtesy of Mildred Brown.)

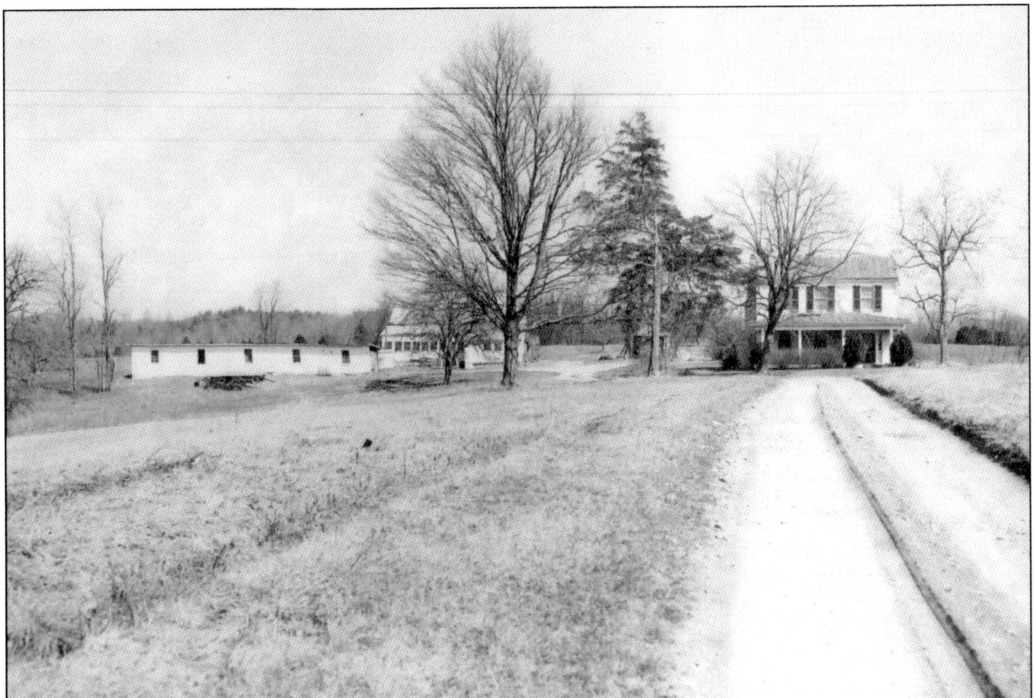

This log home off of King's Church Road used to sit on a farm once owned by a wealthy landowner named S.T. Lloyd. His daughter Alice married Samuel Wallace, and they inherited the farm. Their daughter Myrtle married Everett Fidler, and they resided there for several years. The farm is also known as the Zelia Williams Farm and Evergreen Bee Farm. The home and property sustained severe damage from a tornado in 1927; the house survived, but several trees lining the driveway were destroyed. (Courtesy of Carolyn Quebbeman.)

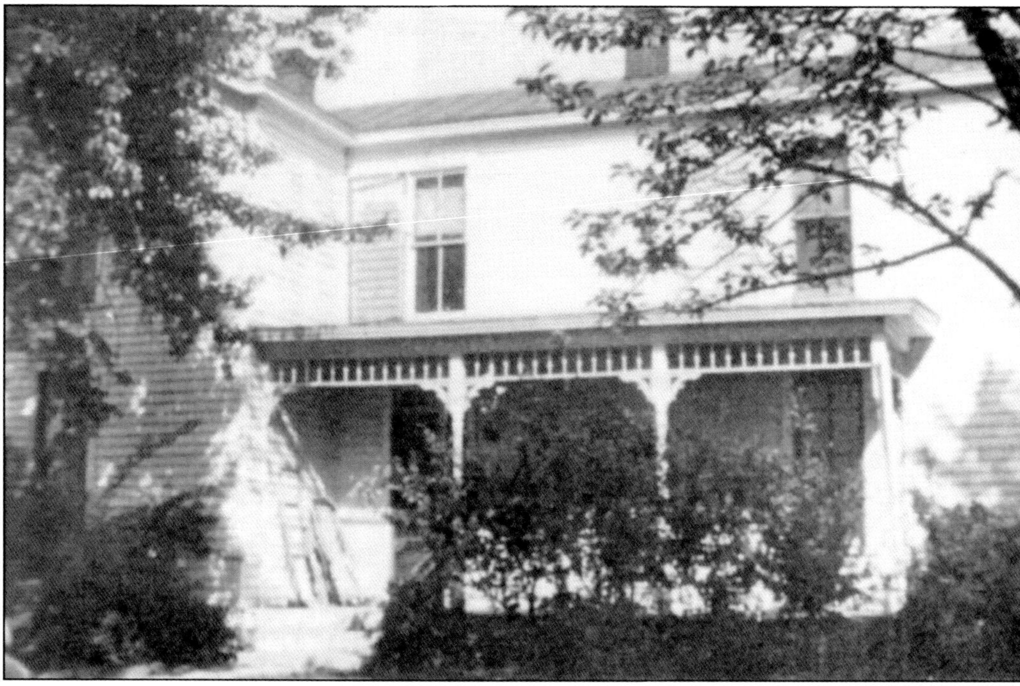

William A. King, the prolific builder, lived in this simple, two-story farmhouse on Stringer Lane close to where he grew up. He later built a modern home on Snapp Street where he lived the rest of his days. (Author's collection.)

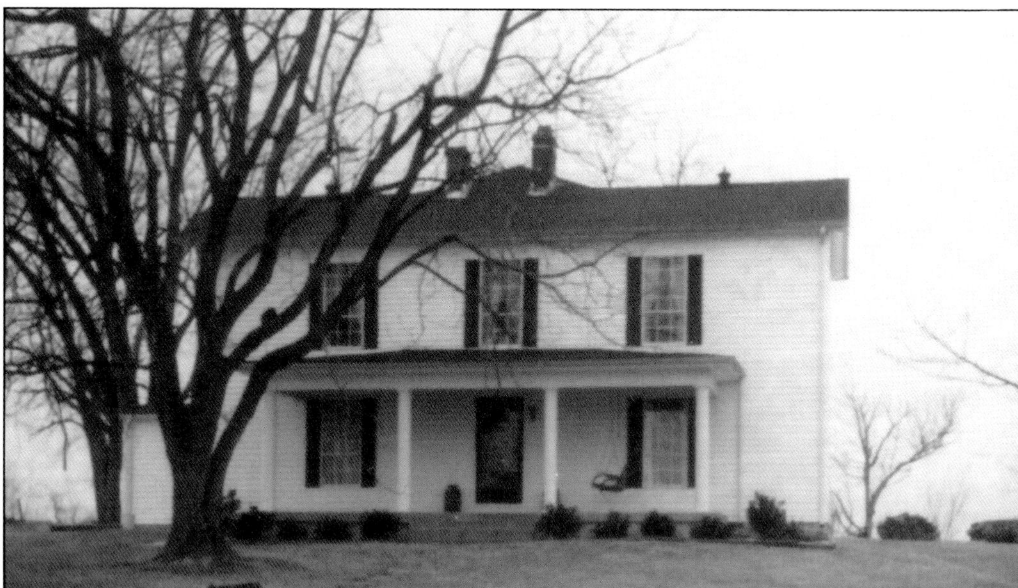

Arson Moore and his wife, Dona Meza (Harris), lived in this farmhouse off of Stringer Lane in their early years, a departure from the two-room shack they lived in immediately after they married. Some of their children and family lived there afterwards. Philip Moore was renovating the house in the late 1980s when the house caught fire and burned. Arson was judge of Bullitt County from 1970 to 1981 and was the last to hold the office. (Courtesy of Paula Ashe.)

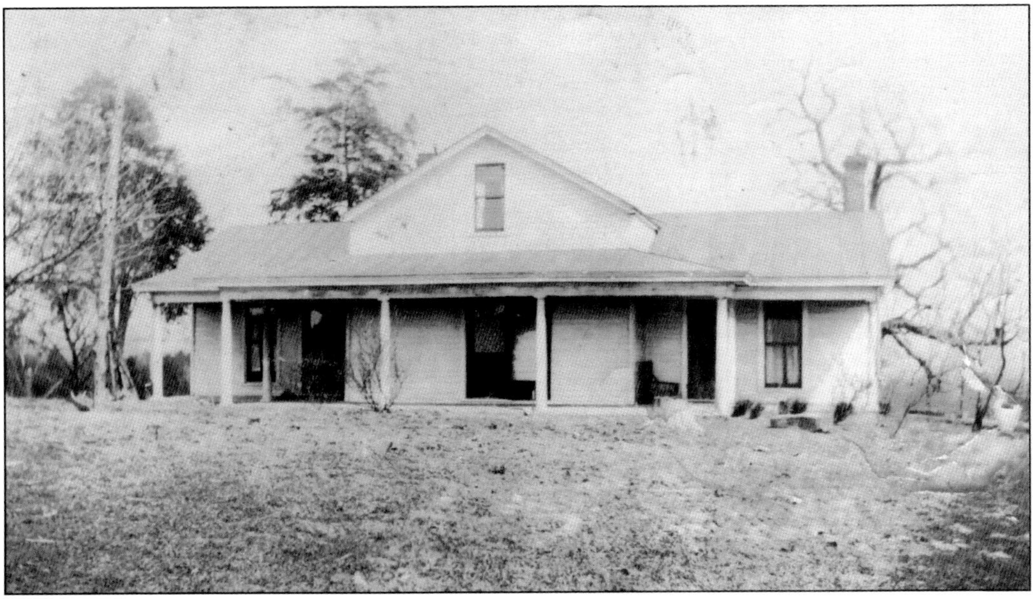

Off of Stringer Lane stood a log home secured with square nails that belonged to the Yancey family in the 1930s. William Robert Cornell bought the house and farm in the mid-1940s and rented it to several families, including Bill and Eve Richardson. Two of his sons lived there, Frank first, then Roy Vernon and his wife, Shirley, who continue to live and farm the property. The old house was torn down several years ago and replaced with a modern home. (Courtesy of Louise Cornell.)

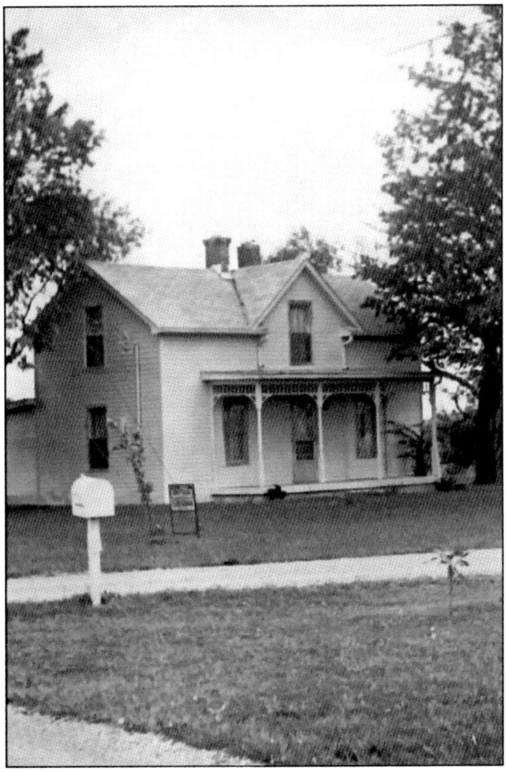

The home of Edward and Rose Mothershead located on Valley View Drive was once on a circular road paralleling Stringer Lane with a few others that no longer exist. Their son Vernon Mothershead became a teller at the Mt. Washington Peoples Bank around 1930 and was eventually promoted to executive vice president before retiring in 1982 with over 50 years of service. (Author's collection.)

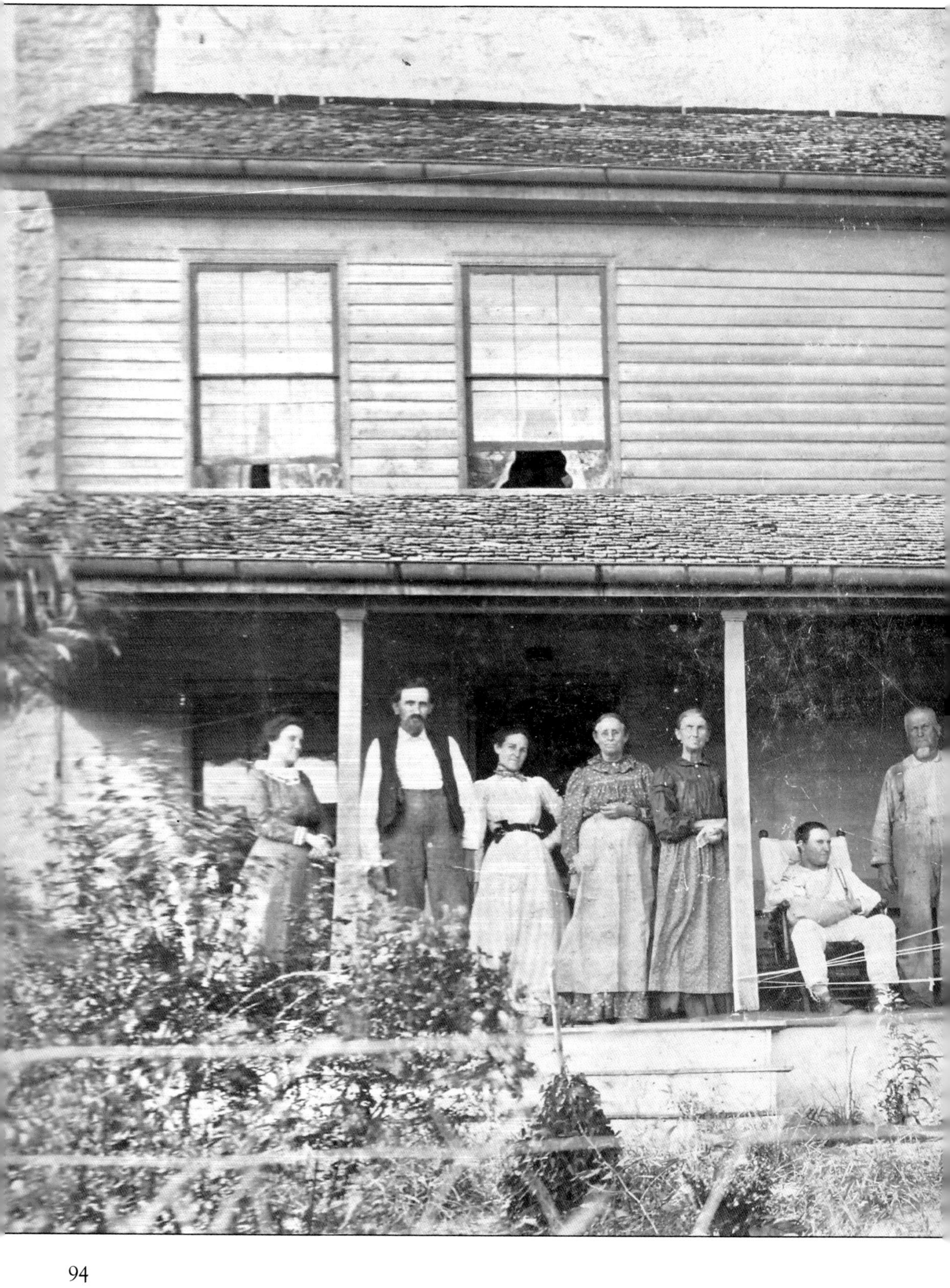

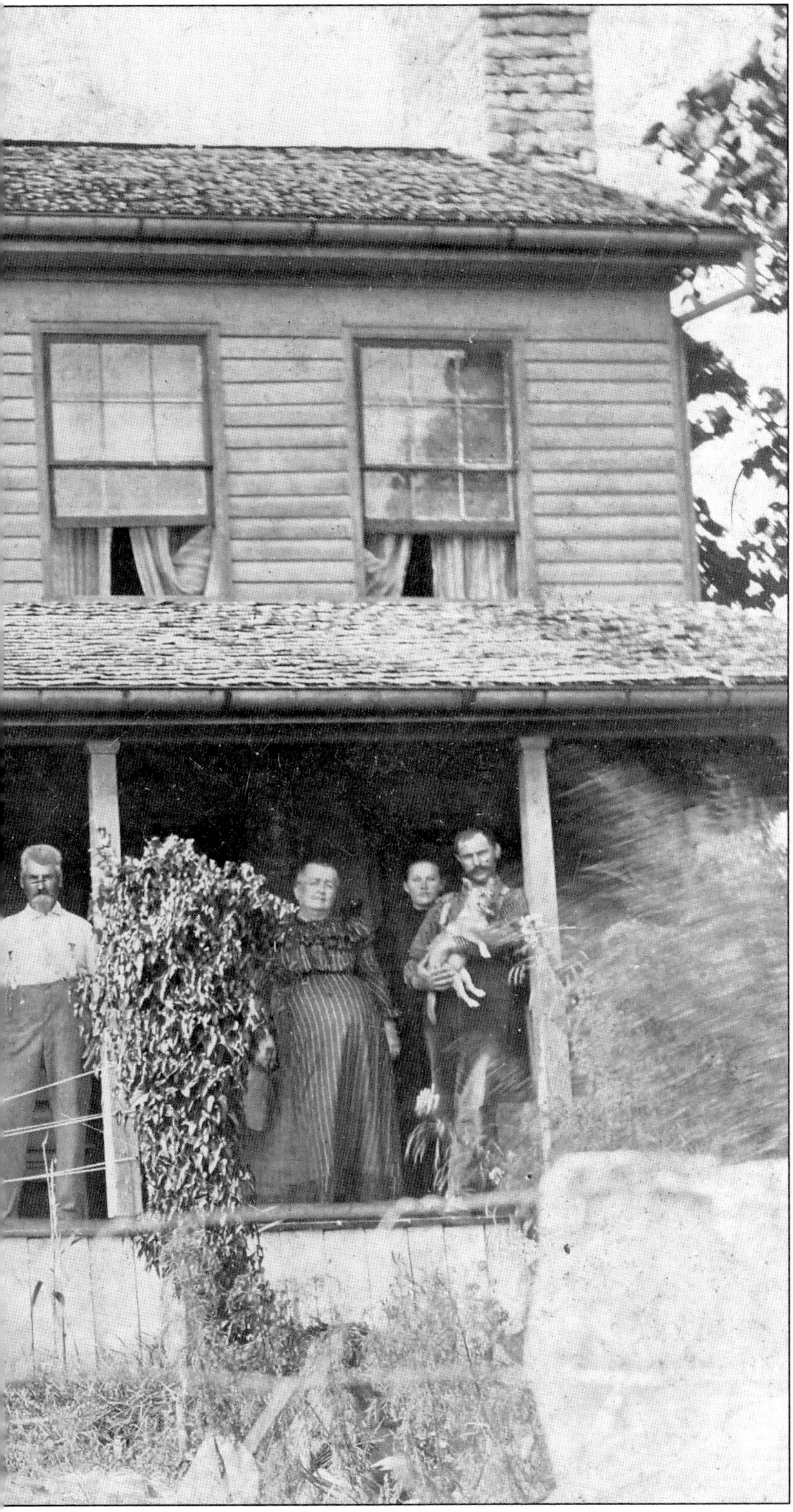

One of the earliest families to settle in the Mt. Washington area was the Harris family. Thomas Harris had two sons, Zedekiah and Simeon, half-brothers, who bought land in the Salt River bottoms near Stringer Lane. The families grew quickly and before long had acquired hundreds of acres between them. Pictured here are members of both sides of the family from left to right: Gillie (Harris) daughter of Brinton; her husband, Dr. H.F. Crenshaw; Birta J. Harris, Brinton's niece; Liz Jones, a relative; Brinton's wife, Elgiva; Brinton's son David; Brinton Harris (Simeon's son); William Levi (Zedekiah's grandson); his first wife, Rebecca (Rouse); William's daughter Tallahassee "Hassie" Parrish; and her husband, Preston Parrish. An astounding number of their descendants still live in the Mt. Washington area. Also, the house on Stringer Lane, which was Brinton's, is still standing. (Courtesy of Anita Harris.)

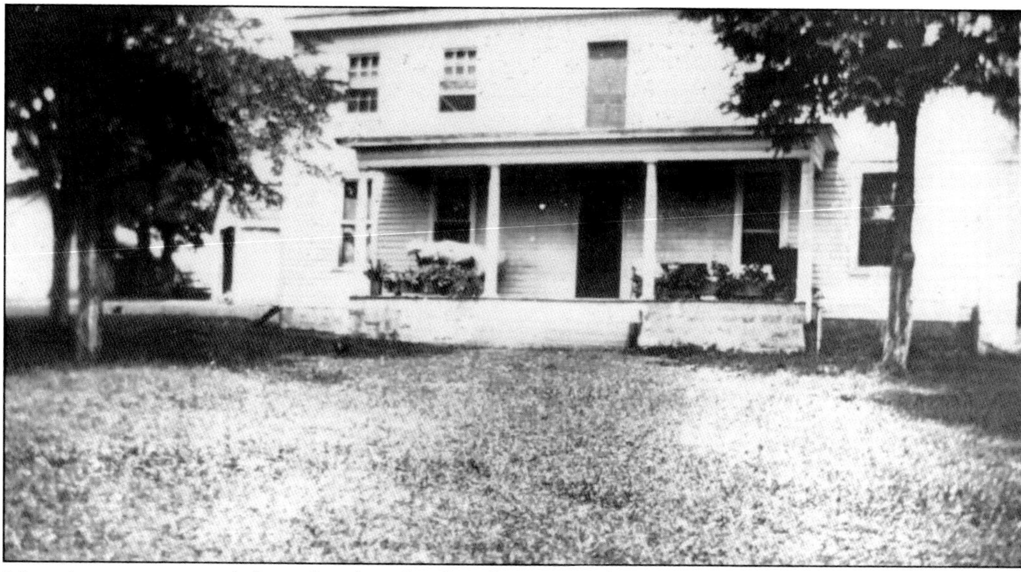

Many important people have lived in this farmhouse a mile west on Highway 44. Thomas McAfee of the McAfee Funeral Home family was an early resident. A Dr. Snyder owned the home and remodeled the exterior by adding stone to the outside walls and extending the porch around the left side of the house. Hubert Armstrong bought the home and farmed the land as did the next owner, Harry F. Roggencamp. When Harry passed away, his widow, Ardelia, married Marvin Moore who was once president of the Peoples Bank of Mt. Washington. The home remains in that family's possession. (Courtesy of Louise Cornell.)

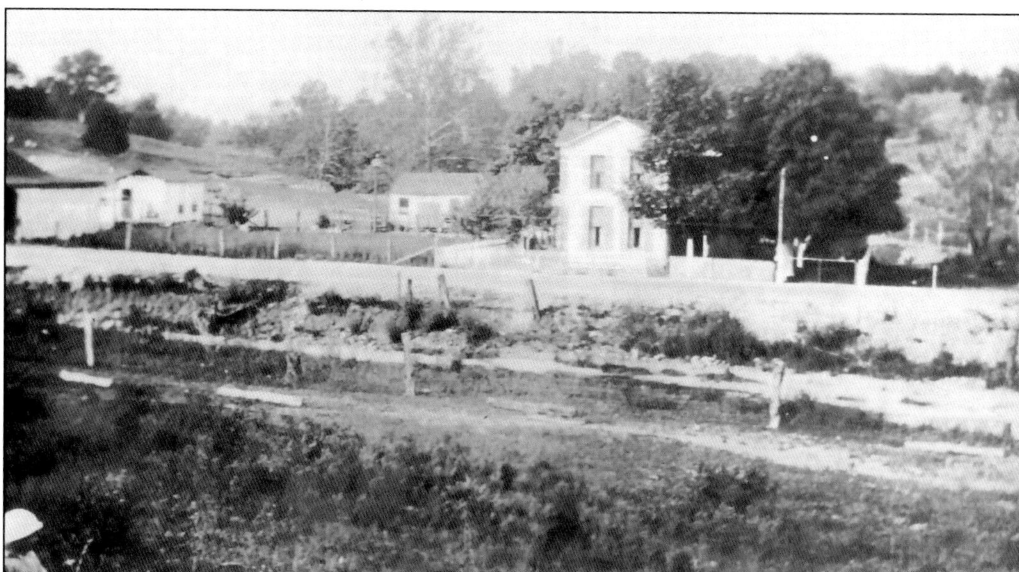

This house was once the residence of Frank Carrithers Porter, who bought it around the turn of the century. The house was in Sugar Valley on South Bardstown Road with Mulberry Run Creek flowing behind it. Frank and his wife, Fannie, moved into town into an even larger home and sold the house to his daughter Aileen and her husband, Sammy Smith. Local entrepreneur and Bullitt County magistrate Billy Couch and his wife, Trulaverne, would eventually live in the home. (Courtesy of Louise Cornell.)

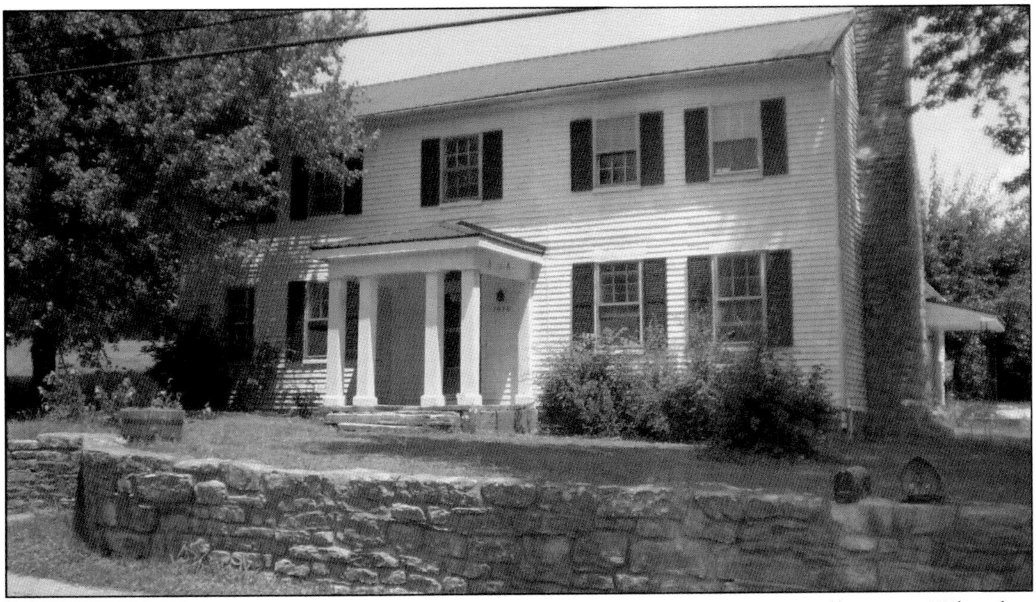

This stately home, built well before the Civil War, was located in Sugar Valley near Whitaker Run Creek. It was first owned by Zachary Stansbury and then his son James D. Stansbury. James's son Clarence "Boss" Stansbury, a president of the Mt. Washington Peoples Bank, and his wife, Lida, a longtime local schoolteacher, lived in the home until she sold it and moved to an assisted-living facility. She passed away at the grand age of 104. A stagecoach stop and tavern were once located nearby. (Author's collection.)

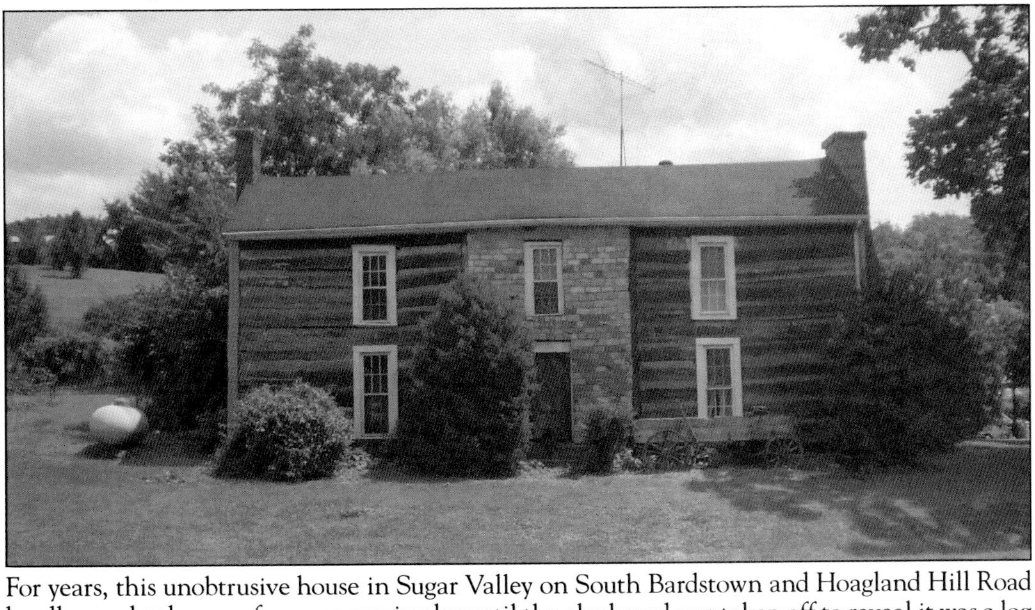

For years, this unobtrusive house in Sugar Valley on South Bardstown and Hoagland Hill Road hardly caught the eye of anyone passing by until the clapboard was taken off to reveal it was a log cabin. Built in the late 1700s, it was constructed in the dogtrot style, which had an open passageway through the center of the house. The house was active during the Civil War, occasionally serving as a hospital for wounded soldiers. Union soldiers ransacked the home often for provisions. One of the first residents was a Swearingen, and Louis Roby and his wife, Maylene, lived in the home for many years. (Author's collection.)

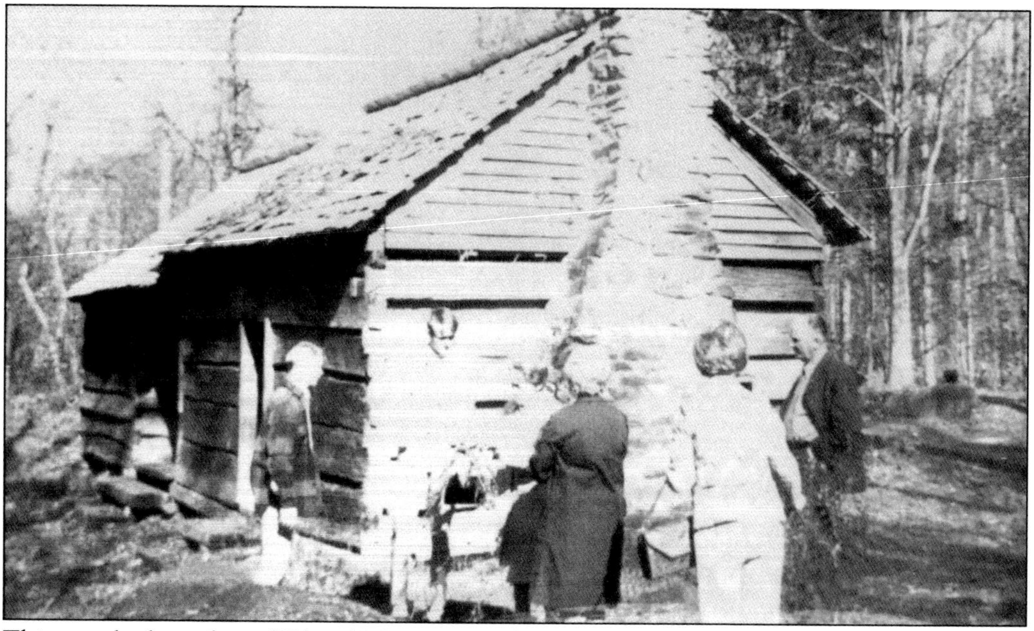

This was the log cabin of Ed and Mae Weaver, located near the intersection of Greenwell Ford Road and Stringer Lane, one of the earliest known passages into Mt. Washington. The cabin could easily have been 200 years old when it was torn down in the 1990s. Ed and Mae raised a large family in the humble three-room cabin. Their children were Beulah, Lester "Slim," Edward, Elizabeth, Dorsey, Florence, Margie, Frank, and Joanne. (Courtesy of C.N. Tichenor.)

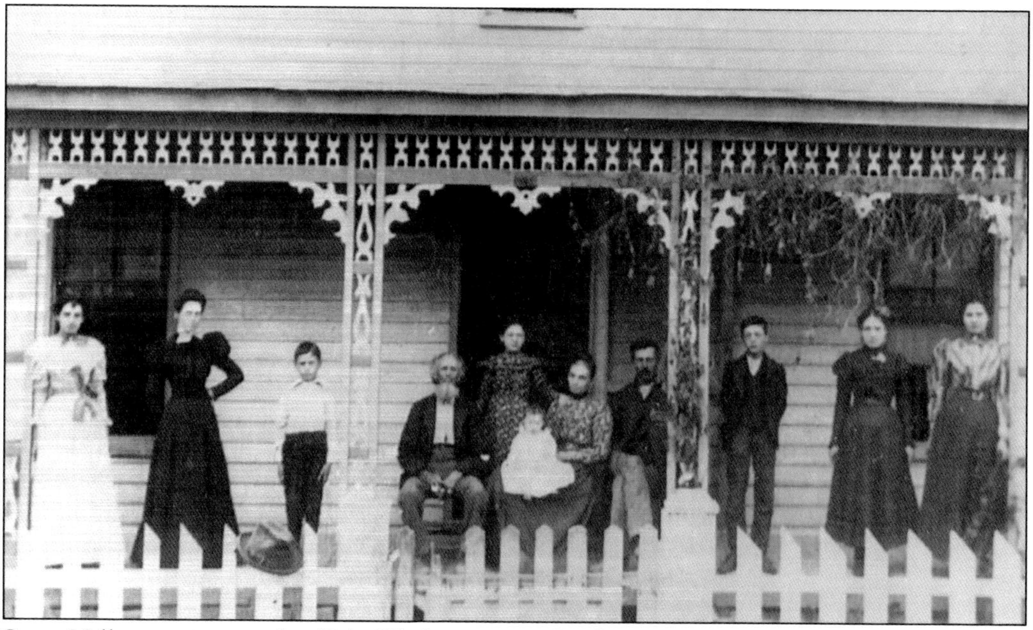

Sugar Valley was just south of Mt. Washington on Bardstown Road with Whitaker Run Creek flowing beside it into the Salt River. As many as five distilleries operated in the area during the 1800s. This house near Hoagland Hill Road was the home of Joseph Hardy. Pictured here from left to right are his family members Emma, Lula, Alex, Lydia, Joseph, Edith (with baby), Thomas, Ben, Hattie, and Ida. (Courtesy of Rita Trent.)

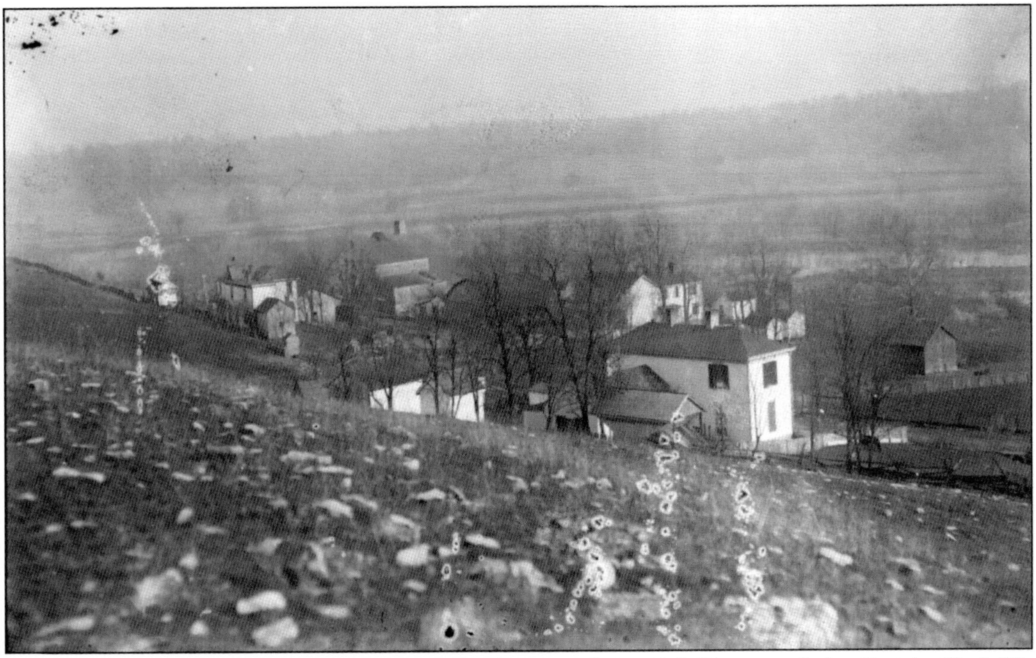

Smithville was a small, quiet community built around the Salt River and the Smithville Mill. Founded around the time of the Civil War, it once featured several large homes, a store, blacksmith shop, and for a time their own post office. It was also a popular place to swim, and local baseball teams would play in the cornfields in the 1920s. (Courtesy of the Mt. Washington Historical Society.)

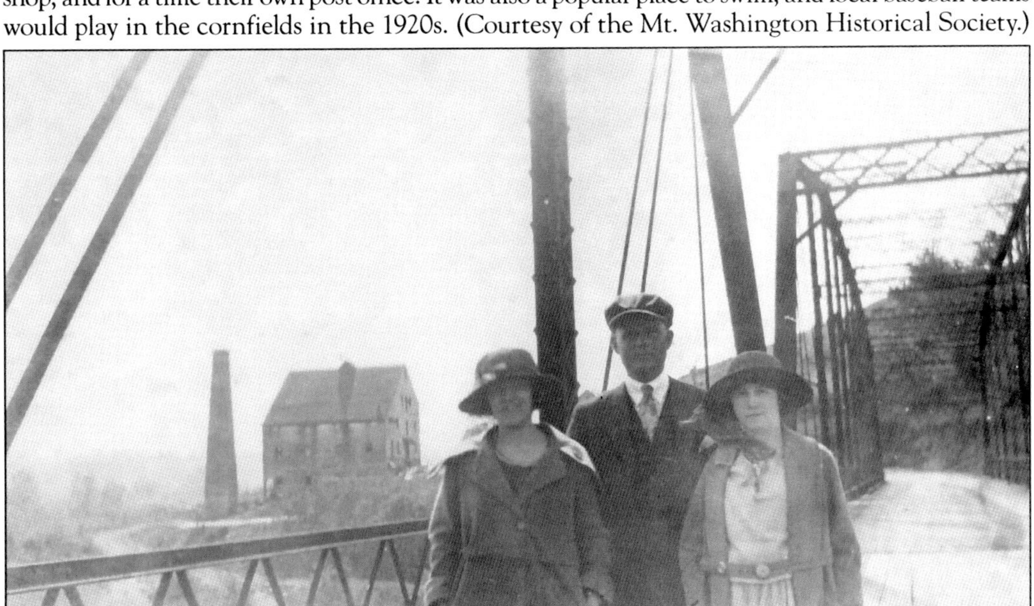

The Smithville mill was an expansive building south of Mt. Washington on the Salt River. It was built around the 1850s and owned by a man named Col. Dick Goode, who lived in a large home on Snapp Street, according to historian Statira McFarland. Many others owned the mill over the years, including S.T. Lloyd, until Warren Troutman bought the property in the 1920s. The top floor was demolished due to age and deterioration. Warren's son Clyde built a home on the property and used the mill as a barn for his livestock. (Courtesy of Gayle and Eleanor Troutman.)

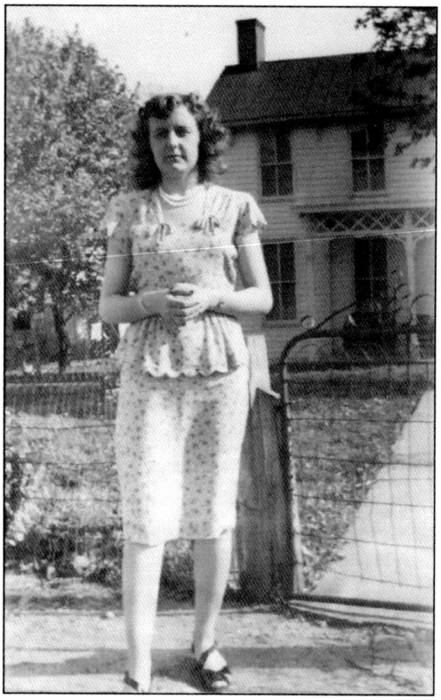

Warren Troutman bought this home, farm, and the old mill on Salt River in the 1920s. Warren's son Clyde and then Clyde's son Mac also lived there. The house burned February 8, 1958, with many of their belongings. It was later replaced with a modern brick house. Clyde's daughter Clyann is standing in front of the original house. (Courtesy of Emma Mae Armstrong.)

Sitting on a hillside near Salt River on Bardstown Road, this estate that must have caught the eye of many passersby. The Sheckles family once owned the home, and E.J. and Ella Hilbert were among the last to live there. The building was torn down for the expansion of Bardstown Road and a new bridge. The old post office used to sit to the right of the house. Pat Troutman is pictured here in front of the fence that surrounded the property. (Courtesy of Emma Mae Armstrong.)

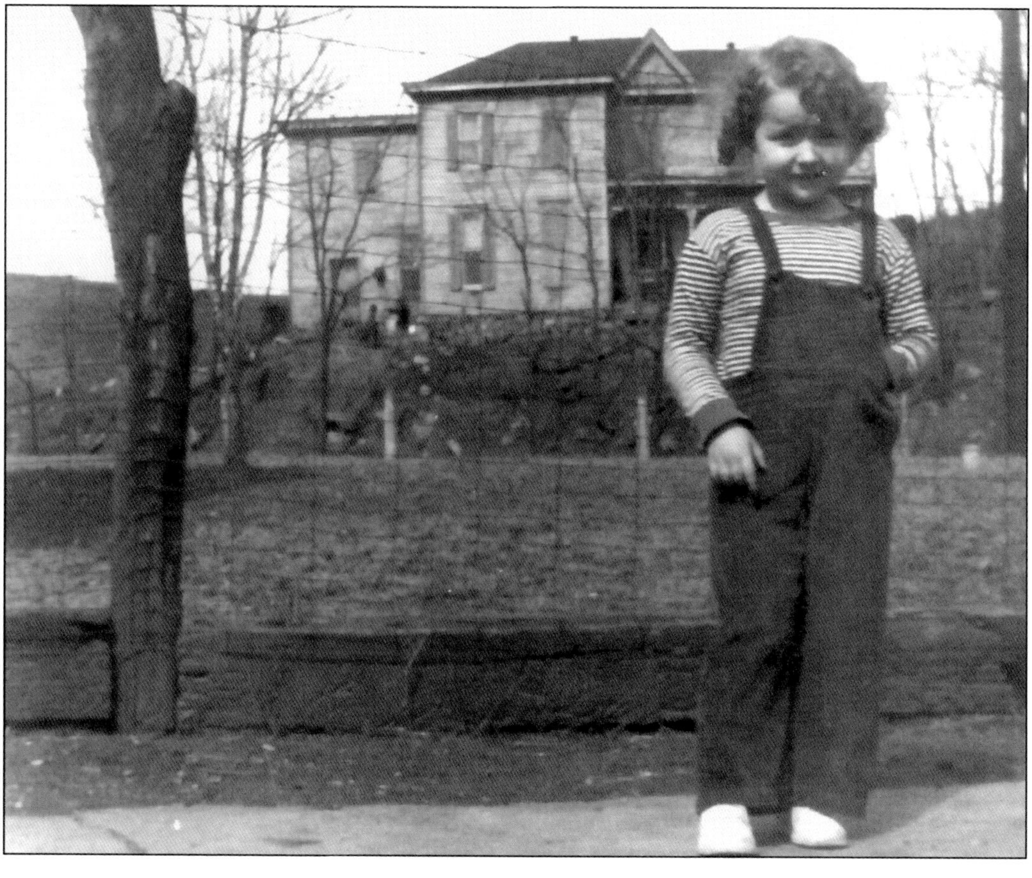

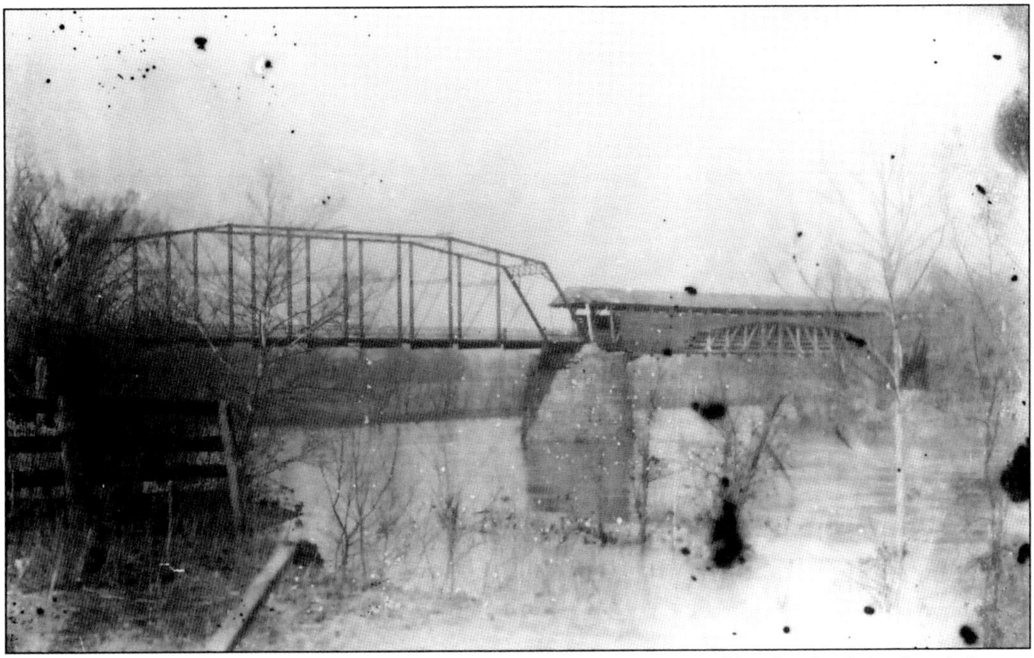

The first bridge to span the Salt River at Smithville was a covered bridge built by locals James Carothers and his brother Samuel in 1832, but it was burned down during the Civil War. The covered section of this bridge was built in 1866, and part of it was replaced with a steel span in 1908 due to damage. The remainder was replaced with steel a few years later. (Courtesy of the Mt. Washington Historical Society.)

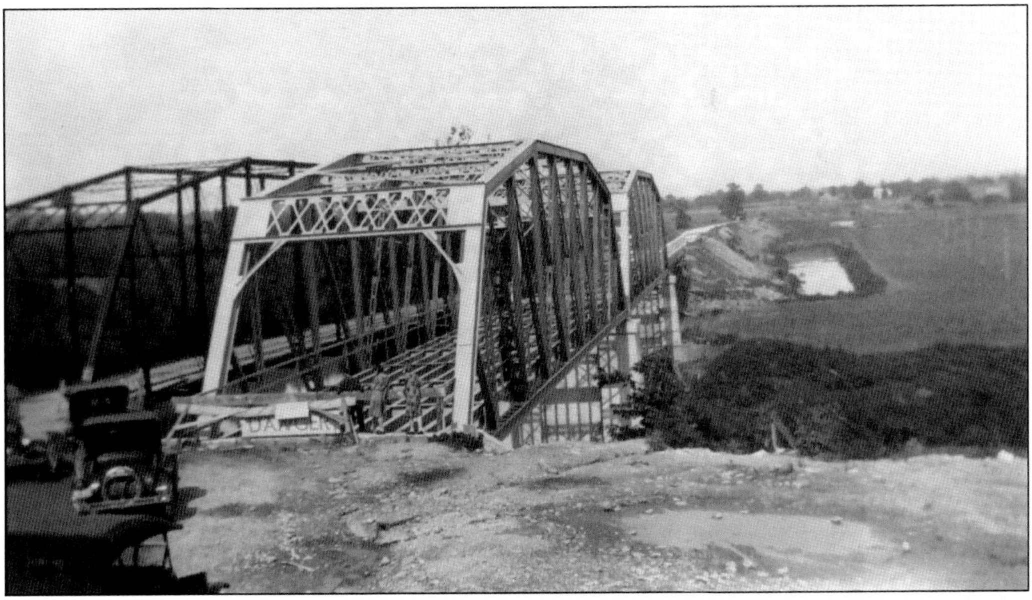

During the reconstruction and initial paving of Bardstown Road from 1923 to 1926, a new bridge was built over the Salt River in Smithville. The old bridge was removed and rebuilt at Lilly Pike in Spencer County. A young man from Arkansas by the name of Garner Dooley was working for the Vincennes Bridge Co. and met his future wife, Bertha Lloyd, while grocery shopping in town, and thus began a family well known to many. (Courtesy of Gayle and Eleanor Troutman.)

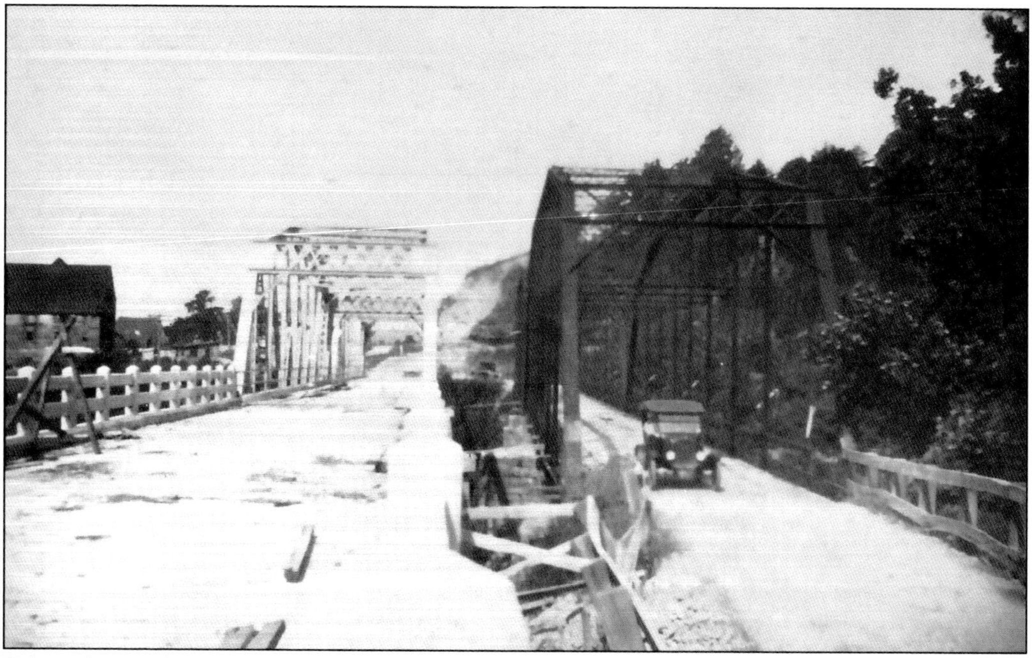

Taken during the construction of the bridge from 1923 to 1925, this photograph contrasts the old with the new. With the paving of Bardstown Road there would certainly be an increase in traffic, and a new bridge was a necessity. It would be nearly 60 years before it would be replaced. (Courtesy of Gayle and Eleanor Troutman.)

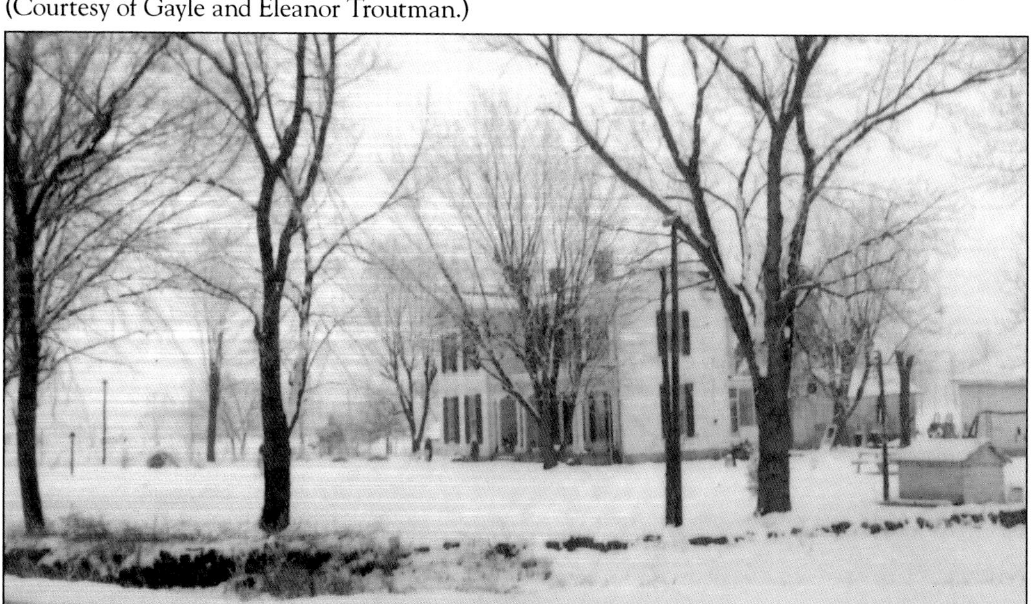

Although this home is in Spencer County, its former occupants have strong ties to Mt. Washington. Located on Dutchman's Creek Road, this house near Salt River was once home to Herman and Mamie "Ganky" Rouse. With a family of seven, the large home served them well. A few of their children lived there after they married. Lester and Hattie (Hardy) Porter bought the home in the early 1950s and had quite a large family of five daughters, with two sets of twins. (Courtesy of Rita Trent.)

Six

Medicine Men of Mt. Washington

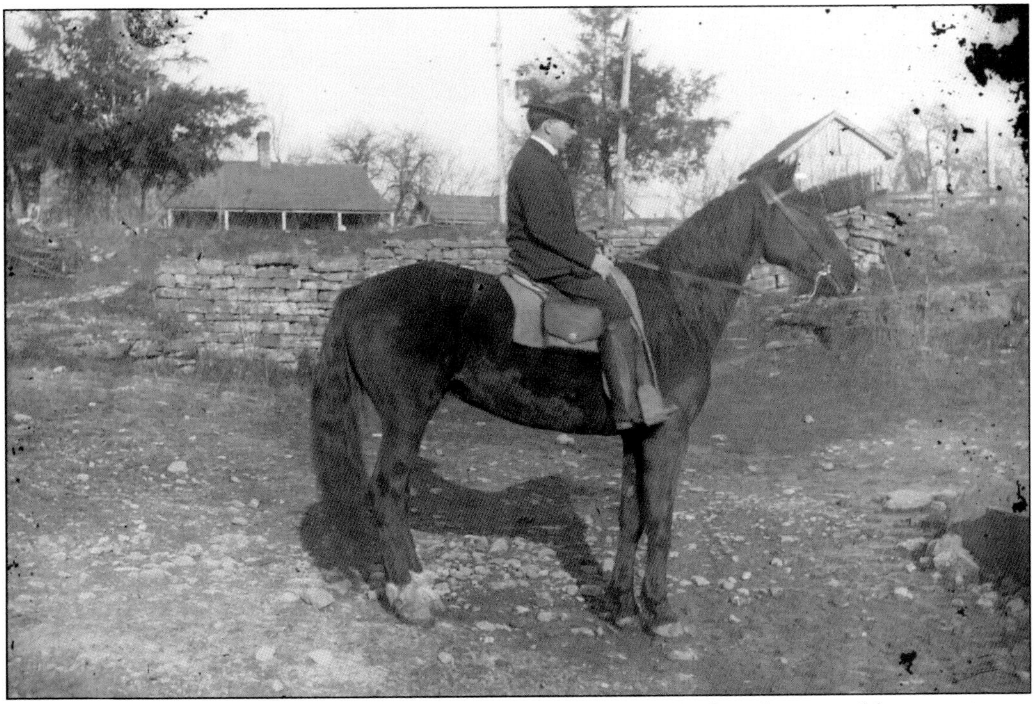

Dr. Asa C. Overall came to serve the city from 1900 to 1913 when he moved his practice to Lawrenceburg, Kentucky. His brother James was also a doctor. While here, he married schoolteacher Maude Harris. His practice was in an office on the first floor of Maccabee Hall, and he and his wife resided in an apartment in the Henry J. Barnes mansion. He was the first doctor to use a mode of transportation other than the horse—a motorbike. He bought the contraption in 1905, but apparently it did not last. This 1910 photograph shows him firmly on the back of a horse. (Courtesy of the Mt. Washington Historical Society.)

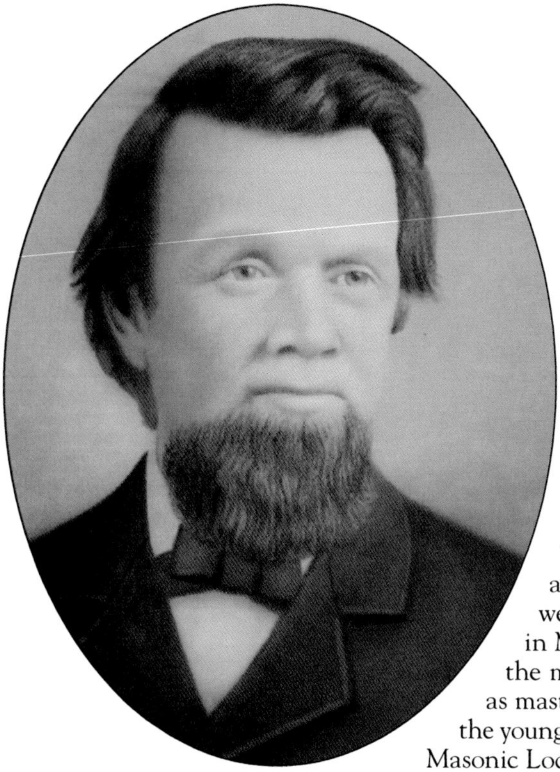

Smith M. Hobbs and his son Nick M. Hobbs were doctors from the mid- to late 1800s. Their office was between the Lewis Hotel and Elmo Jasper's store on Main Street. There were at least seven to eight doctors practicing in Mt. Washington at that time, but they were the most popular of them all. They both served as masters at the Masonic lodge, and Nick died at the young age of 38. (Courtesy of the Mt. Washington Masonic Lodge 180.)

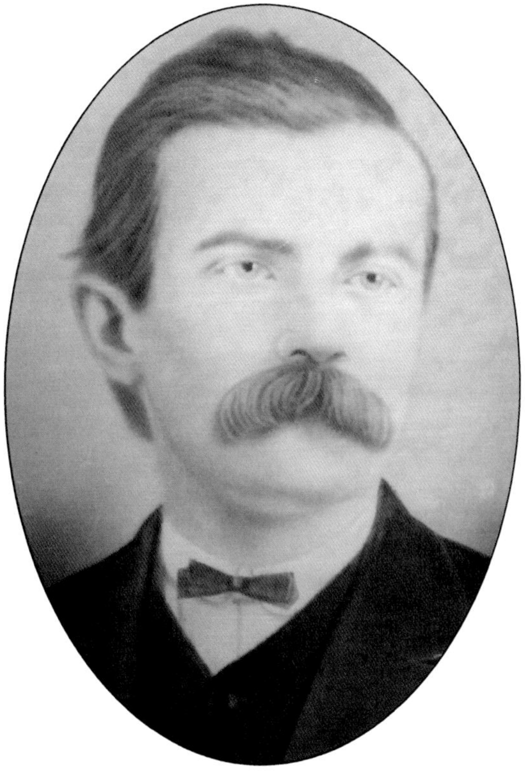

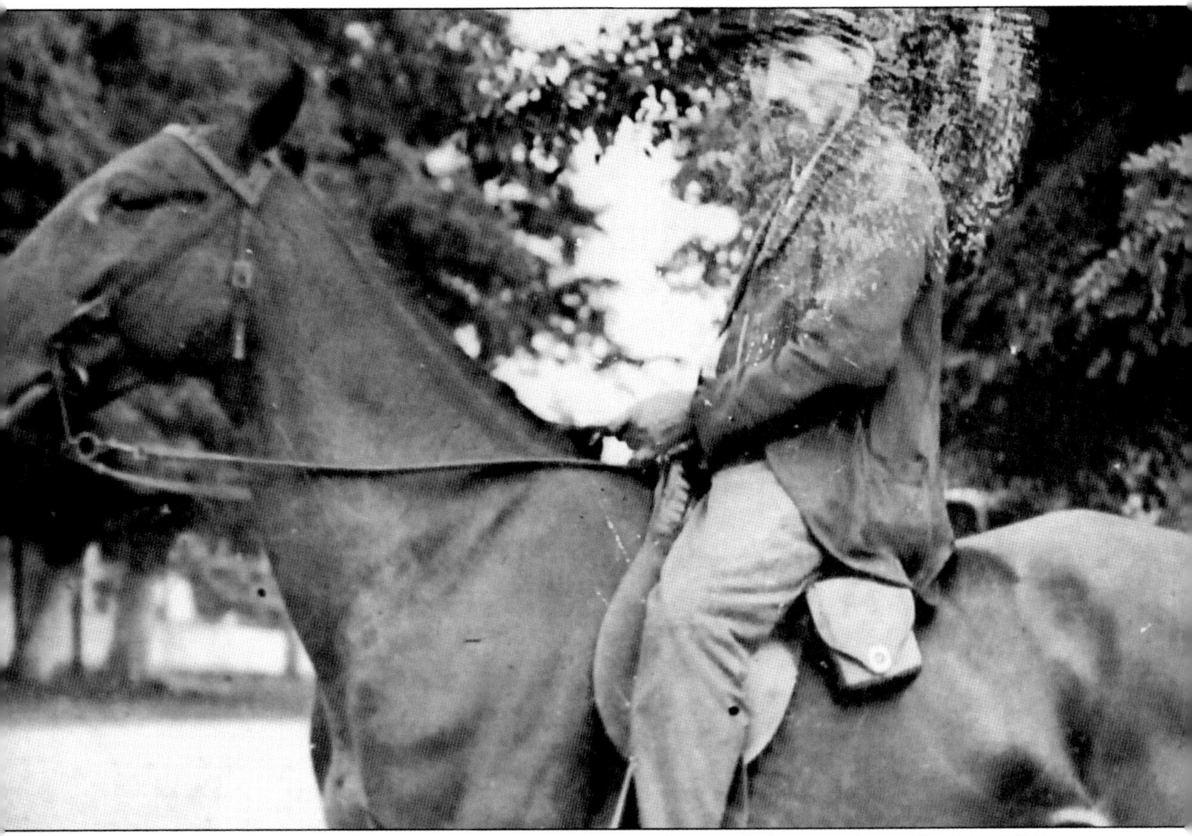

Dr. H.F. Crenshaw was a Mt. Washington native and served the city from the Civil War era until his passing in 1905. He lived and had his practice at his home on the corner of Main Street and Collings Street. He was married twice, first to America Landers and then to Gilley Harris. Dr. Crenshaw is pictured here on his trusty horse, Deck. (Courtesy of the Mt. Washington Historical Society.)

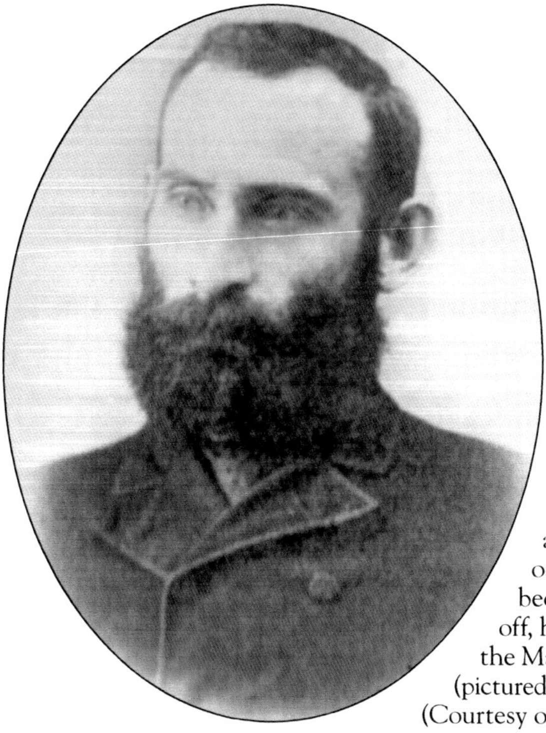

Dr. William W. Coleman served Mt. Washington from the late 1800s until his death at the age of 55. He lived in a small home across from Flatlick Road on Main Street. He owned property behind his place and was preparing to build a new home when one cold day he was unloading lumber and became overheated. When he sat down to cool off, he contracted pneumonia. He was a master at the Masonic lodge and had just opened a new office (pictured below) at the corner of Main and West Streets. (Courtesy of the Mt. Washington Masonic Lodge 180.)

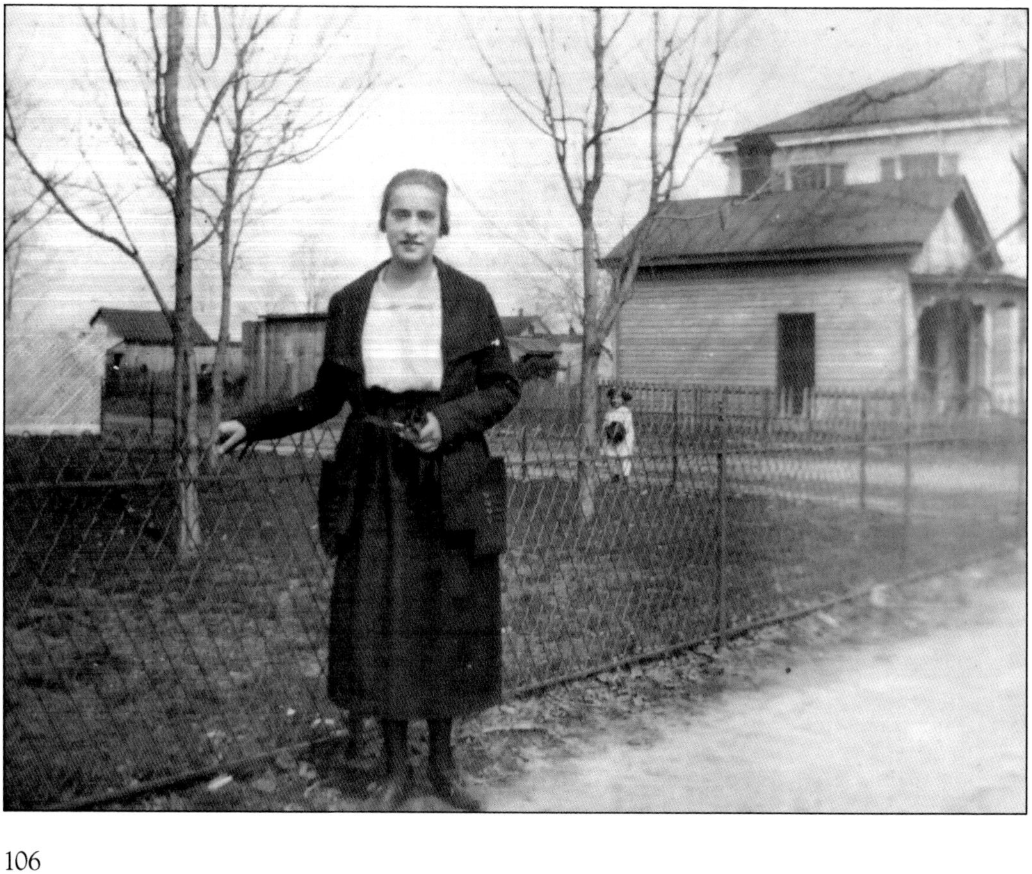

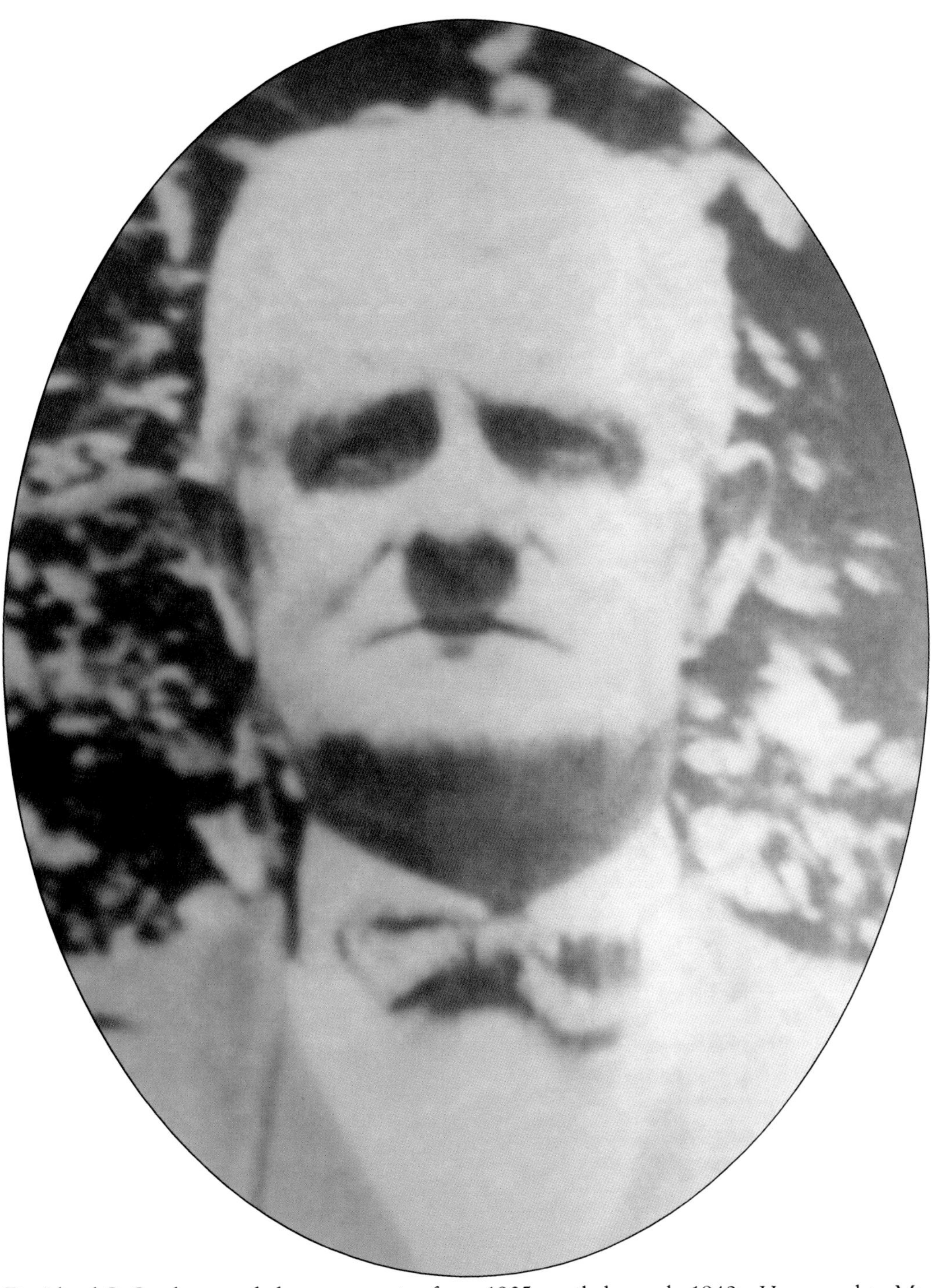

Dr. Lloyd S. Settle served the community from 1905 until the early 1940s. He moved to Mt. Washington from Botland, Kentucky. He was one of the city's most popular doctors, delivering most of the city's babies until Dr. Hill came in 1923. Even though Dr. Settle had a severe handicap, a missing left hand, it never affected his abilities as a doctor. (Courtesy of the Mt. Washington Masonic Lodge 180.)

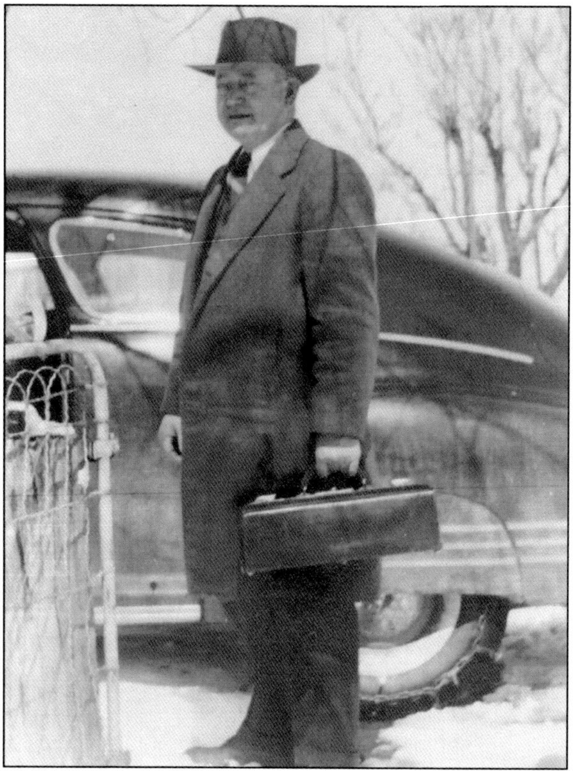

Dr. George B. Hill and his wife, Anna, sister to Edna McGee, came to town in 1923 not long after he graduated from the Medical College at the University of Louisville. They were a very popular couple with the locals, and Dr. Hill gained the respect of the local residents. Dr. Settle had a strong foothold in the city for many years. He delivered a lot of children, and many parents gave their sons the middle name Hill to honor him. (Courtesy of the Mt. Washington Historical Society.)

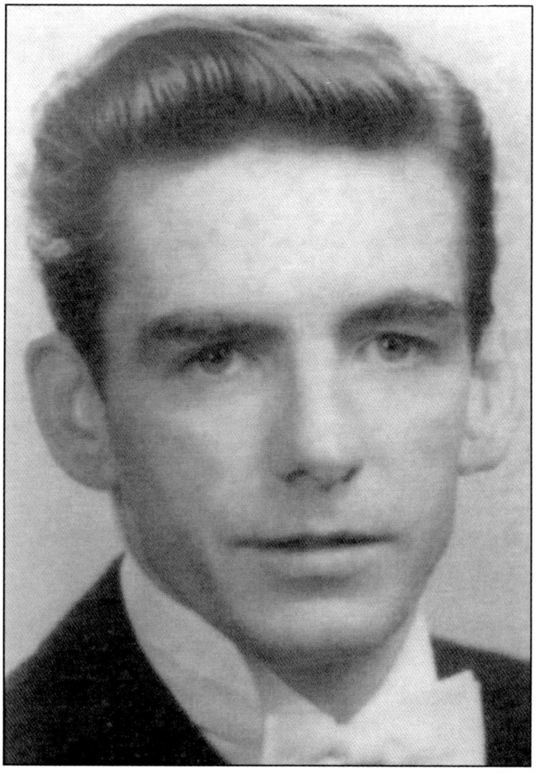

Dr. R. Stephen Bowen came to Mt. Washington from Elizabethtown after attending the Medical College at the University of Louisville in 1953. His office was a few doors down from the Towne Pharmacy drugstore, which was convenient for patients. He was virtually the only doctor in the city before retiring after 35 years of service in 1989. (Courtesy of the Mt. Washington Historical Society.)

Six

Athens of This Section

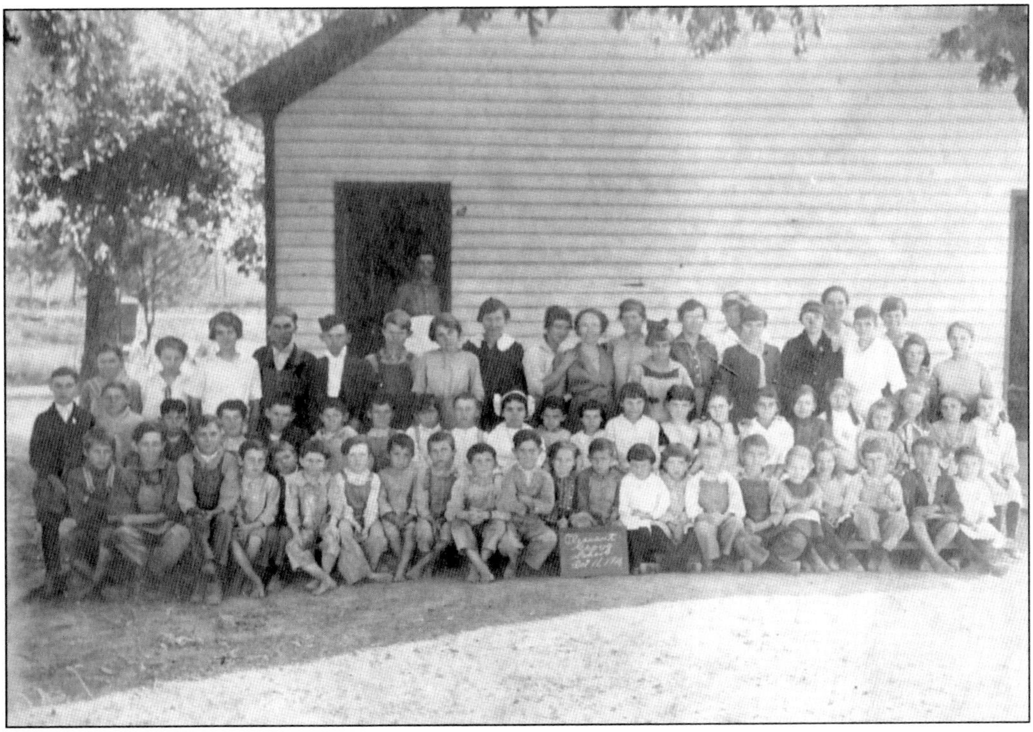

The first mention of a school in Mt. Washington was in 1818. Education has been a vital key element in the city's success. It prides itself on the accomplishments of those who have prospered and become relevant leaders of our community thanks to the guidance and nurturing of so many wonderful instructors. During the early 1900s, there were seven small, public schools. By the 1940s, all had condensed into one. With the population ever increasing, there are again seven schools to handle the multitude of students. This photograph of the Pleasant Grove School was one of the small public schools. (Courtesy of Arbidella Dooley.)

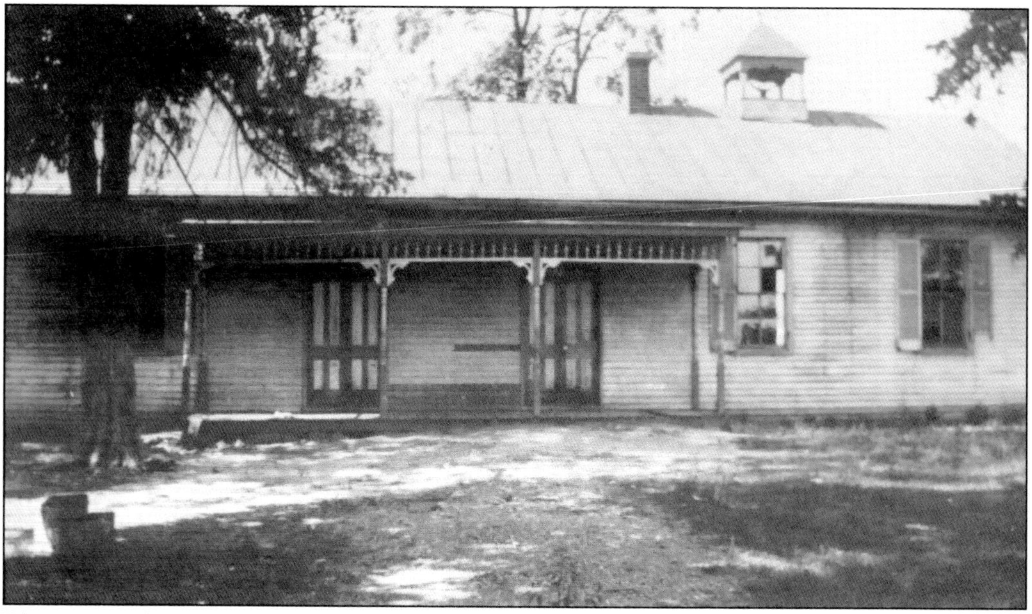

The Mt. Washington Academy was established sometime in the 1840s and located across from Porter Avenue on South Main Street. It was so highly acclaimed that it prompted someone to label Mt. Washington "the Athens of this section." Pictured below, students from many parts of the state attended the academy and boarded in a large, two-story home near the school. In 1850, the school had nearly 100 students in attendance. By 1910, the academy was barely alive with only a handful of students, likely due to the rising availability of public schooling. Soon thereafter, the school became the public Mt. Washington School and operated until 1916 when the new school was built on Water Street. The school was converted to a home occupied by the Ellabys. (Courtesy of Carolyn Quebbeman.)

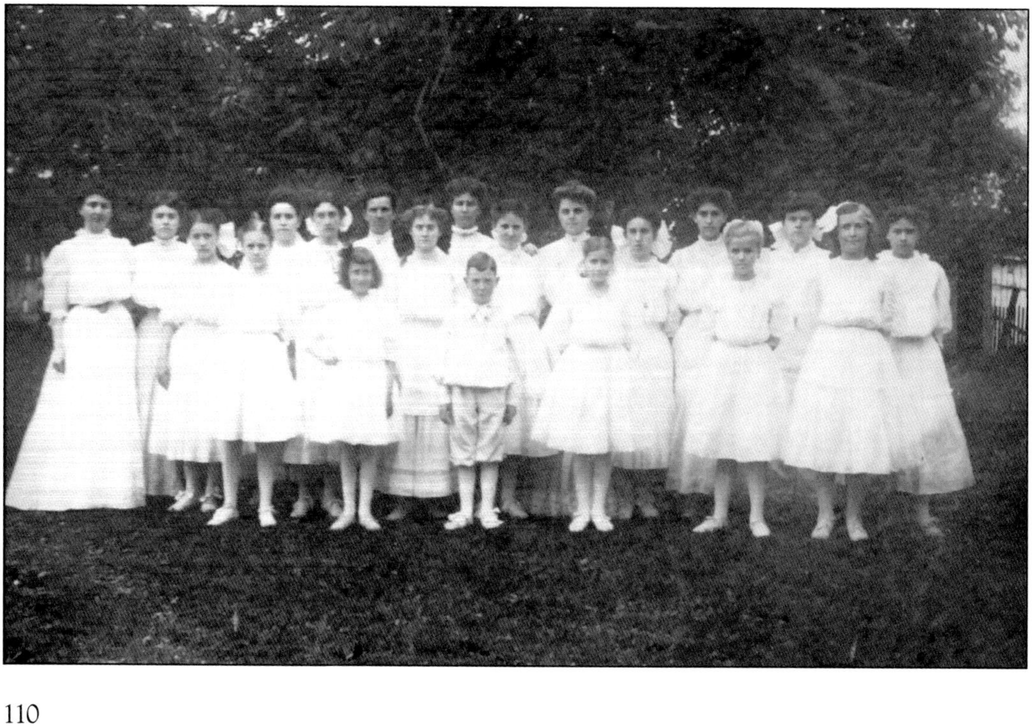

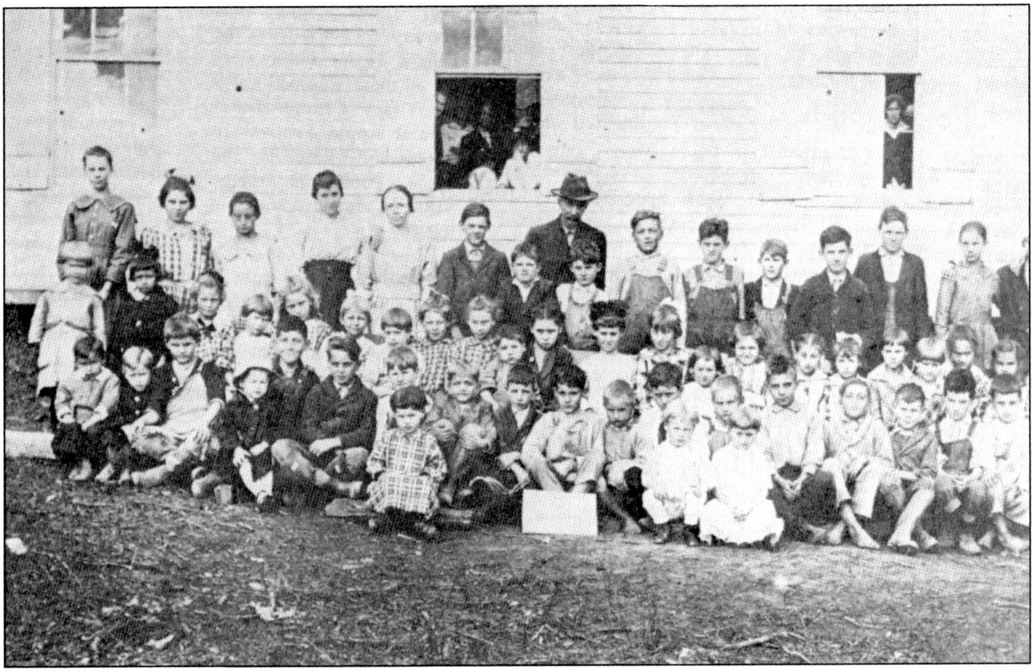

The Greenbriar School, a small public school that served the Flatlick Rood area, was located on Greenbriar Road and operated until the early 1940s. Bethel Church School was also located in the area and served children from the Highway 44 and Armstrong Road area. (Courtesy of the Mt. Washington Historical Society.)

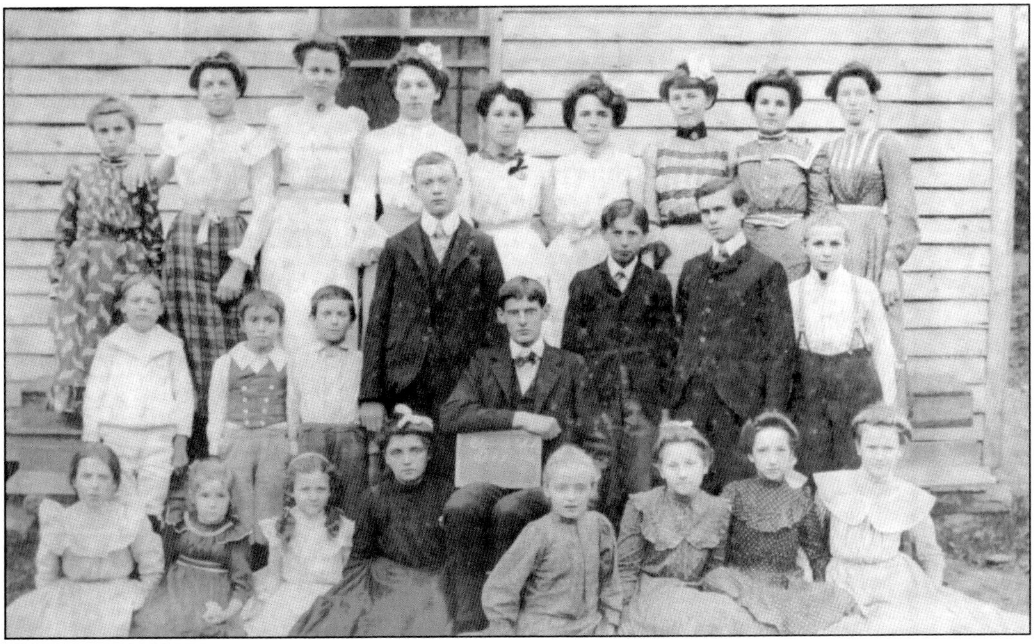

Edgewood School was located on Waterford Road about a mile west of Kings Church Road. George Threlkeld (not pictured) taught there a short time before he became a doctor. Branham, Walls, Fidler, Shake, and Markwell would be some familiar names that would have attended the small school. The photograph was taken in 1902. (Courtesy of the Mt. Washington Historical Society.)

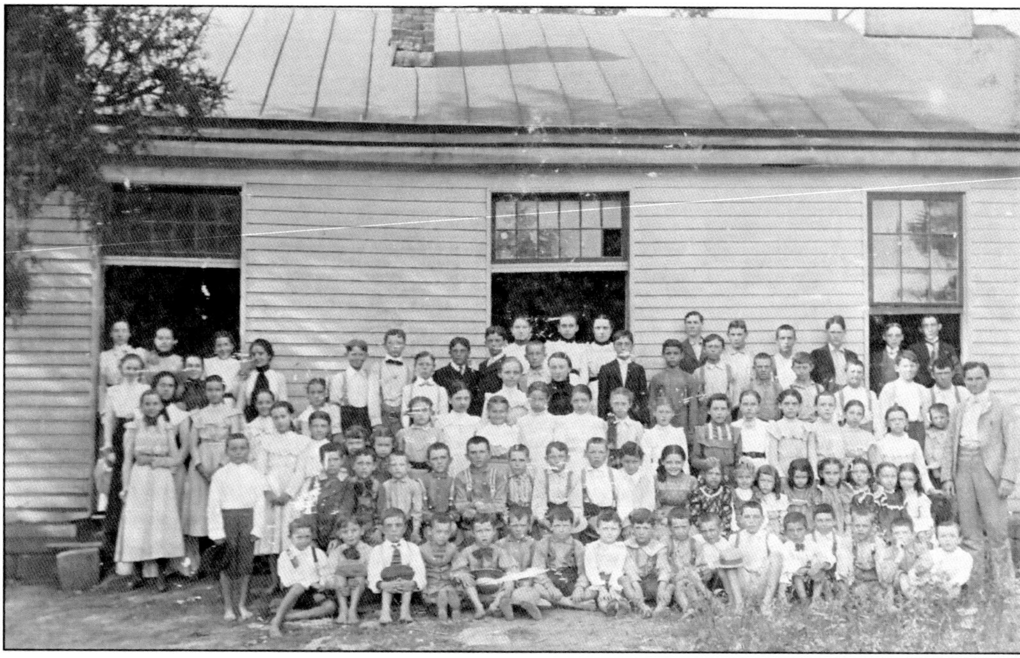

Sugar Valley started sometime in the mid-1800s. The area, including Smithville, had a thriving community with numerous farms and industry due to the nearby Salt River. As many as 100 students attended the small school during its heyday. Almost all of the students transferred to Mt. Washington High School by the late 1930s, and it eventually became a school for black students. The attractive schoolhouse was remodeled into a home that is still in use. (Courtesy of Mildred Brown.)

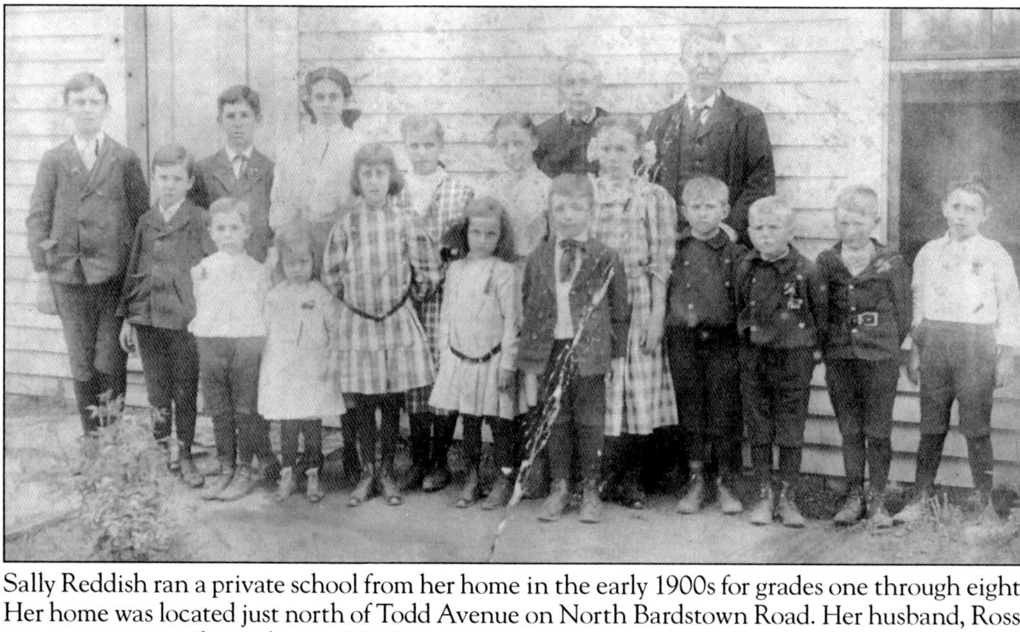

Sally Reddish ran a private school from her home in the early 1900s for grades one through eight. Her home was located just north of Todd Avenue on North Bardstown Road. Her husband, Ross, was a minister and ran the Mt. Washington Creamery from there. Two significant individuals are captured in this image from 1902: Stuyler Harris (far left) and Wiley Blount Rutledge (on his right). Stuyler's younger brother Leo is standing in front of him. (Courtesy of Stuart Tichenor.)

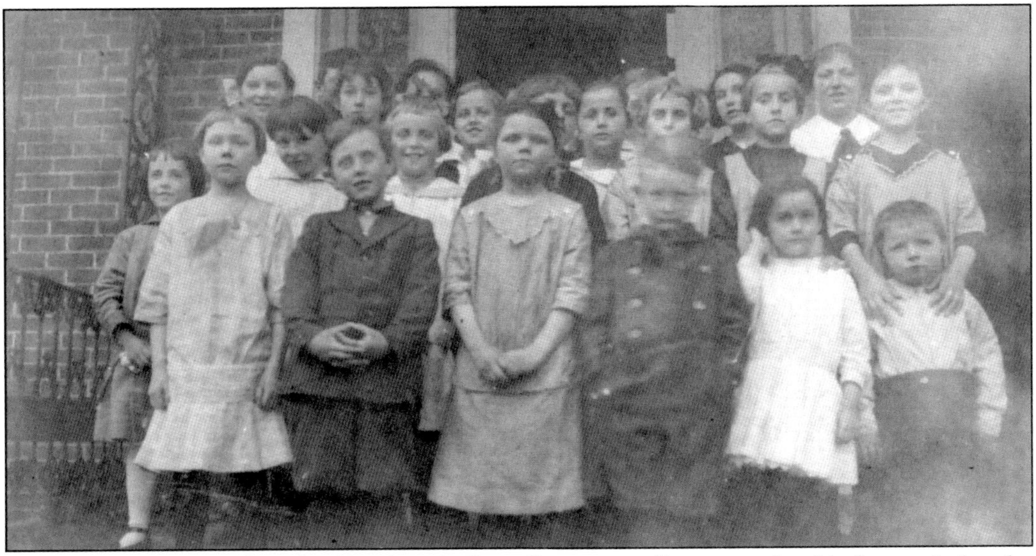

Maude (Harris) Overall, wife of Dr. Asa C. Overall, ran a small private school before and after she married. In the image, her students are standing on the front porch of the H.J. Barnes mansion where she and her husband lived. Her previous school was on South Bardstown Road in Sugar Valley. Maude is not pictured. (Courtesy of Chris Rothman.)

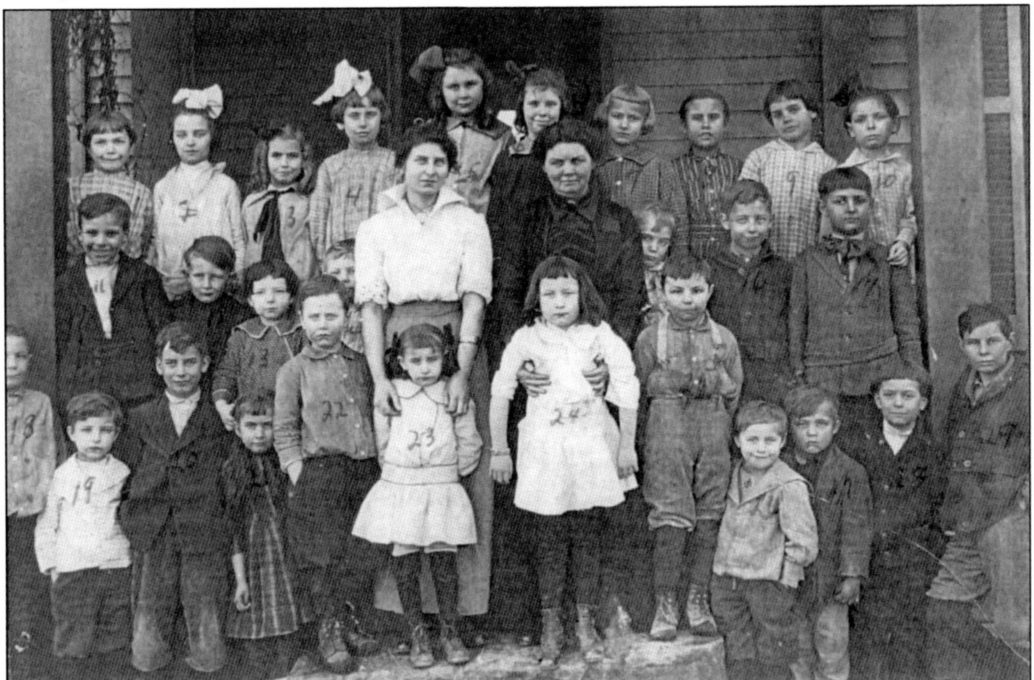

Pictured here around 1916 are students at the new Mt. Washington High School. Many of the students came from the old Mt. Washington School on South Main Street, but some may have come from other schools such as Sugar Valley, Bethel, or Greenbriar if they could find transportation there. There were classes for high school-aged students at the new school; however, they could not graduate because the school did not have accredited tutors. They had to travel to other schools quite a distance away if they wanted their diploma. (Author's collection.)

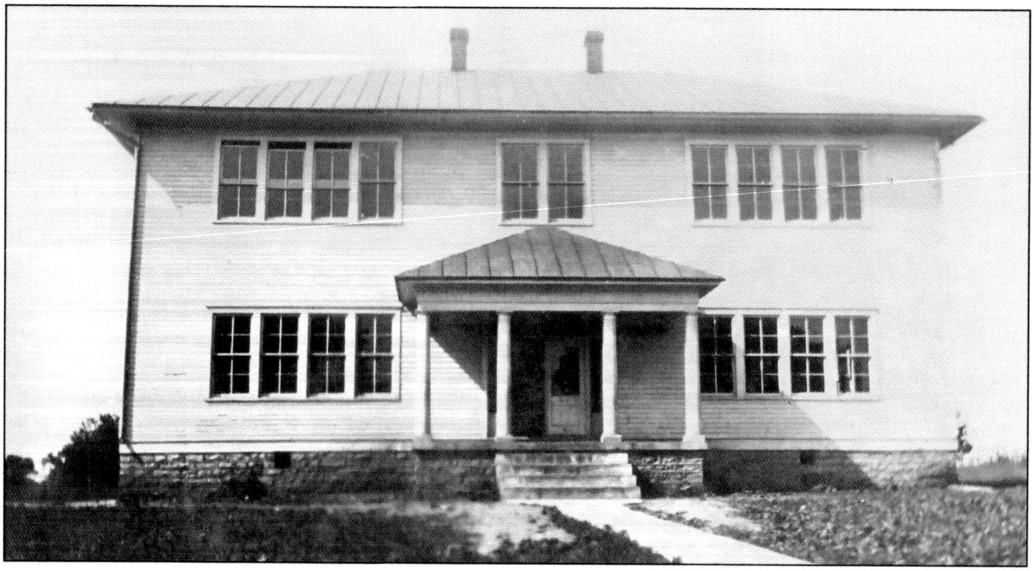

In 1916, a two-story school building that cost $4,000 was erected on Water Street across from Collings Street. The school did not have an accredited program for high school students until 1928 when Beatrice Lutes became the school's first graduating senior. In 1937, the Work Projects Administration granted funds to build a much needed gymnasium that included locker rooms and an auditorium (below). After a fire broke out in the school in December 1940, chutes were attached to the front of the building for quick evacuations. (Author's collection.)

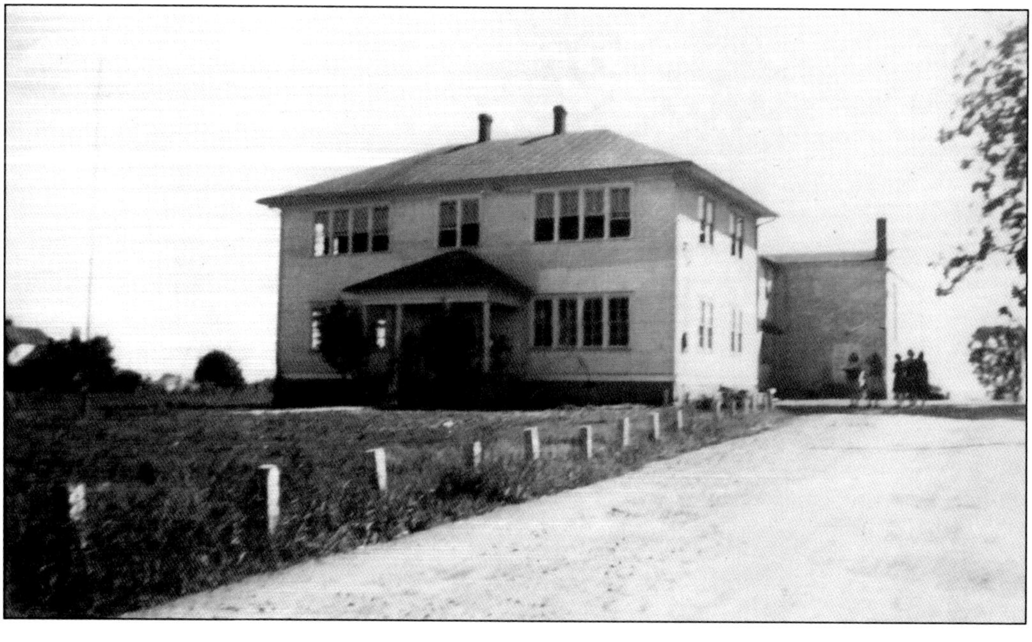

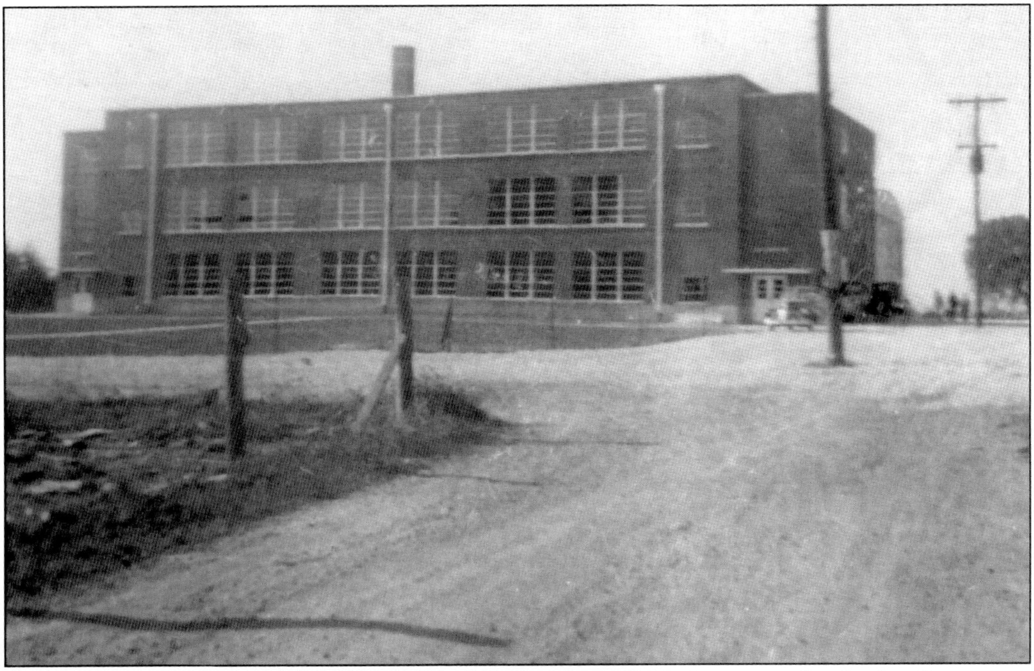

In 1948, the old two-story schoolhouse was moved and a modern three-story brick schoolhouse was built in its place, the gymnasium remained. Over the years, several additions and modifications have taken place, including a cafeteria that was once in a crowded basement under the old gymnasium. It last hosted high school students in 1970, when a centralized high school was built called Bullitt Central. The building now serves as the Mt. Washington Middle School. (Author's collection.)

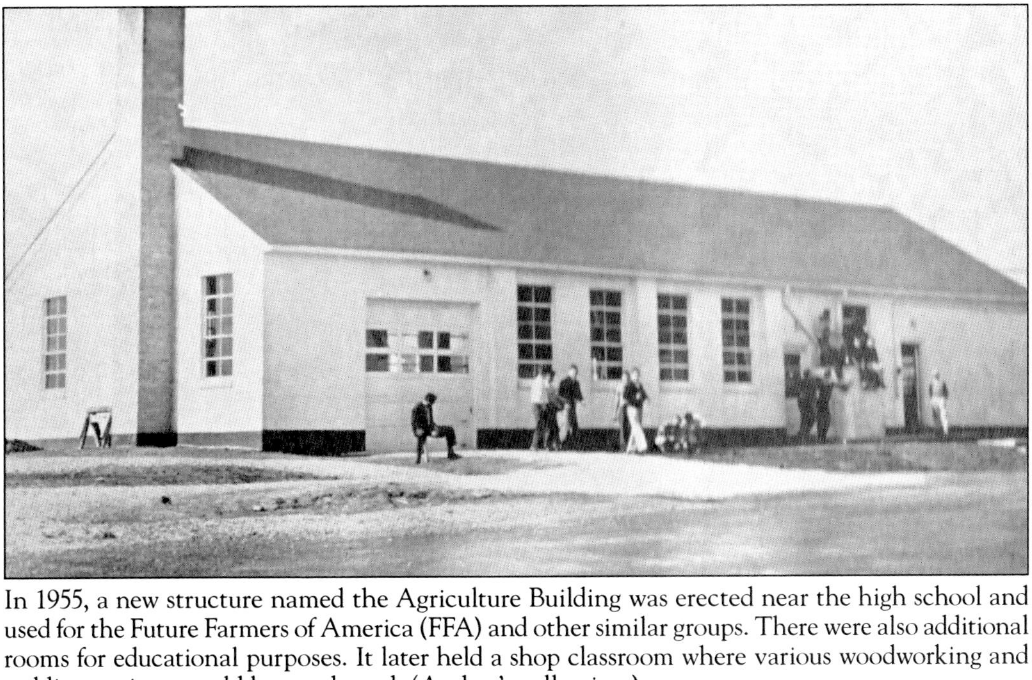

In 1955, a new structure named the Agriculture Building was erected near the high school and used for the Future Farmers of America (FFA) and other similar groups. There were also additional rooms for educational purposes. It later held a shop classroom where various woodworking and welding projects could be conducted. (Author's collection.)

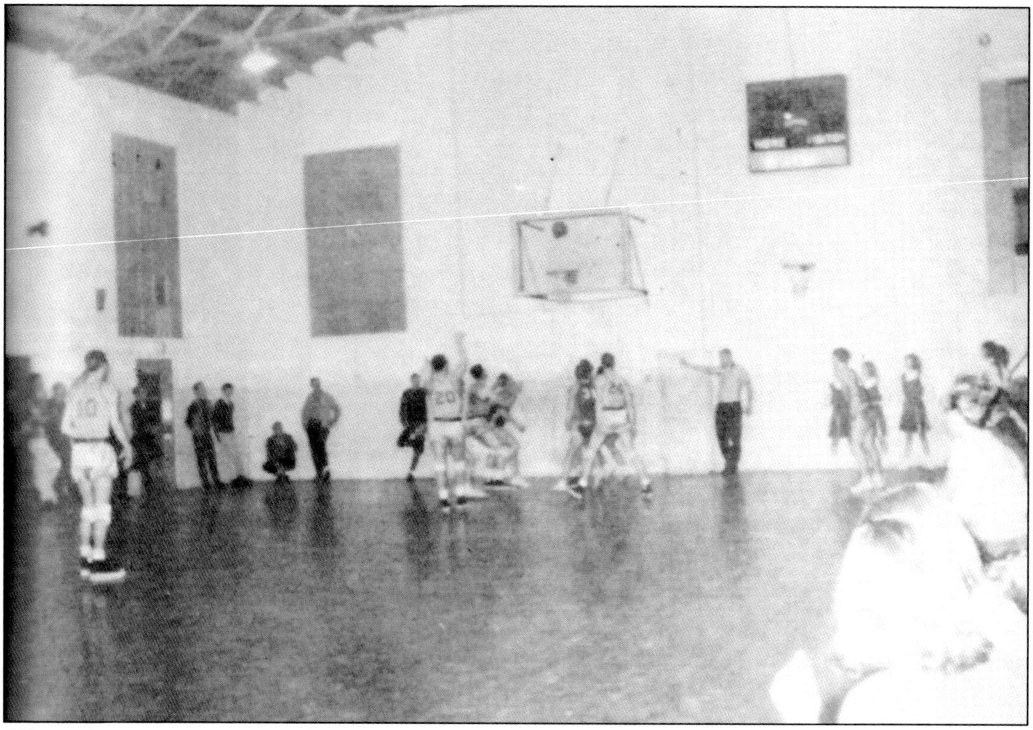

When the gymnasium was added in 1937, it was a boon to sports aficionados, primarily basketball, but allowed for a multitude of events to happen indoors. It also enabled physical education classes to continue through winter months. When the old school building was torn down, the new one was built on the same foundation and connected to the gymnasium by a breezeway. Pictured below, the auditorium, or stage as it was often called, was where school plays, talent contests, movies, and more took place. During basketball games, people would arrive early to get a seat on the front of the stage. (Author's collection.)

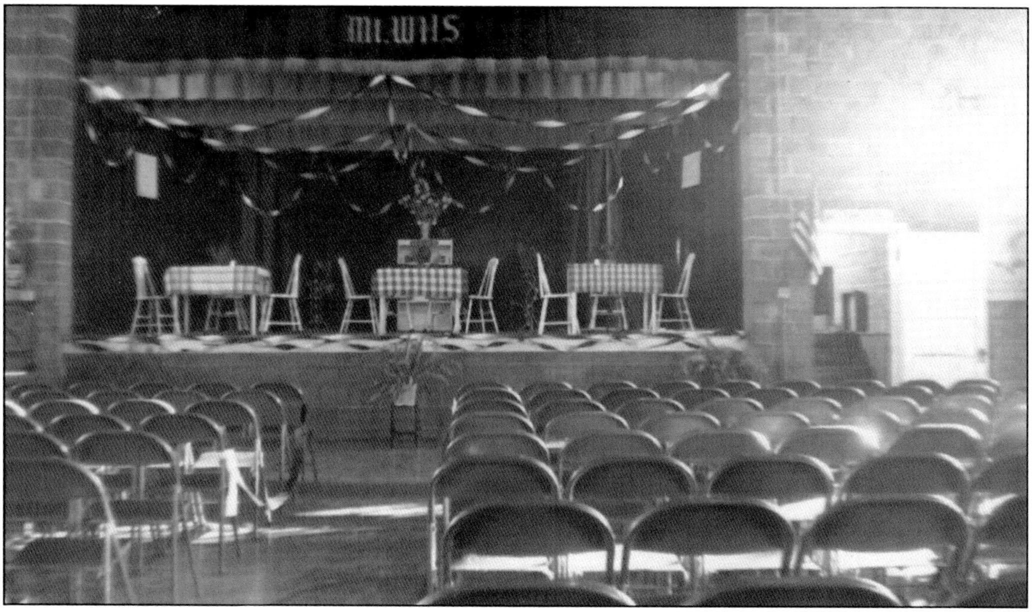

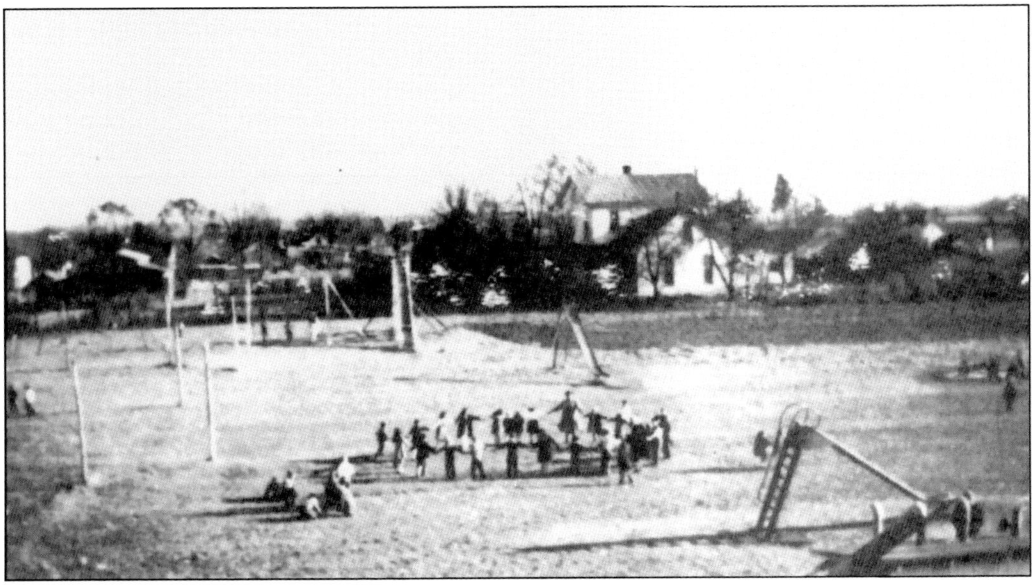

Recess was always a highly anticipated part of the school day, when children would converge on the playground and take their minds off of schoolwork. The playground was a special place just behind the school that featured a small slide for younger students and a large slide for older children or little daredevils. It also included swing sets, a merry-go-round, jungle gym, and a field to play all types of ball. This photograph from 1950 captures all types of activity, even a group playing some type of handholding game led by the teacher. (Author's collection.)

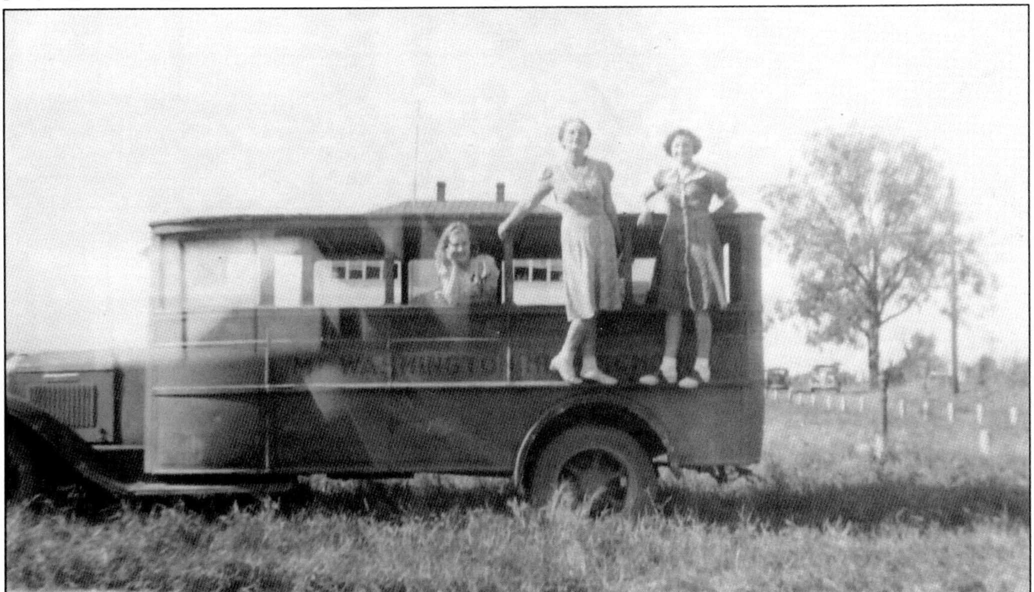

Early transportation was hard to come by, considering there was not enough funding for buses. The options were either catch a ride or walk to school. Billy Rouse, a teacher at Mt. Washington High School, picked up as many children as he could on his way to work in his Model T Ford. Finally, in the late 1920s, the school could afford their first bus, shown here, which lasted for nearly 20 years before it was retired. Students Dorothy Dean Swearingen, Anna Joyce Jasper, and Ruby Donaldson are posing with the bus. (Courtesy of Dorothy D. Porter.)

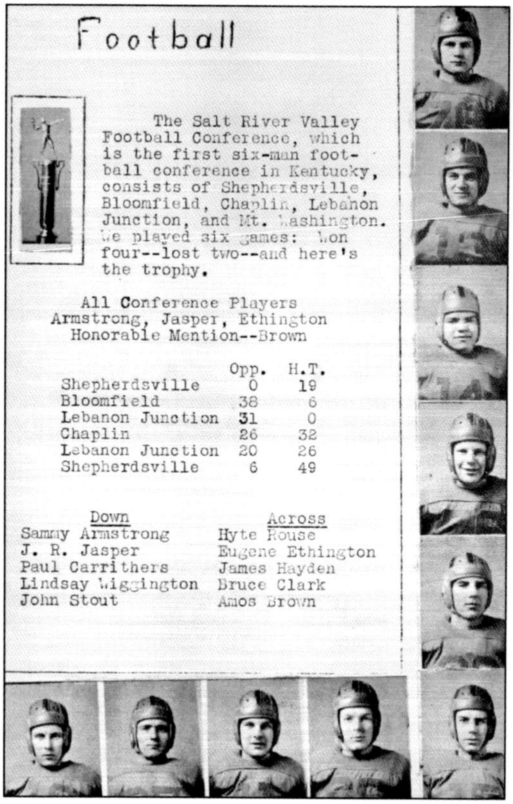

Football

The Salt River Valley Football Conference, which is the first six-man football conference in Kentucky, consists of Shepherdsville, Bloomfield, Chaplin, Lebanon Junction, and Mt. Washington. We played six games: Won four--lost two--and here's the trophy.

All Conference Players
Armstrong, Jasper, Ethington
Honorable Mention--Brown

	Opp.	H.T.
Shepherdsville	0	19
Bloomfield	38	6
Lebanon Junction	31	0
Chaplin	26	32
Lebanon Junction	20	26
Shepherdsville	6	49

Down	Across
Sammy Armstrong	Hyte Rouse
J. R. Jasper	Eugene Ethington
Paul Carrithers	James Hayden
Lindsay Wiggington	Bruce Clark
John Stout	Amos Brown

In the late 1930s and early 1940s, the Mt. Washington High School sported a six-man football team. Several members of this team became important figures in Mt. Washington's future. J.R. Jasper took over Central Garage business from his father, Maynard. Lindsay Wigginton did the same for his father, Hubert, running his grocery and retail store. Amos Brown also ventured into the grocery business with his IGA store, and Bruce Clark would one day become Mt. Washington's first mayor. (Author's collection.)

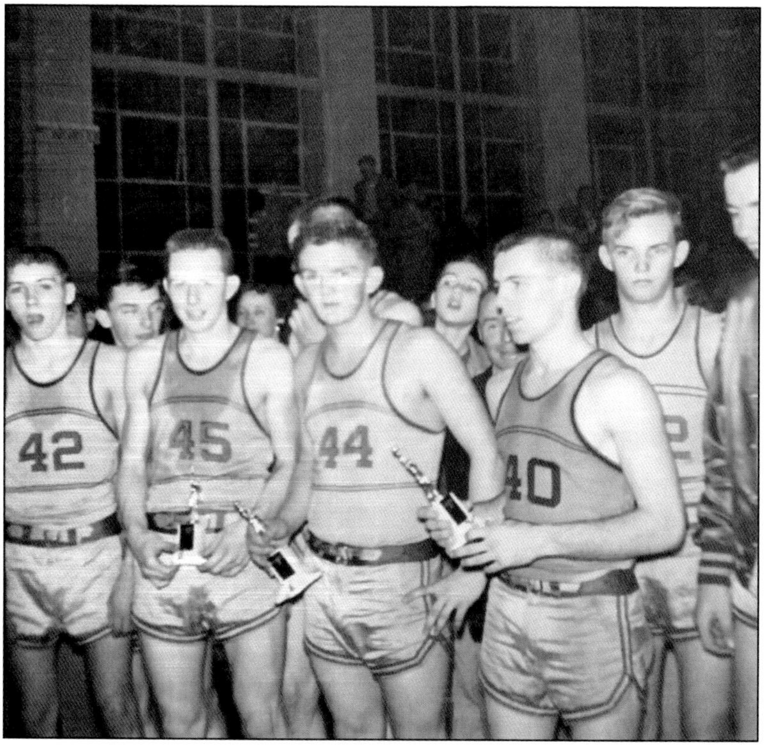

Henry "Skip" Hatfield was probably the most gifted and dominant athlete to participate in sports at Mt. Washington High School. He scored as many as 40 points in a basketball game as a junior on a talented team and threw a number of no-hitters in baseball. The Brooklyn Dodgers and Kansas City Athletics tried to recruit him when he graduated, but Skip chose the quiet life at home instead. In the photograph, Skip is wearing number 44 (center). (Courtesy of Gayle and Eleanor Troutman.)

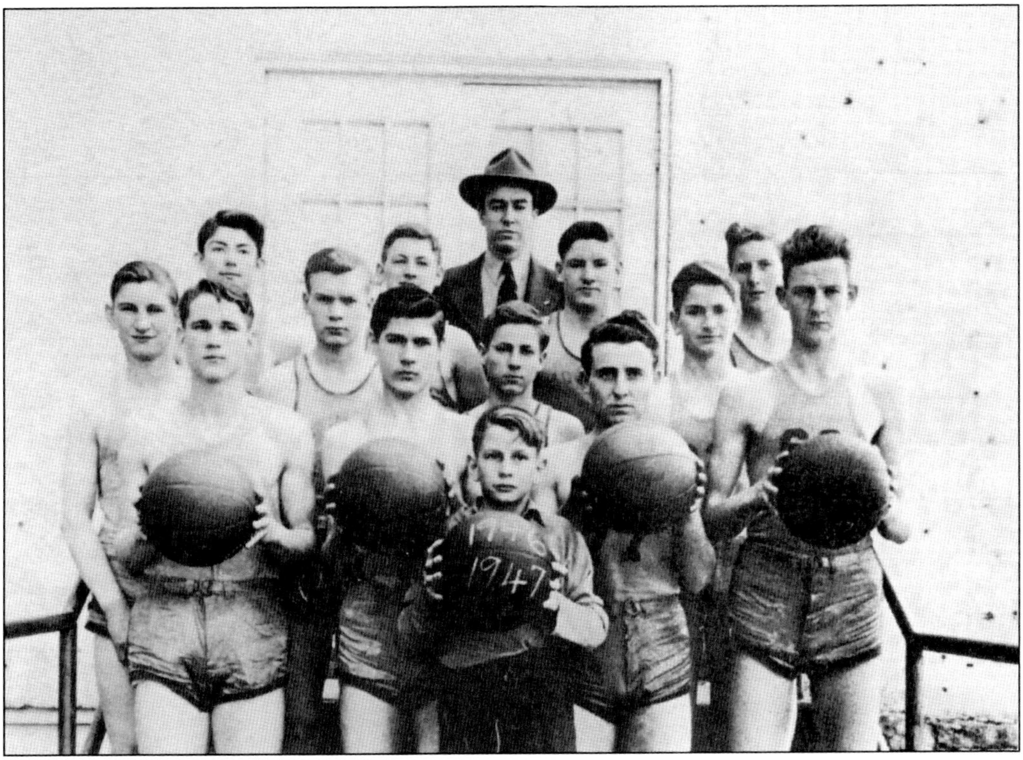

Clyde Troutman began a dynasty of Mt. Washington basketball players. His son Mac (first row on right) played on the varsity team as an eighth grader. That talent has been passed along to at least 20 family members, boys and girls alike, who excel at high school basketball and other sports. Several others in this group made names for themselves. Also pictured here are Lloyd Dooley (forefront, Bullitt County sheriff); Ralph Lutes (mayor of Mt. Washington); Tommy Jasper (Central Garage); Frank Cornell (Cornell Realty). Quite a team. (Author's collection.)

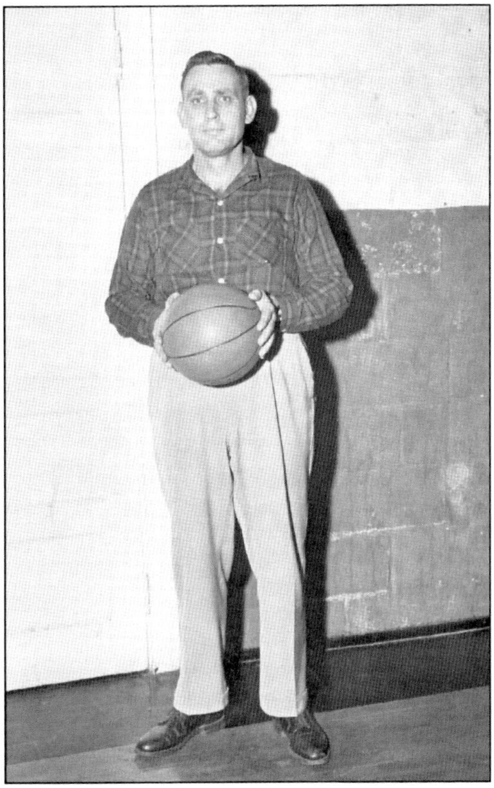

Lloyd Mullins was one of the most popular coaches Mt. Washington High School ever had. He came to the school to teach physics and quickly took on the coaching duties of the basketball and baseball teams. His personality won over many, and he had a successful career there. He gave up coaching when he became the vice principal. When Bullitt Central became the primary high school for Bullitt County, Lloyd worked as a substitute teacher before moving to Spencer County. (Author's collection.)

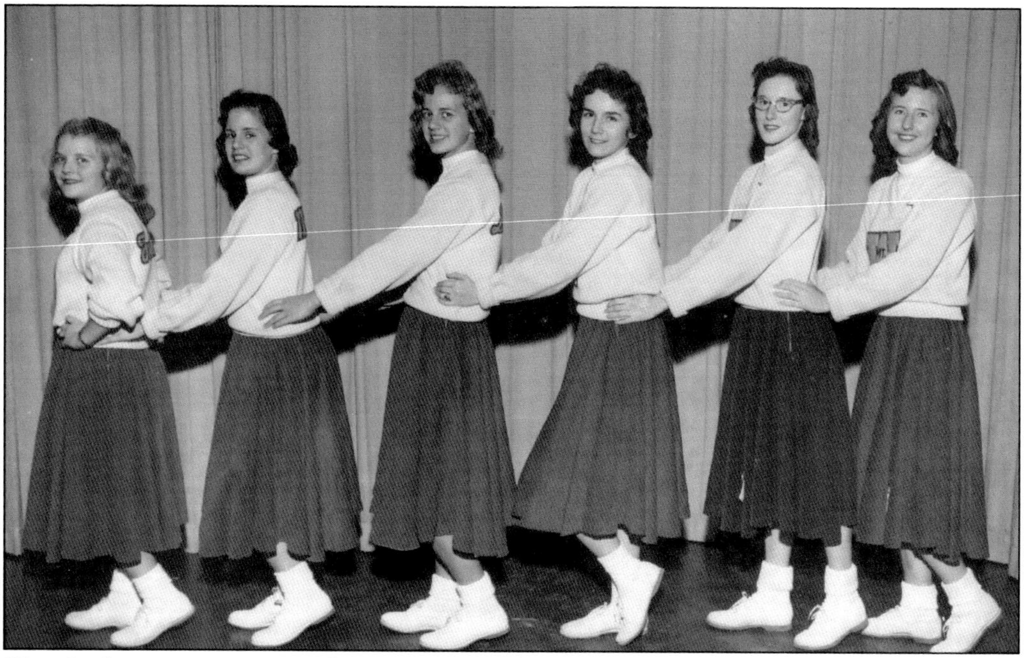

Cheerleaders were instrumental in maintaining the intense excitement of the crowd going, which certainly benefitted the team. They had to be athletes themselves, spending hours practicing their cheers and routines. Pictured here from left to right are Fonda Nutt, Maxine Armstrong, Linda Bleemel, Judy Shields, Eleanor McFarland, and Bonnie Robinson. (Author's collection.)

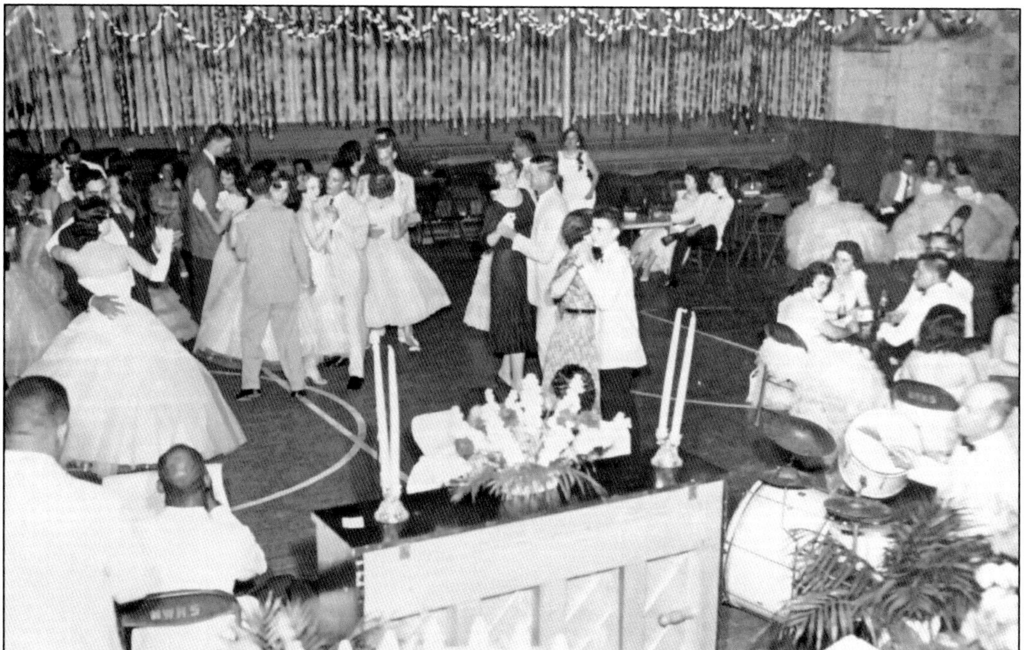

Proms did not take place at the high school until 1958, but they certainly did it in style with the decorated gymnasium and live music provided by a small jazz band. (Courtesy of Gayle and Eleanor Troutman.)

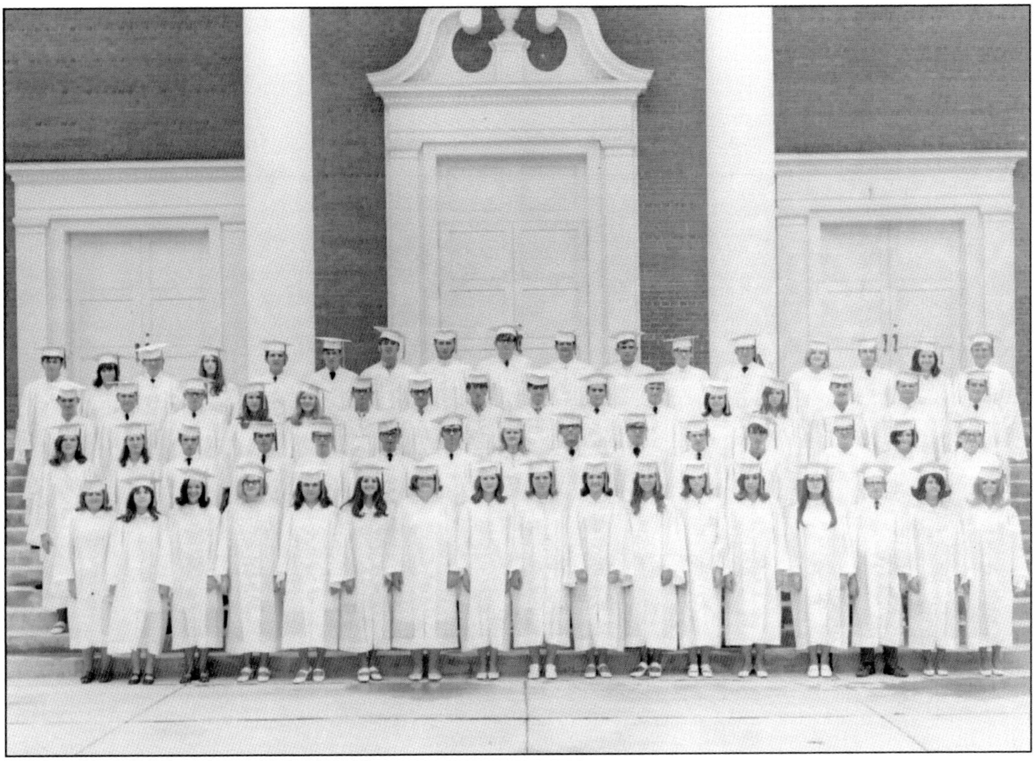

The 42nd, and last, graduating class of Mt. Washington High School poses for this bittersweet moment in 1970. In 1928, there was only one graduating senior; in 1970, there were 65. Within the next ten years, all high school students attended a consolidated school in Shepherdsville called Bullitt Central. (Author's collection.)

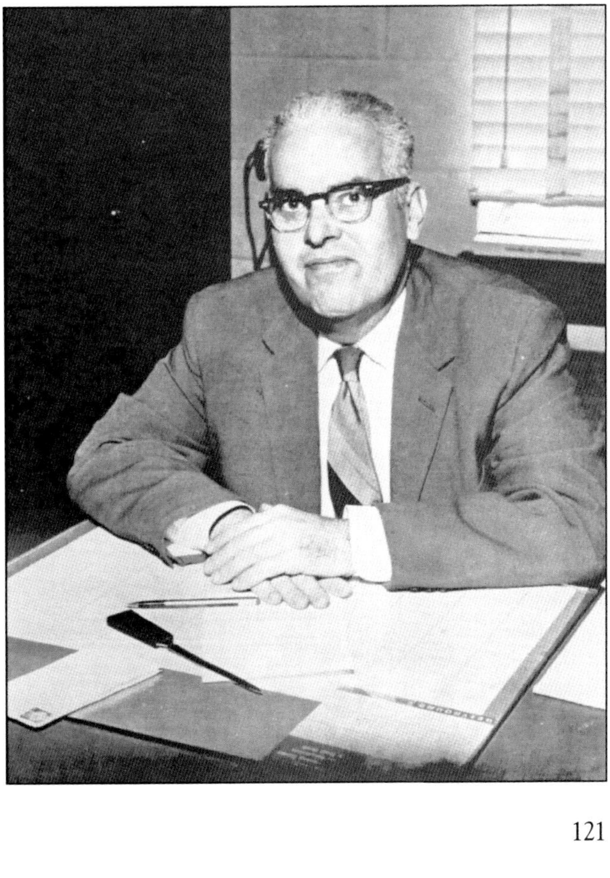

C.L. Francis was principal of Mt. Washington High School from 1954 to 1969, during its largest years of growth. With a scowl and a paddle that could put fear into the bravest of hearts, he ruled the hallways and kept the school in well order. Underneath his gruff demeanor, he was a kind and gentle man that cared for his students. He and his wife, Virginia, a popular first grade teacher, will be remembered in the annals of education. (Author's collection.)

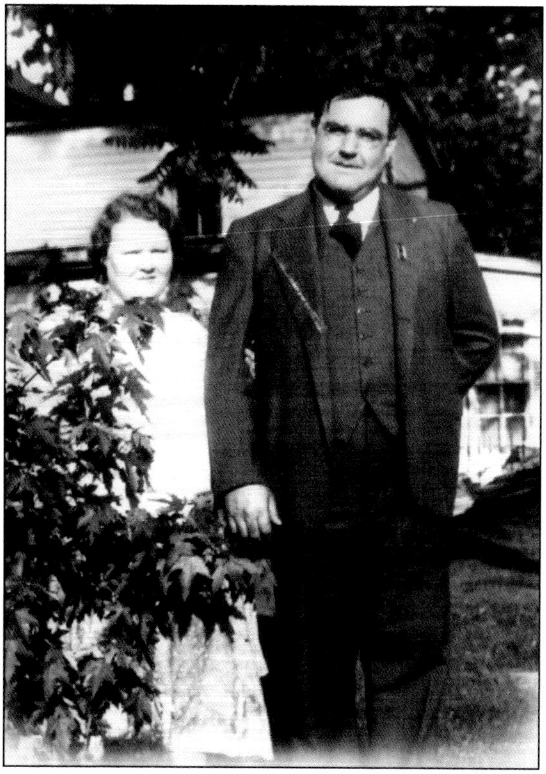

William H. McFarland was an Owensboro native who came to Mt. Washington with his wife, Louella, to be the school's third principal after it had received accreditation. He also taught history and social studies. During his tenure from 1930 to 1934, the school thrived and many new programs were spearheaded. In 1934, he was elected superintendent of Bullitt County schools. After World War II, he returned to teaching in the mid-1950s. In 1963, he became ill and passed away in July of the following year. He was also a Mason and former president of the Mt. Washington Lions Club. (Author's collection.)

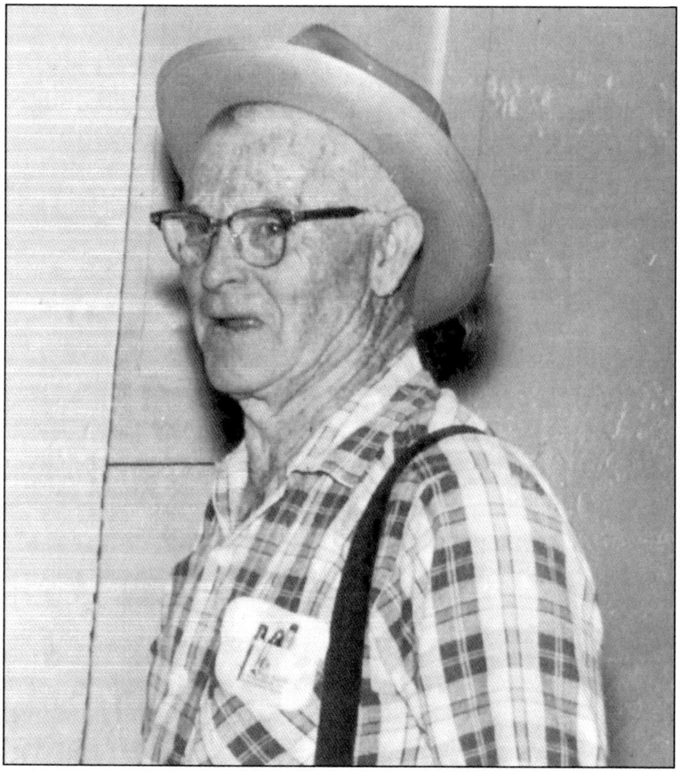

Murrell "Spec" Owens was not only the janitor of the Mt. Washington High School but also a friend to everyone he met. Spec was endeared to many by his friendly smile, and he worked at the school throughout the 1960s. (Author's collection.)

Eight

People, Places, and Polly the Parrot

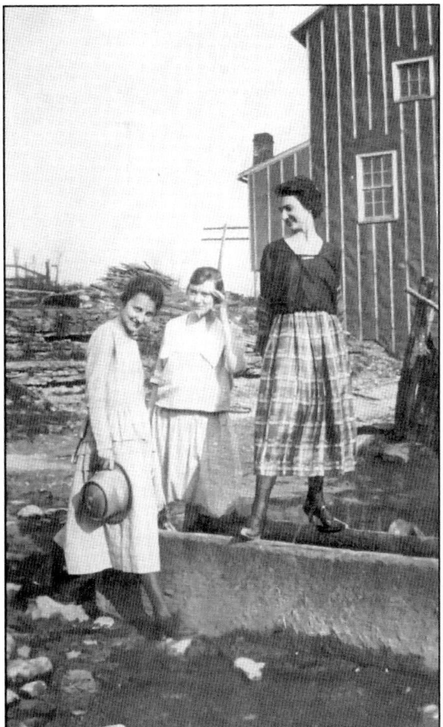

Spout Spring was vital part of Mt. Washington's early development. Located near the crossroads, the spring provided a constant water supply for the city's residents and the industries that prospered in the area. Legend had it that if anyone drank from the spring they would never leave Mt. Washington. According to Statira McFarland, "If anyone drank from the spring today, they certainly wouldn't leave," as the polluted waters have been deadly since the 1930s. (Courtesy of the Mt. Washington Historical Society.)

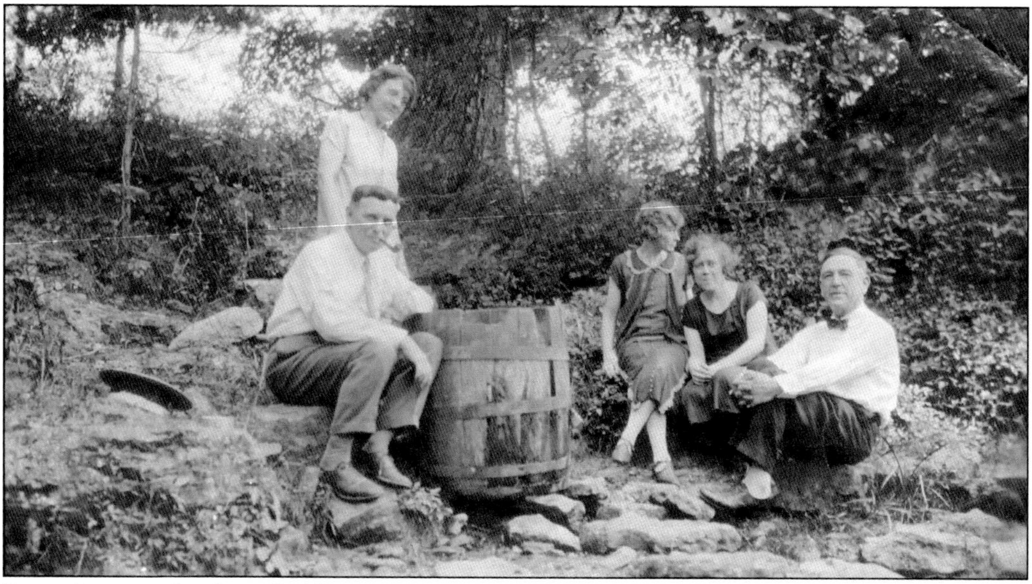

Evans Lane used to be called Evans Spring Lane, due to the crystal clear spring near the end by the old Evan's place. For years, it was a popular gathering place and picnic spot for locals. Dr. George W. Threlkeld owned the property for some time and entertained many of his friends there. (Courtesy of Leda Barnes.)

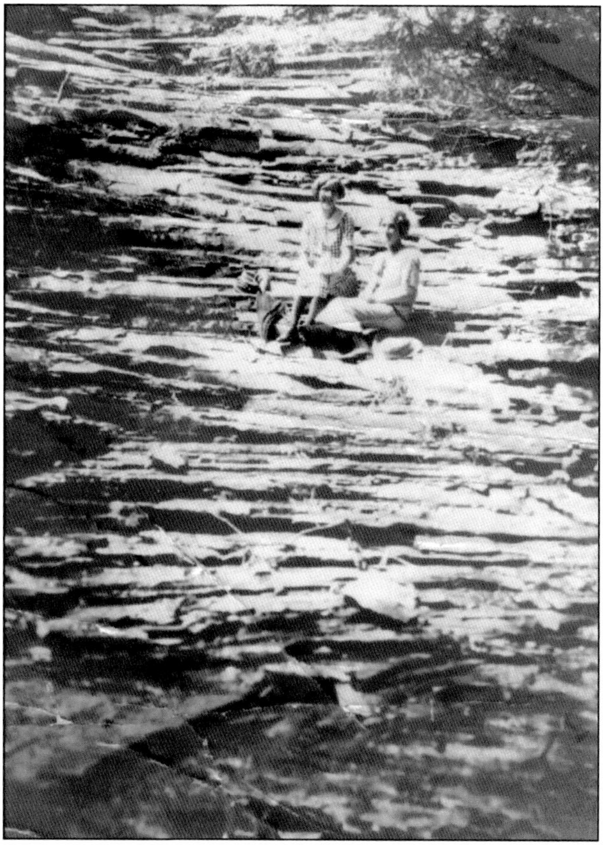

Lovers Leap was another attraction near Evans Spring, more for teenagers than adults, to gather and enjoy the day. It was a pretty, gradual waterfall instead of a severe drop. The story of its name came from a legend about two Indians who were in love and jumped to their deaths over the falls. Maybe slid. (Courtesy of Leda Barnes.)

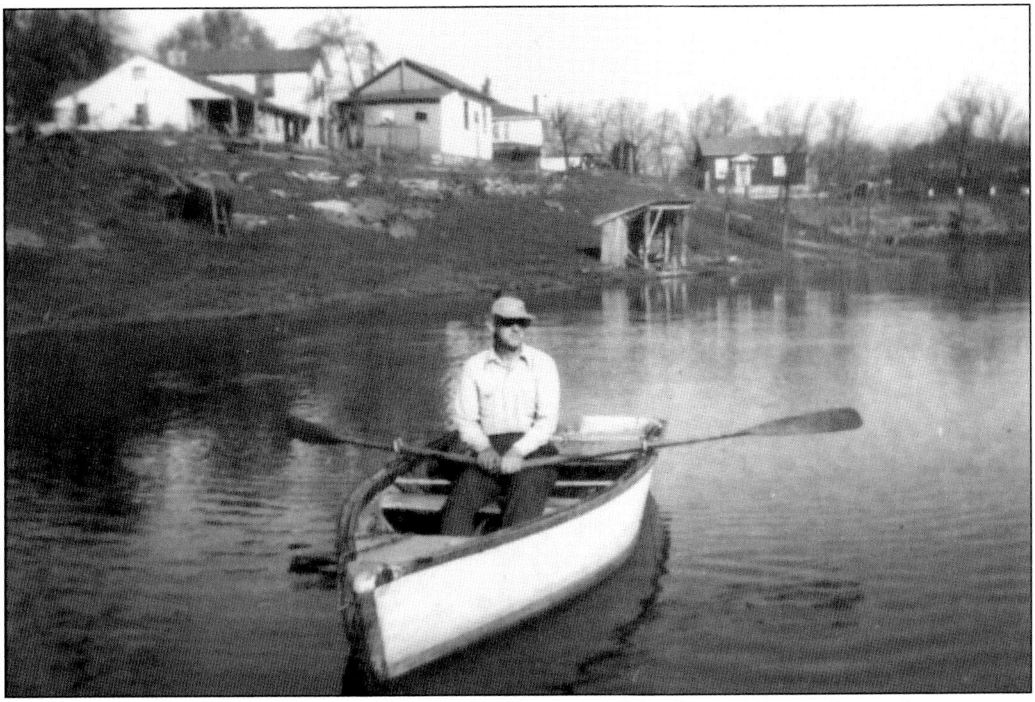

There was a lake just west of the Crossroads that was fed by the old Spout Spring but remains somewhat of a mystery. It was a manmade lake that may have been built as early as 1935, possibly with the help of WPA funds. However, by 1968 Jack Barnes had other plans to develop the property, drained the pond, and had it filled in. (Courtesy of Leda Barnes.)

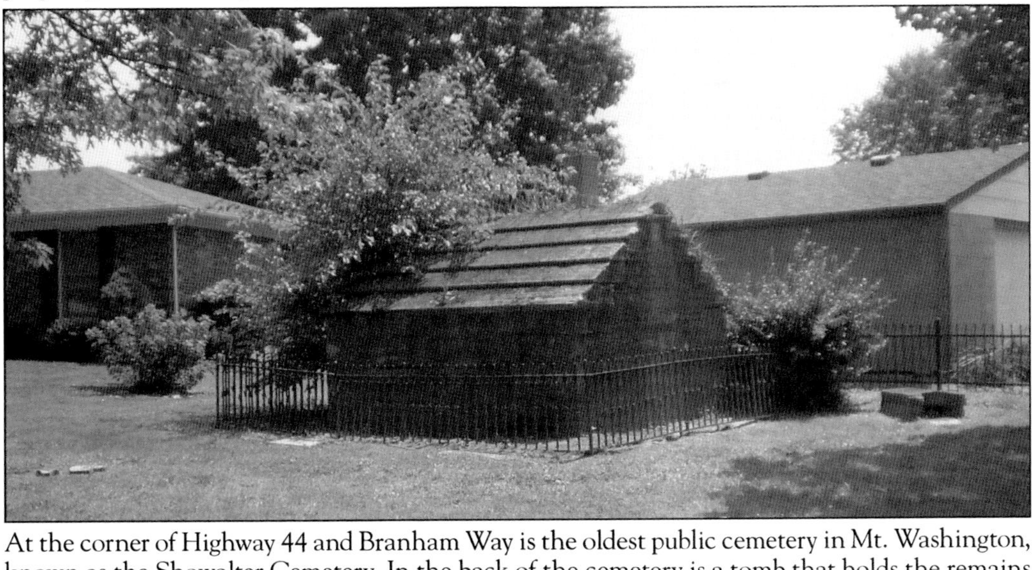

At the corner of Highway 44 and Branham Way is the oldest public cemetery in Mt. Washington, known as the Showalter Cemetery. In the back of the cemetery is a tomb that holds the remains of Edward (1787–1866) and Catherine Hessey. The tomb was constructed from stone hewn by a Canadian named Jonathan Braithwaite. Edward was a veteran of the War of 1812 and lived near the small cemetery, where many of the oldest names can be seen: Peacock, Stevens, and Stringer. According to Hassie Parrish, who lived nearby, Union soldiers would camp there. (Author's collection.)

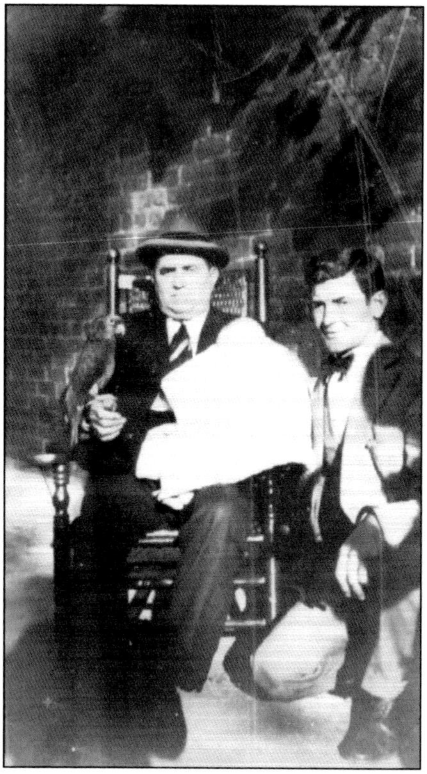

Kenny Snyder, who once owned a clothing store in Maccabee Hall, had a pet parrot named Polly that delighted many of his customers and brought in business. Polly had quite a vocabulary and could confuse anyone into thinking he was a human if they did not know he was there. He could also sing hymns, which he did on a daily basis. Pictured here is Snyder sitting with Polly along with his son-in-law Vernon Troutman and Vernon's infant daughter Jewell. (Courtesy of Jewell Lutes.)

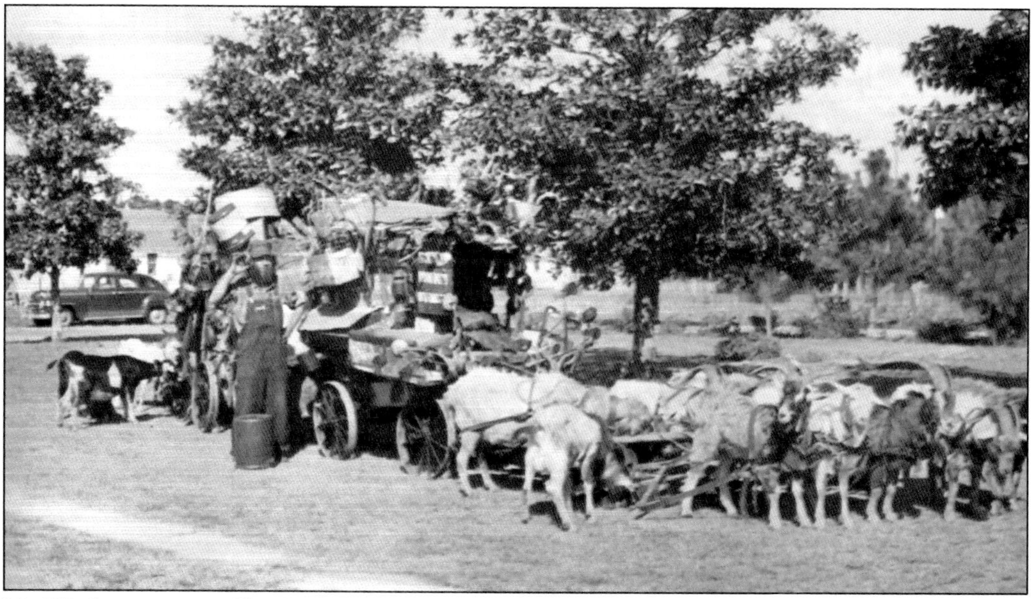

Mt. Washington saw Ches McCartney "The Goat Man" travel through town occasionally. People could hear the bells ringing on the goats that pulled his cart full of whatever he could find to sell and make enough money to survive. Ches started on a religious journey in the 1930s that did not end until 1968. Siblings Robert and Virginia Grigsby would give him a place to sleep and feed him at their small diner. He is revered and endeared in the memories of many. Ches claimed to have traveled every state in the continental United States. (Author's collection.)

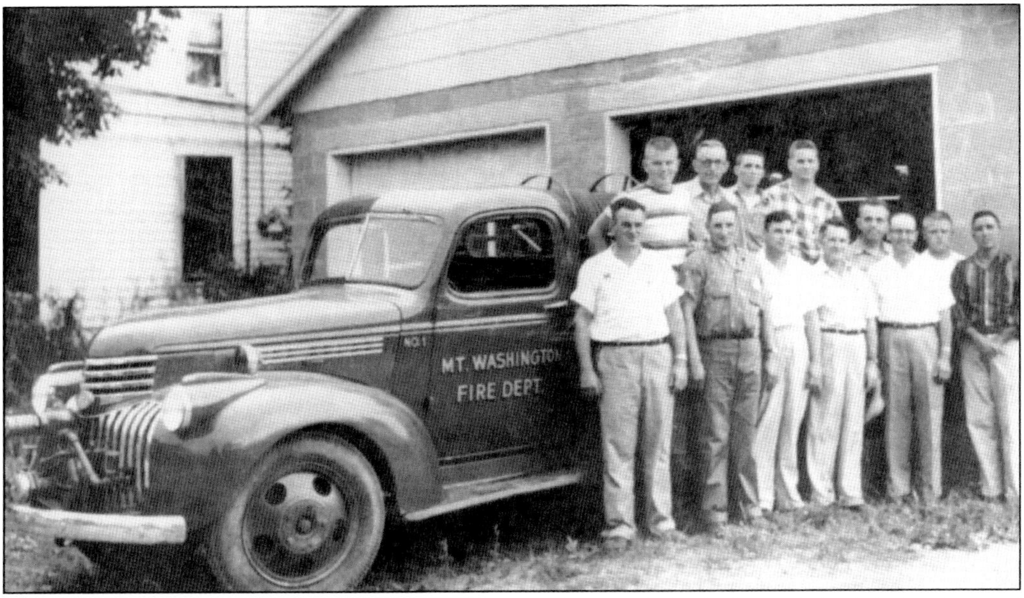

After two devastating fires, one on June 2, 1933, that destroyed Wilder Harris's Ford dealership and another that destroyed Maccabee Hall and threatened to raze the business district on November 18, 1940, the city decided it was time to buy a fire engine. They acquired one in April 1941 and built a garage on Porter Avenue to house it. The city now has an outfitted complex with several fire engines and other specialized equipment. (Courtesy of E.L. Ryan.)

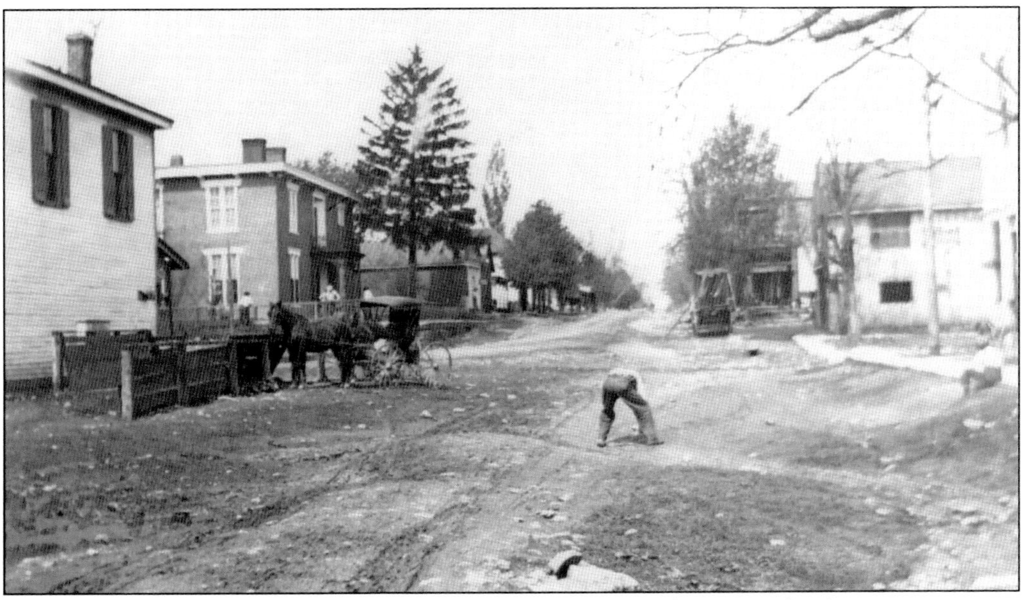

Well, we're right back where we started at the Crossroads. Hope the journey has been entertaining. Have to say so long because I have to get back to picking these rocks up out of the road. Sure can't wait 'til they pave this thing. Have a great day! (Courtesy of the Mt. Washington Historical Society.)

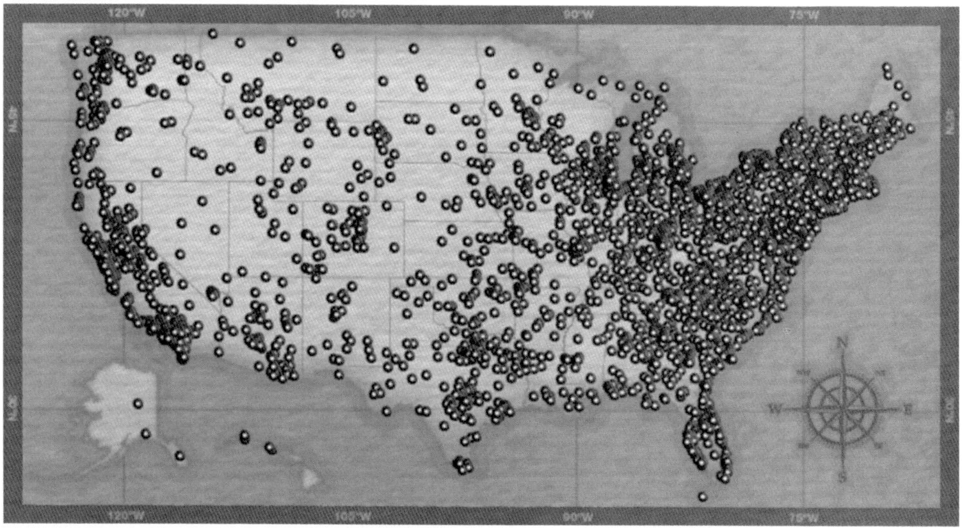